An Introduction To
WRITTEN JAPANESE

C000156846

Teach Yourself

JAPANESE

C. J. DUNN
&
S. YANADA

'The grading of the vocabulary, the correlation of the exercises with the lessons, and the preparation of the conversation pieces have been carried out with skill and care by the two authors, who have clearly drawn on extensive practical teaching experience.'

Bulletin of the School of Oriental and African Studies, University of London.

An Introduction to

WRITTEN JAPANESE

P. G. O'NEILL, Ph.D.

Professor of Japanese
School of Oriental and African Studies
University of London

and

S. YANADA, M. Econ. (Tokyo)

formerly Senior Lecturer in Japanese
School of Oriental and African Studies
University of London

Hodder & Stoughton

A MEMBER OF THE HODDER HEADLINE GROUP

British Library Cataloguing in Publication Data

A catalogue for this title is available from the British Library

ISBN 0 340 204 71 0

First published 1963
Impression number 24 23 22 21 20 19 18 17 16 15
Year   1999 1998 1997 1996 1995

Copyright © 1963 S. Yanda and P. G. O'Neill

All rights reserved. No part of this publication may be reproduced or transmitted in any form or by any means, electronic or mechanical, including photocopy, recording, or any information storage and retrieval system, without permission in writing from the publisher or under licence from the Copyright Licensing Agency Limited. Further details of such licences (for reprographic reproduction) may be obtained from the Copyright Licensing Agency Limited, of 90 Tottenham Court Road, London W1P 9HE.

Printed in Great Britain for Hodder & Stoughton Educational, a division of Hodder Headline Plc, 338 Euston Road, London NW1 3BH by Athenæum Press Ltd, Gateshead, Tyne & Wear.

CONTENTS

PREFACE

THE Japanese language and its writing system were described by early Christian missionaries as inventions of the devil, designed to prevent the spread of the Gospel. Understanding of them has improved somewhat in the last 400 years, but it remains true that written Japanese is unique in its complications.

This book was compiled in the hope of providing the student with a way through the difficult early stages. Designed as a self-contained course, it is intended to take the complete beginner to a stage at which he can handle character dictionaries and the like with some facility and otherwise fend for himself in dealing with modern written Japanese.

To this end, the main body of the book consists of sixteen graded reading exercises using a total of 680 Chinese characters. All these exercises are written in the present-day simplified script, and each is preceded by a list of new characters in the order in which they appear in the text and followed by a Romanized version of the text and notes on grammatical points. Four more lessons, in which no new characters are introduced, use variant forms of the characters and the old, traditional *kana* spellings, and show printed and semi-cursive handwritten forms of the script. Introductions to each of these two main sections explain briefly the points necessary for an understanding of the script used in the following lessons, and English translations are given for the texts of all twenty lessons, followed by a glossary and an index to notes on grammatical points. Finally, a character index has been compiled which lists all the 1,878 Chinese characters in standard use (*tooyoo kanzi*) and their variant forms; it shows where they are to be found in character dictionaries and which of them have been used in this book.

From the publishers' point of view, the production of such a book was far from straightforward, and we should here like to thank them for the understanding they have shown throughout the work.

The lessons are based on material used during the first-year course in Japanese at the School of Oriental and African Studies, University of London, and are intended for use with C. J. Dunn and S. Yanada's *Teach Yourself Japanese*, published by Hodder & Stoughton. The student is recommended to work through about ten lessons of

[vii]

this grammar before starting on the written exercises in this book, so that he will find little difficulty with grammatical constructions or vocabulary and will be free to concentrate on the written form of the language.

The list of 680 characters used in this book has its origin in a selection of 714 compiled for first-stage use by Mr. F. J. Daniels, Professor of Japanese in the University of London, and introduced into the beginners' course at the School of Oriental and African Studies in 1942. Since then it has been continually revised by S. Yanada in the light of teaching experience and developments in Japan. Of the 680 characters used in this book, 564 (83%) are retained from the original list of 714; 584 (86%) are in the Japanese Ministry of Education's list of 881 basic characters to be learned during the years of compulsory schooling; and all are among the 1,878 *tooyoo kanzi*.

Learning to read and write Japanese is a laborious business, and there are no short cuts to memorizing a large number of Chinese characters, for example. On the other hand, there is no need to despair. In recent years *kana* spelling has been simplified and the number of characters in common use substantially reduced, and on the inevitable occasions when the student feels that he is making little or no progress, he should find reassurance in a backward glance at earlier exercises and in the thought that the same hard path has been followed by everyone—foreigner and Japanese alike—who has learned to read and write the language.

P. G. O'N.
S. Y.

London, 1963

INTRODUCTION

MODERN Japanese is written in a mixture of Chinese characters (*kanzi*) and syllabic signs (*kana*) developed from the characters by the Japanese. It is usually written vertically, in columns running from top to bottom and following on from right to left across the page. Equal space is allowed for the writing of each character and *kana*, but no space is left between words.

Until recent years the number of characters available for use in written Japanese was virtually unlimited (a standard dictionary has entries under 15,000 different characters, for example), and changes in pronunciation over the centuries without corresponding changes in the writing often resulted in the same sound being represented in writing by combinations of *kana* which differed from word to word. In November 1946, however, the Japanese Government issued a list of 1,850 characters and a set of simplified *kana* spellings which were recommended for use to the exclusion of all others. Since that time nearly all Japanese publications of a non-specialist nature have conformed to these recommendations. To date the only subsequent development has been a suggestion by an official committee that 28 of the chosen characters be replaced by 28 different ones. This change has not yet been given government approval, but the effect has been to bring the extra characters into general use too. Thus, in practice, the total number of characters in standard use (*tooyoo kanzi*) at the present time is 1,878.

Chinese Characters

These were the first means of writing known to the Japanese and, lacking any alternative, they tried to use them to write their own language, using them at first on their own and later in combination with *kana*.

Classification. Each Chinese character either is or contains one of 214 basic elements known as radicals, and is traditionally classified under that radical in character dictionaries. The various characters coming under any particular radical are subdivided according to the number of strokes with which they are written, exclusive of the radical element itself. For example, 木 'tree', is radical 75, and 村 'village' is classified under the same radical 75 with three extra strokes. These two characters may therefore be described as being 75/0 and in the group 75/3 respectively. It is these radical and stroke numbers which appear beside each character in the lists in this book.

Unfortunately, it is not always easy to discover which part of a character is the radical and, in fact, the traditional arrangement of characters under this system is both inefficient and illogical if the aim is to facilitate the finding of unknown characters. In his *Beginners' Dictionary of Chinese–Japanese Characters and Compounds*, Arthur Rose-Innes arranged the characters in a more practical way by always regarding the most obvious element as the radical. This system was further developed in Nelson's *The Modern Reader's Japanese–English Character Dictionary*, Tuttle, and since this dictionary is now in general use among foreign students of Japanese, the characters listed in this book have been given their radical and stroke numbers according to the Nelson system.

One further complication arises from the existence of variant and simplified forms of characters. The 1946 revision of the writing system brought a large number of these into standard use, but since publications before that date normally used the earlier full forms of characters, the serious student will sooner or later need to recognize these forms too. Because of this, these full forms and common variants etc. have been included where appropriate in the character lists in this book.

Readings. Almost every character used in Japanese has at least two readings, and most of them have three or more. They are of two kinds. The first, known as ON (literally 'sounds'), are forms of the original Chinese pronunciations imitated by the Japanese when they learned the characters from teachers from the mainland. The second, known as *kun* (literally 'readings'), are native Japanese words which indicate the meaning, or one of the meanings, of a character. They are, as it were, Japanese translations of the meanings of the Chinese characters. (In listing readings it is a useful convention to distinguish ON by giving them in block capitals.) Thus, the character 村 has an ON reading SON, which is the present-day Japanese version of the original Chinese pronunciation, and a *kun* reading *mura*, which is the native Japanese word for the meaning of the character, 'village'.

Only experience will tell whether a character is to be read in the ON or the *kun*, but a character used independently will in most cases be read in the *kun*, and one used in combination with one or more other characters will be more likely to be read in the ON. For example, 村 occurring as a single character would be read *mura*, but the two-

[2]

character compound it makes when followed by TYOO 長 'chief, head' is read SONTYOO 'village head'. To give some help with characters which do not conform to this general rule, ON readings which are used alone as independent words in normal colloquial Japanese have been marked in the character lists with an asterisk, thus: 本 HON*, to show that the reading in question covers the meanings given up to the first semi-colon or full stop; and the few *kun* readings which are not independent words but exist only as parts of compound words have been put in brackets, thus: 相 (*ai*).

One further general point about readings remains to be mentioned. In 1948 an official list of ON and *kun* readings for the *tooyoo kanzi* was issued, but until that time a character had not been restricted to a definite, limited number of readings. Its *kun* readings, in particular, were often indeterminable and, conversely, the same Japanese word could be found used with several different characters of similar, but subtly different, meanings. The 1948 list recognizes comparatively few readings for each character, and those used in this book have been kept within much the same limits. In a word, the readings given are selective, not exhaustive.

(i) *ON readings*. In Chinese a character normally has only one reading in any particular dialect at any particular time, but the Japanese were taught the readings of characters by teachers who came from widely separated parts of the mainland and spanned many centuries of time. As a result, most of the characters used by the Japanese have collected two or three different ON readings each.

Sometimes one particular meaning of a character will be restricted to a particular ON reading. For example, the character 行, which has two common ON readings, KOO and GYOO, and several possible meanings, will always be read GYOO when used in the meaning of 'row, column'. In most cases, however, all the ON readings can cover all the various meanings of a character, the choice of which is used in a particular word having been determined by the origin and associations of the word.

(ii) Kun *readings*. A few Chinese characters can be regarded as having a single meaning which is adequately covered by one Japanese word; but since a *kun* is usually a 'translation' of only one of several different ideas represented by the same character, it is generally more limited in meaning than the ON. 行, for example, is read as the first part of the Japanese verb *i(ku)* when used to mean 'go'; and as the first part of the verb *okona(u)* when used to mean 'act, carry out'.

When the *kun* of a character is a Japanese noun not derived from a verb, the character alone will be read as the whole of the word. Thus

[3]

人 will be read as *hito* 'person'. But in other cases—adjectives, verbs and, usually, nouns derived from verbs—the character itself will account for only the first part (the base or stem) of the *kun* word, and the ending will be shown by adding the appropriate *kana*. *I(ku)*, for example, is written 行く and *okona(u)*行う. In the character lists preceding the lessons, as in the examples above, the part of a word which is written in *kana* has been shown by enclosing it in brackets.

Kana

The 47 basic syllables of the *kana* tables are usually arranged in what is known as the *gozyuuon* '50 sounds' order, three of the sounds being regarded as occurring twice each. This arrangement, shown in the tables below, consists of five vowels in the order *a, i, u, e, o* and then the same five vowels preceded in turn by nine consonants in the order *k, s, t, n, h, m, y, r, w*. 'Thickening marks' (*nigori*) in the form of two small strokes added to the *kana* for sounds beginning with *k, s, t*, and *h* represent 20 further syllables beginning with the voiced consonants *g, z, d*, and *b* respectively; and a semi-voicing sign (*han-nigori*) in the form of a small circle added to the *kana* for sounds beginning with *h* represents the same five vowel sounds preceded by the consonant *p*. There is also a separate sign for the consonant *n* alone, used to write the final *n* of a syllable, making a total of 48 different basic signs.

In addition to being used to write particles, adjective and verb endings etc., *kana* is sometimes given in small print beside Chinese characters to show how they are to be read. This *hurigana*, as it is called, has been shown on p. 66 against certain place and proper names.

There are two different sets of *kana* signs, one known as *hiragana* and the other as *katakana*. Both were derived from Chinese characters, *hiragana* (literally 'level, flat *kana*') being cursive forms of whole characters, and *katakana* (literally 'side *kana*') being small parts of characters. The Chinese character 加, which has the ON reading KA, for example, represents the sound *ka* in *hiragana* in the form か and in *katakana* in the form カ.

Hiragana. This is the kind of *kana* normally used in books, letters, newspapers, etc. In addition to the 48 basic signs, a number of variant forms used to be current, but these are now rarely used, and then only in handwriting.

Katakana. This is always used to write foreign words, including personal and place names. It is also found used at times to spell out the reading of a Chinese character which, for some reason, has not been used itself; to write words which are required to be distinctive or

[4]

emphatic; or to show that certain sounds within a word are not full syllables but form part of a diphthong (e.g. チョット *tyotto*), when they are often written smaller than the rest of the *kana*.

In all these cases *katakana* appears among what is mainly *hiragana*, but it is regularly used with Chinese characters in place of *hiragana* for official notices and proclamations, for orders and regulations in the Armed Services, and for private diaries and the like—in short, for formal, official writings or for the sake of clarity. (*Katakana* has been used to write certain texts in this book, however, not because it is appropriate to their subject-matter, but in order to give practice in reading this syllabary.)

In the writing of foreign words and names in Japanese the sound of the consonant *v* is represented either by adding *nigori* to the *katakana* sign for *u*, thus ヴ ; or by using the sign for the appropriate syllable beginning with *b* (*ba* for *va*, *bi* for *vi*, etc.).

Diphthongs. Instead of each *kana* sign being read as a full syllable, two or more may combine to form a diphthong when the first ends in the vowel -*i* and the second begins with a *y*-; for example, きよ may have to be read *kyo* and びや *bya* in some words, instead of *kiyo* and *biya.*

Long Vowels. In *katakana* a vowel can be lengthened by following any of the syllabic signs with a short vertical line (see 'Miscellaneous Signs' below); but in both types of *kana* all vowels can be lengthened by adding the *kana* for the vowel in question: *nee*, for example, is written ねえ *ne* + *e*. The *oo* sound, however, is usually written *o* + *u* (e.g. *soo* そう; *desyoo* でしよう), and is only written *o* + *o* in a few words in which the second *o* was traditionally written *ho* ほ (e.g. *ooi* 'numerous' (formerly written おほい) is now おおい, and *koori* 'ice' (こほり) is now こおり).

Double Consonants. In both *kana* writing and combinations of Chinese characters, within a word:

(i) a final *n* before a syllable with an initial *n* will always double the consonant, e.g. どんな *donna*;

(ii) *ku* or *ki* before a *k* may give a double consonant, e.g. (学) がく *gaku* + (校) こう *koo* = *gakkoo*;

(iii) *tu* before *k*, *s*, *t*, or *p* will usually double the consonant in question, e.g. はっきり *hakkiri*; and before an initial *h* it will sometimes give a double *p* sound, e.g. (出) しゆつ *syutu* + (発) はつ *hatu* = *syuppatu.*

Irregular *Kana*. The particles *wa*, *o*, and *e* are written with the *kana* signs for *ha* は (ハ), (*w*)*o* を (ヲ), and *he* へ (ヘ) respectively; and

INTRODUCTION

HIRAGANA

	A あ	I い	U う	E え	O お
K	ka か	ki き	ku く	ke け	ko こ
S	sa さ	si (shi) し	su す	se せ	so そ
T	ta た	ti (chi) ち	tu (tsu) つ	te て	ro と
N	na な	ni に	nu ぬ	ne ね	no の
H	ha は	hi ひ	hu (fu) ふ	he へ	ho ほ
M	ma ま	mi み	mu む	me め	mo も
Y	ya や		yu ゆ		yo よ
R	ra ら	ri り	ru る	re れ	ro ろ
W	wa わ	(w)i ゐ		(w)e ゑ	(w)o を
Final N	ん				
G	ga が	gi ぎ	gu ぐ	ge げ	go ご
Z	za ざ	zi (ji) じ	zu ず	ze ぜ	zo ぞ
D	da だ	zi (ji) ぢ	zu づ	de で	do ど
B	ba ば	bi び	bu ぶ	be べ	bo ぼ
P	pa ば	pi び	pu ぶ	pe ぺ	po ぽ

KATAKANA

	A ア	I イ	U ウ	E エ	O オ
K	ka カ	ki キ	ku ク	ke ケ	ko コ
S	sa サ	si (shi) シ	su ス	se セ	so ソ
T	ta タ	ti (chi) チ	tu (tsu) ツ	te テ	to ト
N	na ナ	ni ニ	nu ヌ	ne ネ	no ノ
H	ha ハ	hi ヒ	hu (fu) フ	he ヘ	ho ホ
M	ma マ	mi ミ	mu ム	me メ	mo モ
Y	ya ヤ		yu ユ		yo ヨ
R	ra ラ	ri リ	ru ル	re レ	ro ロ
W	wa ワ	(w)i ヰ		(w)e ヱ	(w)o ヲ

Final N ン		V ヴ	

G	ga ガ	gi ギ	gu グ	ge ゲ	go ゴ
Z	za ザ	zi (ji) ジ	zu ズ	ze ゼ	zo ゾ
D	da ダ	zi (ji) ヂ	zu ヅ	de デ	do ド
B	ba バ	bi ビ	bu ブ	be ベ	bo ボ
P	pa パ	pi ピ	pu プ	pe ペ	po ポ

the sounds zi and zu are written じ and ず (and not ち and づ) unless:

(i) the change from an unvoiced ti or tu is due to the formation of a compound word, e.g. *hana* 'nose', *ti* 'blood' > *hanazi* はなぢ 'nosebleed'; or

(ii) they are immediately preceded in the same word by ti or tu respectively, e.g. *tuzuku* つづく 'continue'.

Miscellaneous Signs

(1)　　(2)　　　(1) Shows the square brackets used with quotations
〕　　テ　　as inverted commas, and with the names of books
ヽ　　｜　　etc. which in English would normally be given in
ヽ　　ブ　　italics; and, inside the brackets, the signs for a comma
ヽ　　ル　　and a full stop.
ヽ　　　　　(2) The word *teeburu*, 'table', showing the line
ヽ　　　　which can be used in *katakana* for lengthening a
ヽ°　　　vowel.
⌐

Romanization

There are two main systems for romanizing Japanese, known as the *kunrei-siki* and Hepburn systems, and it is as well for students to be familiar with both. The former has been officially preferred in Japan, but is comparatively little used. It is, however, not without its advantages for teaching purposes, and it has been used in this book in the romanized transcriptions, notes and glossary, and under the signs in the *kana* tables. Where different, the Hepburn spellings for the sounds represented by the *kana* signs have also been given in the tables, in brackets; and since the Hepburn system has for long been familiar as the one in general use, it seemed appropriate to use it in the English translations.

TEXTS, TRANSCRIPTIONS,
AND
NOTES

一	1/0	**ITI,* ITU** hito(tu) one								
	イイ チツ	一								
二	7/0	**NI *** huta(tu) two								
	ニ	一	二							
三	1/2	**SAN *** mit(tu) three								
	サ ン	一	二	三						
四	3 1/2	**SI *** yot(tu) four								
	シ	丨	冂	冗	四	四				
五	1/3	**GO *** itu(tu) five								
	ゴ	一	丁	五	五					
六	8/2	**ROKU *** mut(tu) six								
	ロ ク	丶	亠	六	六					
七	5/1	**SITI *** nana(tu) seven								
	シ チ	一	七							
八	12/0	**HATI *** yat(tu) eight								
	ハ チ	ノ	八							
九	4/1	**KYUU, KU *** kokono(tu) nine								
	キュ ウ	ノ	九							
十	24/0	**ZYUU *** too ten								
	ジュ ウ	一	十							

一。あそこになにがありますか。

　　いすとテーブルがあります。

二。いすはいくつありますか。

　　四つあります。

三。テーブルはいくつありますか。

　　二つあります。

四。そこにフォークがいくつありますか。

　　六つあります。

五。ナイフも六つありますか。

　　ナイフは七つあります。

六。それはなんですか。

　　これはりんごです。

七。いくつありますか。

　　五つあります。

八。あれもりんごですか。

　　あれはオレンジです。

九。オレンジはいくつありますか。

　　十あります。

十。あれはだれのいぬですか。

　　わたしのいぬです。

十一。あなたのねこはどこにいますか。

　　ねこはここにいます。

LESSON 1

ITI

1. Asoko ni nani ga arimasu ka. Isu to teeburu ga arimasu. **2.** Isu wa ikutu arimasu ka. Yottu arimasu. **3.** Teeburu wa ikutu arimasu ka. Hutatu arimasu. **4.** Soko ni fooku (*literally* huooku) ga ikutu arimasu ka. Muttu arimasu. **5.** Naihu mo muttu arimasu ka. Naihu wa nanatu arimasu. **6.** Sore wa nan desu ka. Kore wa ringo desu. **7.** Ikutu arimasu ka. Itutu arimasu. **8.** Are mo ringo desu ka. Are wa orenzi desu. **9.** Orenzi wa ikutu arimasu ka. Too arimasu. **10.** Are wa dare no inu desu ka. Watasi no inu desu. **11.** Anata no neko wa doko ni imasu ka. Neko wa koko ni imasu.

Notes

1 **teeburu**: written in *katakana* because it is recognized to be a foreign word; cf. *fooku, naihu,* etc., below.

2 **ikutu**: general word for 'how many?', used when no other unit-word is appropriate.

6 **nan desu ka**: in combination with unit classifiers and *-yoobi,* 'day (of the week)', *nani* always takes the form *nan* (e.g. *nanbon,* etc.); and as an independent word it likewise becomes *nan* before a word beginning with *n, t,* or *d.*

11 **imasu**: used to refer to the position of something animate, just as *arimasu* is used of something inanimate. Note, however, that *arimasu* can be used with an animate subject when it is purely a matter of existence and not position, e.g. *Sonna ḷito ga arimasu ka,* 'Is there such a person?'

本	75/1	**HON** * book; main, origin; (unit for counting cylindrical objects)							
	ホン	一	十	才	木	本			
親	147/9	**SIN** intimacy; **oya** parent							
	シン	'	亠	立	立	亲	亲	新	親 親
友	29/2	**YUU** **tomo** companion							
	ユウ	一	ナ	方	友				
英	140/5	**EI** Britain, England							
	エイ	一	十	サ	艹	苎	苎	英 英	
国	31/8	**KOKU** **kuni** country, nation							
	コク	國	冂	冂	冋	囯	国	国 国	
人	9/0	**ZIN, NIN** **hito** person							
	ジン ニン	ノ	人						
日	72/0	**ZITU, NITI** **hi** day, sun; (-ka) day							
	ジニ ツチ	丨	冂	月	日				
田	102/0	**DEN** **ta** rice-field							
	デン	丨	冂	冂	用	田			
東	4/7	**TOO** **higasi** east							
	トウ	一	丆	峝	亩	吉	束	東 東	
京	8/6	**KYOO** capital city							
	キョウ	'	亠	亠	古	古	宁	京 京	

[13]

何	9/5	KA nani, nan what								
	カ	ノ	イ	仁	仁	伍	伍	何		
語	149/7	GO * word, language								
	ゴ	`	㇗	言	言	言	言	訂	訂	語	語
勉	4/9	BEN diligence								
	ベン	勉	ノ	ク	ク	台	台	免	免	免	勉
強	57/8	KYOO, GOO tuyo(i) strong								
	キョゴウウ	強	フ	コ	弓	弓	弘	弥	弹	強	強
旅	70/6	RYO tabi travelling								
	リョ	旅	`	㇗	方	方	方	扩	扩	旅	旅
行	144/0	KOO i(ku) vi go; -yuki bound for. GYOO * line, column								
	コギウウ	ノ	ノ	彳	彳	行	行			
帽	50/9	BOO hat								
	ホウ	l	冂	巾	巾	帕	帕	帽	帽	帽	帽
子	39/0	SI ko child. SI, SU (suffix)								
	シス	㇇	了	子						
鉛	167/5	EN lead (metal)								
	エン	鉛	ノ	㇏	卢	车	令	令	金	釒	鉛
筆	118/6	HITU hude writing-brush								
	ヒツ	ノ	ノ	ド	竹	竹	竺	竺	筆	筀	筆

[14]

二

一。ソレハアナタノ本デスカ。　ワタシノ親友ノ本デス。

二。アナタノ親友ハ英国人デスカ。　英国人デハアリマセン。日本人デス。

三。ダレデスカ。　本田サンデス。

四。本田サンハドコニイマスカ。　東京ニイマス。

五。東京デ何ヲシテイマスカ。　英語ヲ勉強シテイマス。

六。コレモ本田サンノ本デスカ。　ソレハ東サンノ本デス。

七。東サンモアナタノ親友デスカ。　アノ人ハ本田サンノ友ダチデス。

八。東京ニイマスカ。　東京ニハイマセン。英国ヘ旅行シテイマス。

[15]

九。 アソコニアル帽子ハダレノ帽子デスカ。 アレハワタシノ子ドモノ帽子デス。

十。 アナタハ帽子ヲカブリマスカ。 カブリマセン。

十一。 東サンニ子ドモガアリマスカ。 二人アリマス。

十二。 英国ヘ行ッテイマスカ。 一人ハ英国ヘ行ッテイマス。一人ハ日本ニイマス。

十三。 ソコニ鉛筆ガアリマスカ。 鉛筆ハアリマセン。

十四。 筆ガアリマスカ。 筆ハアリマス。

十五。 何本アリマスカ。 三本アリマス。一本ハワタシノ筆デス。二本ハワタシノ子ドモノ筆デス。

十六。 イイ筆デスカ。 ワタシノ筆ハイイデス。子ドモノ筆ハヨクアリマセン。

NI

1. Sore wa anata no hon desu ka. Watasi no sinyuu no hon desu.
2. Anata no sinyuu wa Eikokuzin desu ka. Eikokuzin de wa arimasen.
Nihonzin desu. 3. Dare desu ka. Honda-san desu. 4. Honda-san wa
doko ni imasu ka. Tookyoo ni imasu. 5. Tookyoo de nani o site
imasu ka. Eigo o benkyoo site imasu. 6. Kore mo Honda-san no hon
desu ka. Sore wa Higasi-san no hon desu. 7. Higasi-san mo anata no
sinyuu desu ka. Ano hito wa Honda-san no tomodati desu. 8. Tookyoo ni imasu ka. Tookyoo ni wa imasen. Eikoku e ryokoo site imasu.
9. Asoko ni aru boosi wa dare no boosi desu ka. Are wa watasi no
kodomo no boosi desu. 10. Anata wa boosi o kaburimasu ka. Kaburi-
masen. 11. Higasi-san ni kodomo ga arimasu ka. Hutari arimasu.
12. Eikoku e itte imasu ka. Hitori wa Eikoku e itte imasu. Hitori
wa Nihon ni imasu. 13. Soko ni enpitu ga arimasu ka. Enpitu wa
arimasen. 14. Hude ga arimasu ka. Hude wa arimasu. 15. Nanbon
arimasu ka. Sanbon arimasu. Ippon wa watasi no hude desu. Nihon
wa watasi no kodomo no hude desu. 16. Ii hude desu ka. Watasi no
hude wa ii desu. Kodomo no hude wa yoku arimasen.

Notes

2 **de wa arimasen**: the negative form of *desu*, this itself being a contraction of *de arimasu*. (The plain form *da* has the negative *de (wa) nai*.)

3 **Honda**: a family name, unusual in being a combination of ON and *kun* readings. Japanese names are often difficult—sometimes impossible—to read with certainty, but in general one can expect family names to be read in the *kun*.

5 **Tookyoo de**: *de*, with the meaning 'in', used with a verb of action.

6 **Higasi**: when found as a family name, the character in question may also be read *Azuma*, but, since this is otherwise a very rare reading, the usual reading of *higasi* has been preferred here.

10 **kaburimasu ka**: this form indicates a general question, 'do you wear?'; cf. *kabutte imasu ka* 'are (you) wearing?'

11 **Higasi-san ni ... arimasu**: a standard way of saying 'A has B' is *A ni (wa) B ga arimasu*, 'to A there exists B'.

12 **itte imasu**: since *iku* is a verb of motion, the meaning of this *-te iru* form is not 'is going' but 'is having gone; has gone'.

14 **Hude wa**: *hude* having been mentioned already, *wa* would in any case have been used in its 'echoing' function, as it was in No. 13 above; but, in the context, it has a strong 'isolating' or 'contrasting' force: 'as far as *brushes* are con-cerned (as distinct from pencils), they exist'.

15 **Nanbon**: a combination of the interrogative *nan* (see n. to Lesson 1, No. 6 above) and *hon*, the unit for cylindrical objects.

16 **yoku**: adverbial form from *ii* (or *yoi*), used because the verb is in the negative.

中	2/3	**TYUU** **naka** middle, inside
	チュウ	丶 一 口 中
外	36/2	**GAI** **soto** outside; **hoka** apart (from), other (than)
	カイ	ノ ク タ 夘 外
新	69/9	**SIN** **atara(sii)** new
	シン	丶 亠 立 立 辛 亲 亲 新 新 新
聞	169/6	**BUN** **ki(ku)** *vt* hear, ask; **ki(koeru)** *vi* be audible
	ブン	丨 冂 阝 阝 門 門 門 門 聞 聞
読	149/7	**DOKU** **yo(mu)** *vt* read
	ドク 讀	亠 宀 宀 言 言 計 計 詰 読 読
者	125/4	**SYA** **mono** person
	シャ 者	一 十 土 耂 者 者 者 者
雑	172/6	**ZATU** miscellaneous
	ザツ 雑	九 杂 杂 新 新 新 新 雑 雑 雑
誌	149/7	**SI** (written) record
	シ	亠 言 言 言 計 計 詰 誌 誌 誌
度	53/6	**DO** * degree; **tabi** (number of) times
	ド	丶 亠 广 广 庐 庐 庐 度 度
委	115/3	**I** delegate
	イ	ノ 二 千 禾 禾 秀 秀 委

員	30/7	**IN** personnel									
	イ ン		丶	冖	口	尸	肙	鳥	冒	員	員

会	9/4	**KAI** * society, meeting; **a(u)** *vi* meet						
	カ イ	會	丿	人	스	今	会	

書	129/4	**SYO** **ka(ku)** *vt* write									
	シ ョ		¬	⇁	ヨ	聿	言	聿	書	書	書

類	181/9	**RUI** sort								
	ル イ	類	丶	丷	米	米	米	类	类	類	類

時	72/6	**ZI** **toki** time								
	ジ		丨	冂	日	日	旷	旷	旪	時	時

午	4/3	**GO** noon			
	ゴ		丿	乍	仁	午

前	12/7	**ZEN** **mae** before								
	ゼ ン		丶	丷	丷	产	产	前	肖	前	前

長	168/0	**TYOO** chief, head; **naga(i)** long							
	チョ ウ		丨	厂	F	F	上	토	長	長

放	70/4	**HOO** **hana(su)** *vt* release						
	ホ ウ		丶	亠	方	方	方	扩	放

送	162/6	**SOO** **oku(ru)** *vt* send							
	ソ ウ	送	丶	丷	丷	关	羊	关	送	送

学	39/5	**GAKU** * learning								
	カ ク / 學	丶	゛	'''	'''	兴	学	学	学	
校	75/6	**KOO** school								
	コ ウ	一	十	才	木	朾	朾	朾	栌	校
先	10/4	**SEN saki** tip, (pointed) end; prior (time)								
	セ ン	ノ	丄	生	生	牛	先			
生	100/0	**SEI, SYOO** life; **i(kiru)** *vi* be alive; **u(mu)** *vt* bear; **uma(reru)** *vi* be born								
	セイ ショウ	ノ	丄	牛	牛	生				
駅	187/4	**EKI** * (railway) station								
	エ キ / 驛	l	「	冂	厈	馬	馬	馬	馿	駅
自	132/0	**ZI, SI** self, natural								
	ジ シ	ノ	イ	冂	白	自	自			
動	19/9	**DOO** **ugo(ku)** *vi*, **ugo(kasu)** *vt* move								
	ド ウ	ノ	厶	午	台	台	育	重	重	動
車	159/0	**SYA kuruma** vehicle, car								
	シ ャ	一	厂	百	百	百	亘	車		
売	32/4	**BAI** **u(ru)** *vt* sell								
	バ イ / 賣	一	十	士	十	壴	声	売		
買	122/7	**BAI** **ka(u)** *vt* buy								
	バ イ	丶	冖	冊	罒	罒	罒	買	買	買

[20]

三

一。あなたは「中外新聞」の読者ですか。読者ではありません。

二。ここにある新聞か雑誌のどれかを読みますか。さあ、どれも読みません。その本は一度読みました。

三。どの本ですか。この本ですか。え、それです。

四。「外国語の本を読みますか。いえ、読みません。あなたは読みますか。

五。わたしは英語の本と雑誌を読みます。新聞は読みませんか。

六。読みません。あれはあなたのかばんですか。どれですか。

七。かばんの中に何がありますか。え、あれはわたしのかばんです。あれですか。え、あれはわたしのかばんです。

八。委員会は何時にありますか。委員会の書類があります。午前十一時にあります。

[21]

九。委員会の会長はだれですか。中田さんです。あなたはあの人の放送を聞きましたか。

十。聞きませんでした。あの人は何ですか。学校の先生です。

十一。東京駅へ行くつもりです。あなたはどこかへ行くつもりですか。旅行ですか。

十二。いえ、友だちに会うつもりです。その人は駅の中でまっていますか。

十三。駅の前でまっています。その人は何をしていますか。

十四。自動車などの売買をしています。あなたは新しい自動車を買うつもりですか。

十五。いえ、自動車を売るつもりです。あなたはその雑誌をだれかに送るつもりですか。外国にいる友だちに送るつもりです。

LESSON 3

SAN

1. ANATA wa *Tyuugai Sinbun* no dokusya desu ka. Dokusya de wa arimasen. 2. Koko ni aru sinbun ka zassi no doreka o yomimasu ka. Saa, doremo yomimasen. Sono hon wa itido yomimasita. 3. Dono hon desu ka. Kono hon desu ka. E, sore desu. 4. Gaikokugo no hon o yomimasu ka. Ie, yomimasen. Anata wa yomimasu ka. 5. Watasi wa Eigo no hon to zassi o yomimasu. Sinbun wa yomimasen ka. 6. Yomimasen. Are wa anata no kaban desu ka. Dore desu ka. Are desu ka. E, are wa watasi no kaban desu. 7. Kaban no naka ni nani ga arimasu ka. Iinkai no syorui ga arimasu. 8. Iinkai wa nanzi ni arimasu ka. Gozen zyuuitizi ni arimasu. 9. Iinkai no kaityoo wa dare desu ka. Nakata-san desu. Anata wa ano hito no hoosoo o kikimasita ka. 10. Kikimasen desita. Ano hito wa nan desu ka. Gakkoo no sensei desu. Hon mo kakimasu. Anata wa dokoka e iku tumori desu ka. 11. Tookyoo-eki e iku tumori desu. Ryokoo desu ka. 12. Ie, tomodati ni au tumori desu. Sono hito wa eki no naka de matte imasu ka. 13. Eki no mae de matte imasu. Sono hito wa nani o site imasu ka. 14. Zidoosya nado no baibai o site imasu. Anata wa atarasii zidoosya o kau tumori desu ka. 15. Ie, zidoosya o uru tumori desu. Anata wa sono zassi o dareka ni okuru tumori desu ka. Gaikoku ni iru tomodati ni okuru tumori desu.

Notes

1 **Tyuugai Sinbun**: fictitious name for a newspaper. *Tyuugai* means 'internal and external', hence 'home and foreign'.

2 **Koko ni aru**: an attributive phrase qualifying both *sinbun* and *zassi*. *Ka* between nouns means 'or'.

   doreka: *dore* alone means 'which (of more than two)?', and the addition of *ka* makes it equivalent to 'any(one)'. The last part of the sentence could be translated literally as 'Which perhaps do you read?', i.e. 'Do you read any?' Cf. *dotira* 'which (of two)?', and *dotiraka* 'either, one or the other'.

   doremo: with a negative verb means 'not . . . any'.

5 **Eigo no**: qualifies both *hon* and *zassi*.

   Sinbun wa: the strongly 'isolating' function of *wa* here serves to contrast *sinbun* with the previously mentioned *hon to zassi* (see n. to Lesson 2, No. 14). This sentence clearly shows that, unlike *ga*, which always indicates the grammatical subject of a sentence, *wa* marks off whatever the speaker has uppermost in his mind and intends to refer to in the rest of the sentence; *wa* can therefore follow many different parts of speech.

10 **tumori**: means 'intention', but since it is used more lightly in Japanese, an unobtrusive translation such as 'going to (do)' is often preferable.

12 **Sono hito**: when there is no reference to physical position (*sono* 'that [there by you]'), the use of *sono* implies that the speaker is unfamiliar with the particular person or occasion (e.g. *sono toki*). *Ano* in similar phrases implies the opposite and is sometimes used, as in No. 10 above, because the person referred to is something of a public figure.

   eki no naka de: *de* 'in, at', is used because *matu* is regarded as a verb of action.

[23]

高	189/0	**KOO** taka(i) high, dear	コウ ＇ 亠 六 亠 古 占 高 高 高 高
野	166/4	**YA** no moor(land)	ヤ ＇ 口 日 甲 里 里 野 野 野
山	46/0	**SAN** yama mountain	サン 丨 山 山
来	4/6	**RAI** ku(ru) *vi* come	ライ 來 一 丆 丂 立 平 来 来
週	162/8	**SYUU** * week	シュウ 週 丨 冂 冃 用 用 周 周 週 週
木	75/0	**MOKU** ki tree	モク 一 十 才 木
曜	72/14	**YOO** day of week	ヨウ 曜 日 日 日 日 日 日 日 日 曜
小	42/0	**SYOO** tii(sai) small	ショウ 丨 小 小
説	149/7	**SETU** * opinion, theory; explanation	セツ ＇ 亠 言 言 言 訁 訁 討 詥 説
領	181/5	**RYOO** jurisdiction	リョウ 領 丿 八 今 今 令 令 令 訇 領 領

[24]

事	6/7	**ZI koto** matter, affair								
	ジ	一	一	一	三	三	写	写	事	
父	88/0	**HU titi** father								
	フ	′	ハ	少	父					
母	80/0	**BO haha** mother								
	ボ	く	勾	勾	毋	母				
月	74/0	**GETU** (space of) month; **GATU** month (of year); **tuki** moon, month								
	ゲカ ッツ	ノ	刀	月	月					
承	4/6	**SYOO** assent								
	ショ ウ	フ	了	孑	手	手	承	承	承	
知	111/3	**TI si(ru)** *vt* know								
	チ	ノ	ト	上	矢	矢	知	知	知	
助	19/5	**ZYO tasu(karu)** *vi* be helped, saved; **tasu(keru)** *vt* help, save								
	ジョ	l	冂	月	月	且	助	助		
手	64/0	**SYU te** hand								
	シュ	′	ニ	三	手					
火	86/0	**KA hi** fire								
	カ	、	′	火	火					
水	85/0	**SUI mizu** water								
	スイ	l	기	水	水					

B

都	163/8 トッ 都	**TO** miyako capital city. **TU** all	一	土	尹	才	未	者	者	者ヿ	者阝	都
見	147/0 ケン	**KEN** mi(ru) *vt* see	丨	冂	月	月	目	見	見			
物	93/4 ブ モ ツ ツ	**BUTU, MOTU** mono thing	ノ	ヒ	牛	牛	牜	物	物	物		
住	9/5 ジュウ	**ZYUU** su(mu) *vi* reside	ノ	亻	亻'	仁	什	住	住			
所	63/4 ショ	**SYO** tokoro place	一	㇗	㇗	戸	戸	所	所	所		
残	78/6 ザン 残	**ZAN** noko(ru) *vi* remain; noko(su) *vt* leave behind	一	厂	㇗	㇗	㇗	㇗	歹三	残	残	残
念	9/6 ネン	**NEN** idea, wish	ノ	人	人	今	今	念	念	念		
家	40/7 カケ	**KA, KE** ie, uti, [ya] house, family. **KA** -er, -ist	'	'	宀	宀	宀	㝹	家	家	家	
有	130/2 ユ ウ	**YUU** a(ru) *vi* have, be	ノ	ナ	才	有	有	有				
名	36/3 メミィョウ	**MEI, MYOO** na name	ノ	ク	夕	夕	名	名				

商	8/9	**SYOO** trade									
	ショウ	丶	亠	六	亢	产	产	产	商	商	商
店	53/5	**TEN** mise shop									
	テン	丶	亠	广	广	庐	庐	店	店		
写	14/3	**SYA** utu(su) *vt* copy									
	シャ 寫	丶	冖	写	写	写					
真	24/8	**SIN** truth; **ma-** (emphatic prefix)									
	シン 眞	一	十	市	古	卢	直	直	真	真	
機	75/12	**KI** machine									
	キ	木	杉	杉	棷	槻	椣	機	機	機	
輸	159/9	**YU** transport									
	ユ 輸	一	車	車	軒	軩	軩	輪	輪	輸	
入	11/0	**NYUU** hai(ru), i(ru) *vi* enter; i(reru) *vt* put in									
	ニュウ	ノ	入								
出	2/4	**SYUTU** de(ru) *vi* go (come) out; da(su) *vt* take (send, put) out									
	シツ	丨	屮	屮	出	出					
大	37/0	**DAI, TAI** oo(kii), oo- big									
	ダイ タイ	一	ナ	大							
変	8/7	**HEN** * strange; kawa(ru) *vi* ka(eru) *vt* change									
	ヘン 變	丶	亠	亣	亦	亦	亦	亦	夳	変	

四

一。アナタが高野山ヘ行クノハイツデスカ。　来週ノ木曜日デス。

二。ナゼ高野山ヘ行クンデスカ。　アソコデ小説ヲ書イテイル友ダチニ会ウツモリナンデス。「前田領事ノ父母」ヲ書イタ人デス。

ワタシハ先月行クツモリデシタ。

三。ドウシテ行カナカッタンデスカ。　父が承知シナカッタンデス。

四。オ母サンハ承知シタンデスカ。　母ハ承知シマシタ。

五。ワタシノ助手ハ来週ノ火曜日カ水曜日ニ京都ヘ行キマス。

見物デスカ。

六。イイエ。アノ人ハ京都カラ来テイマス。京都ニハオ父サンがイマス。　ソウデスカ。アナタハ住所ヲ知ッテイマスカ。

七。知リマセン。 ソレハ残念デス。ワタシモ京都ヘ行クカモ知
レナインデス。アナタハ京都ヘ行ッタ事ガアリマスカ。

八。アリマス。アナタノ友ダチノ小説家ハダレデスカ。
ンデス。有名ナ三木商店ノ三木サンノ親類デス。

三木サ

九。三木商店ハ何ヲ売ッテイルンデスカ。 写真機デス。

十。外国ヘモ売ッテイマスカ。 輸入モ輸出モシテイマス。コレ
ガ三木サンノ店ノ写真デス。

十一。ドレガ三木サンデスカ。 帽子ヲカブッテイル小サイ人デ
ス。

十二。アノ人ハ英語ガ大変ヨク出来マス。 エ、ヨク
アナタハ三木サンヲヨク知ッテイルンデスカ。
知ッテイマス。

十三。三木サンハドコニ住ンデイマスカ。 中野ニアル新シイ家
知ッテイマス。タビタビ店ヘ行ッテ三木サンノ手ツダイヲシマス。

[29]

ニ住ンデイマス。

十四。　アナタハ三木サンノ家ノ中ヘ入ッタ事ガアリマスカ。　モ
チロンアリマス。　大キナ家デス。　ココニ三木サンノ家ノ写真ガア
リマス。

十五。　コノ変ナ物ハ何デスカ。　　ソレハ手デス。　ダレカガ写真機
ノ前ヘ手ヲ出シタノデス。　ココニモ写真ガアリマス。　高イ木ノカ
ゲデ三木サンガ月ヲ見テイルンデス。

十六。　コレハ何デスカ。　　山ノ中ニアル小サイ家デス。

十七。　コレハサカナデスカ。　　エ、ソウデス。水ノ中ノサカナデ
ス。

十八。　ソレハ何ノ写真デスカ。　　コレハワタシガ生レタ家ノ写真
デス。

LESSON 4

SI

1. Anata ga Kooya-san e iku no wa itu desu ka. Raisyuu no mokuyoo-bi desu. **2.** Naze Kooya-san e ikun' desu ka. Asoko de syoosetu o kaite iru tomodati ni au tumori nan' desu. *Maeda Ryoozi no Hubo* o kaita hito desu. Watasi wa sengetu iku tumori desita. **3.** Doosite ikanakattan' desu ka. Titi ga syooti sinakattan' desu. **4.** Okaasan wa syooti sitan' desu ka. Haha wa syooti simasita. **5.** Watasi no zyosyu wa raisyuu no kayoo-bi ka suiyoo-bi ni Kyooto e ikimasu. Kenbutu desu ka. **6.** Iie, ano hito wa Kyooto kara kite imasu. Kyooto ni wa otoosan ga imasu. Soo desu ka. Anata wa zyuusyo o sitte imasu ka. **7.** Sirimasen. Sore wa zannen desu. Watasi mo Kyooto e iku ka mo sirenain' desu. Anata wa Kyooto e itta koto ga arimasu ka. **8.** Arimasu. Anata no tomodati no syoosetuka wa dare desu ka. Miki-san desu. Yuumei na Miki syooten no Miki-san no sinrui desu. **9.** Miki syooten wa nani o utte irun' desu ka. Syasinki desu. **10.** Gaikoku e mo utte imasu ka. Yunyuu mo yusyutu mo site imasu. Kore ga Miki-san no mise no syasin desu. **11.** Dore ga Miki-san desu ka. Boosi o kabutte iru tiisai hito desu. Ano hito wa Eigo ga taihen yoku dekimasu. **12.** Anata wa Miki-san o yoku sitte irun' desu ka. E, yoku sitte imasu. Tabitabi mise e itte Miki-san no tetudai o simasu. **13.** Miki-san wa doko ni sunde imasu ka. Nakano ni aru atarasii ie ni sunde imasu. **14.** Anata wa Miki-san no ie no naka e haitta koto ga arimasu ka. Motiron arimasu. Ooki na ie desu. Koko ni Miki-san no ie no syasin ga arimasu. **15.** Kono hen na mono wa nan desu ka. Sore wa te desu. Dareka ga syasinki no mae e te o dasita no desu. Koko ni mo syasin ga arimasu. Takai ki no kage de Miki-san ga tuki o mite irun' desu. **16.** Kore wa nan desu ka. Yama no naka ni aru tiisai ie desu. **17.** Kore wa sakana desu ka. E, soo desu. Mizu no naka no sakana desu. **18.** Sore wa nan no syasin desu ka. Kore wa watasi ga umareta ie no syasin desu.

Notes

1 **Kooya-san:** a mountain in Wakayama Prefecture, famous for its many Buddhist temples and monasteries. (The more usual reading of the first two characters, as in family and other place names, is *Takano*.)

iku no wa itu desu ka: literally 'the going is when?' This common construction consists of a verbal noun (*iku no* 'the going') used with *wa*, or occasionally *ga*, and any appropriate complement (e.g. *naze desu ka*; *zannen desu*); and it can be used when there is no doubt in the speaker's mind that the action of the verb is going to take place. The sentence in question is thus virtually the same in meaning as *Itu iku no desu ka*, 'When is it that (you) go?' Cf. the first sentence of No. 2 below.

2 ikun' desu ka: a colloquial contraction of *iku no desu ka*.

au tumori nan' desu: a contraction of ... *na no desu*. *Na* is invariably used to replace the verb *da* (plain form of *desu*) before *no desu*, etc., just as it is before the conjunctions *no de* and *no ni*. The *no desu* construction has an explanatory force when used in answer to a question, and the whole phrase could therefore be rendered literally as 'It is that (-*n' desu*) it is the intention ...'

Maeda: family name. Note that, in Japanese, descriptive titles and ranks such as *ryoozi* follow the name of the person to whom they apply.

4 Okaasan: the first speaker uses the polite word for the mother of the other person; but he, speaking of her to someone outside the family, uses the plain word *haha*. Note the emphatic 'isolating' force of *wa* in both sentences.

6 kite imasu: *kuru* being a verb of motion, the meaning of the *-te iru* form here is 'is having come; is (from)'.

7 ka mo siremasen: expresses an idea of possibility like the English 'may (do, go, etc.)', since it means literally 'There is no knowing even whether ...' The construction is preceded by the plain forms of verbs and adjectives, but when the verb is *da* it is usually omitted, *e.g. Kyooto ka mo siremasen*, 'It may be Kyoto.'

itta koto ga arimasu ka: literally 'Does (your) having gone exist?'; this is the standard way of saying in Japanese, 'Have you ever (gone etc.)?' Note that the reply in Japanese is normally just some form of *aru*.

8 Anata no tomodati no syoosetuka: note the two different uses of *no* here, the first possessive ('of you; your'), and the other descriptive ('the novelist *who is* a friend').

10 ... mo ... mo: means 'both ... and ...' with a positive verb (and, hence, 'neither ... nor ...' with a negative).

11 Eigo ga ... dekimasu: *dekiru* is an intransitive verb in Japanese, but it can conveniently be thought of as meaning 'accomplish; achieve' both in the sense of 'finish; complete' and also, as here, 'manage (to do); succeed in ...'

12 itte: like the English '-ing' form, the *-te* form in Japanese has a connection with the following main verb which may range from the very weak, as here (little more than 'go ... and [help]'), to the causal, *e.g. Tenki ga yokute sanpo simasita*, 'The weather being good, I went for a walk.'

15 no desu: note its explanatory force (see n. to No. 2, *au tumori nan' desu*, above).

18 watasi ga umareta ie: the first three words being a clause qualifying the noun *ie*, the meaning is 'the house where I was born'. In such attributive clauses the subject of the verb is often followed by *no* instead of *ga*, with no change in meaning. *Watasi no umareta ie*, for example, is an alternative here.

金	167/0	**KIN** * gold; **kane** money, metal									
	キン	ノ	人	人	今	全	全	余	金		
銀	167/6	**GIN** * silver									
	ギン	ᄼ	ᄐ	全	金	釒ᄀ	釒ᄀ	釒ᄏ	鈤	銀	銀
文	67/0	**BUN** *, **MON** writing, literature									
	ブモンン	'	亠	宀	文						
部	163/8	**BU** * part, section									
	ブ	'	亠	立	立	立	产	音	咅ᄀ	�ᄀ	部
省	4/8	**SYOO** (government) Ministry									
	ショウ	ノ	小	小	少	少	省	省	省	省	
後	60/6	**GO** * **noti** after; **usi(ro)** rear, behind									
	ゴ	'	ᄼ	彳	彳	袳	袳	後	後	後	
公	12/2	**KOO** public									
	コウ	ノ	八	公	公						
園	31/10	**EN** park									
	エン	丨	冂	冂	国	冑	閨	園	園	園	園
土	32/0	**TO**, **DO** **tuti** earth, soil									
	トド	一	十	土							
市	8/3	**SI** * city									
	シ	'	亠	宀	宁	市					

[33]

役	60/4	**YAKU *** (official) post, use, role; government service
	ヤク	′　彡　彳　彳′　彳⁁　役　役
兄	30/2	**KEI, KYOO ani** elder brother
	ケ キョ イ ウ	丶　ロ　口　尸　兄
弟	12/5	**TEI, DAI otooto** younger brother
	テ ダ イ イ	丶　ゝ　ㅛ　芭　兰　弟　弟
電	173/5	**DEN** electricity
	デ ン	一　⼧　⼾　帀　帀　雨　雷　雷　電
話	149/6	**WA hana(su)** *vt* speak
	ワ	亠　宀　言　言　言　言　訁′　訁′　訐　話
合	9/4	**GOO a(u)** *vi* agree with, fit; **a(waseru)** *vt* join, combine
	ゴ ウ	ノ　人　今　今　合　合
朝	130/8	**TYOO** Imperial court; **asa** morning
	チョ ウ	一　十　十　古　卓　車　朝　朝　朝　朝
論	149/8	**RON *** discussion, thesis
	ロ ン	亠　言　訁　訡　訡　訡　諭　諭　論
編	120/9	**HEN** compile; **a(mu)** *vt* knit
	ヘ ン	′　幺　幺　糸　糸　系　糸′　紵　紵　編
集	172/4	**SYUU atu(maru)** *vi*, **atu(meru)** *vt* gather
	シ ウ	′　亻　亻′　什　什　件　伴　隹　隹　集

姉	38/5	**SI** **ane** elder sister
シ	く	く	女	女	女	如	姉	姉
妹	38/5	**MAI** **imooto** younger sister
マ イ	く	く	女	女	妒	奸	妹	妹
船	137/5	**SEN** **hune** ship
セ ン	′	ſ	ń	ń	舟	舟	舟	船	船	船
余	9/5	**YO** **ama(ri)** excessively, too
ヨ	ノ	八	人	今	余	弁	余
計	149/2	**KEI** -meter; **haka(ru)** vt measure, plan
ケ イ	'	二	亠	言	言	言	言	計
考	125/2	**KOO** **kanga(eru)** vt consider
コ ウ	一	十	土	耂	耂	考
古	24/3	**KO** **huru(i)** old
コ	一	十	古	古	古
非	175/0	**HI** not
ヒ	ノ	ナ	ヲ	ヲ	킈	非	非	非
常	42/8	**ZYOO** usual
ジョ ウ	'	''	'''	尚	尚	学	常	常	常
表	2/7	**HYOO** * list; reveal; **omote** surface, front
ヒョ ウ	一	十	丰	主	丰	表	表	表

紙	120/4	**SI** **kami** paper								
	シ	㇉	纟	幺	纟	纟	糸	糺	紅	紙	紙
今	9/2	**KON** the present, this; **ima** now								
	コ ン	ノ	人	亽	今						
晩	72/8	**BAN** * evening, night								
	バ ン	冂	日	日′	日″	日‴	昕	晰	晼	晩	晩
映	72/5	**EI** shine, reflect								
	エ イ	㇑	冂	冃	日	日	旷	肌	映	映	
画	1/7	**GA** picture. **KAKU** plan								
	カ ク 畫	一	𠃍	冂	襾	襾	甴	画	画		
館	184/8	**KAN** building								
	カ ン	ノ	今	亽	飠	食	食	飣	飵	飿	館
間	169/4	**KAN** aida interval, space, among; **ma** interval, space, room								
	カ ン	丨	ㄏ	阝	門	門	門	門	門	間	
整	77/12	**SEI** regulate								
	セ イ	一	弓	束	束	敕	敕	敕	整	整	
理	96/7	**RI** principle, reason								
	リ	一	丁	王	玗	玾	玾	玾	理	理	
方	70/0	**HOO** * direction; region; **kata** person (hon.)								
	ホ ウ	`	亠	方	方						

五

一。金曜日には何をしましたか。

午後は公園と動物園へ行きました。

午前は銀行と文部省へ行って

二。市役所へはいつ行きましたか。

土曜日に行って田山さん兄

弟に会いました。電話で都合を聞いてから行ったのです。

三。市長の田山さんは兄さんですか。

いえ、兄さんの田山さん

は「朝野新論」を編集しています。

四。「朝野新論」は雑誌ですか。

そうです。あの人は小説も書き

ます。あなたはあの人の「姉妹船」を読みましたか。

五。その小説は聞いた事もありません。わたしは読んだ事があ

りませんが、兄は大変ほめています。

六。余計な事ですが、あの変な物は何ですか。

さあ、何だかわ

たしは知りません。わたしの兄の子の物なんです。考古学を勉強していて、ときどき変な古い物を買うんです。その本はあなたのですか。

七。これですか。これは姉のです。

姉さんのですか。見てもいいですか。

八。もちろんいいです。

これは非常にめずらしい本です。表紙はありませんが中の紙は大変きれいです。あなたはいつか読むつもりですか。

九。え、日曜日の朝に読むつもりです。わたしはよく古本を買いますが、この本は店で見た事がありません。姉さんはこれを売るつもりでしょうか。

十。さあ、知りません。わたしが買ってもいいです。

十一。姉に話しましょう。あなたは今晩外へ出かけますか。

十二。いえ、出かけません。映画館へ行きましょうか。

十三。行ってもいいですが。時間がありませんか。

十四。今晩は書類を整理するつもりだったんです。長くかかり

ますか。

十五。余り長くはかからないでしょう。午後電話をかけましょ

うか。

十六。その方がいいです。わたしは行かなくてもいいんです。

十七。いいえ、行きましょう。映画は何時にはじまりますか。

八時にはじまります。あなたはうちを七時に出ても間に合うでし

よう。

十八。どこで会いましょうか。映画館の前がいいでしょう。

[39]

GO

1. Kɪɴʏᴏᴏ-ʙɪ ni wa nani o simasita ka. Gozen wa ginkoo to monbu-syoo e itte, gogo wa kooen to doobutuen e ikimasita. **2.** Siyakusyo e wa itu ikimasita ka. Doyoo-bi ni itte Tayama-san kyoodai ni aimasita. Denwa de tugoo o kiite kara itta no desu. **3.** Sityoo no Tayama-san wa niisan desu ka. Ie, niisan no Tayama-san wa *Tyooya Sinron* o hensyuu site imasu. **4.** *Tyooya Sinron* wa zassi desu ka. Soo desu. Ano hito wa syoosetu mo kakimasu. Anata wa ano hito no *Simaisen* o yomimasita ka. **5.** Sono syoosetu wa kiita koto mo arimasen. Watasi wa yonda koto ga arimasen ga, ani wa taihen homete imasu. **6.** Yokei na koto desu ga, ano hen na mono wa nan desu ka. Saa, nan da ka watasi wa sirimasen. Watasi no ani no ko no mono nan' desu. Kookogaku o benkyoo site ite, tokidoki hen na hurui mono o kaun' desu. Sono hon wa anata no desu ka. **7.** Kore desu ka. Kore wa ane no desu. Neesan no desu ka. Mite mo ii desu ka. **8.** Motiron ii desu. Kore wa hizyoo ni mezurasii hon desu. Hyoosi wa arimasen ga naka no kami wa taihen kirei desu. Anata wa ituka yomu tumori desu ka. **9.** E, nitiyoo-bi no asa ni yomu tumori desu. Watasi wa yoku huru-hon o kaimasu ga, kono hon wa mise de mita koto ga arimasen. Neesan wa kore o uru tumori desyoo ka. **10.** Saa, sirimasen. Watasi ga katte mo ii desu. **11.** Ane ni hanasimasyoo. Anata wa konban soto e dekakemasu ka. **12.** Ie, dekakemasen. Eigakan e ikimasyoo ka. **13.** Itte mo ii desu ga. Zikan ga arimasen ka. **14.** Konban wa syorui o seiri suru tumori dattan' desu. Nagaku kakarimasu ka. **15.** Amari nagaku wa kakaranai desyoo. Gogo denwa o kakemasyoo ka. **16.** Sono hoo ga ii desu. Watasi wa ikanakute mo iin' desu. **17.** Iie, ikimasyoo. Eiga wa nanzi ni hazimarimasu ka. Hatizi ni hazimarimasu. Anata wa uti o sitizi ni dete mo ma ni au desyoo ka. **18.** Doko de aimasyoo ka. Eigakan no mae ga ii desyoo.

Notes

2 Siyakusyo e wa: on this use of *wa*, see n. to Lesson 3, No. 5.

denwa de: 'by phone', this being the 'instrumental' use of *de*.

tugoo o kiite kara: *tugoo* means 'circumstances; convenience', usually in the sense of one's situation in regard to other arrangements or commitments. The *-te kara* construction means 'after ——ing' and must be distinguished from (*kii*)*ta kara*, '(ask)ed and so'.

3 niisan: polite form of *ani*, used here of a third person who is not present to show respect to him.

4 **Tyooya Sinron**: *New National Review*, a fictitious name for a periodical. The first two characters are read *Asano* as a family name etc., but read *tyooya* they mean 'the Court and the wilds', i.e. 'the capital and the country; the whole nation'.

5 **mo**: used here with a negative form of the usual (*kiita*) *koto ga aru* construction, it can be translated as '(have never) even'.

homete imasu: the *-te iru* construction is used here to convey much the same idea of constant or habitual action as the English present form 'praises it'. In No. 6 below, however, *benkyoo site ite* clearly indicates continuing action.

6 **Yokei na koto**: is 'something superfluous, uncalled-for', and the clause expresses the idea that 'This is nothing to do with what we were talking about, but . . .'

7 **Neesan**: the brother has used the plain word *ane* of his own sister, but the other person, not a member of the family, refers to her with respect as *neesan*; cf. n. to Lesson 4, No. 4.

Mite mo ii desu ka: literally 'Is even looking all right?' The *-te (mo) ii* construction (the *mo* is sometimes omitted) expresses the meaning '(You) may . . .; it is all right if (you) . . .' or, with reference to oneself (see the second sentence of No. 10 below), 'I would not mind . . .'

8 **ituka**: 'at some time (or another)'.

9 **yoku**: in addition to 'well', it can mean 'a lot; often', as it does here.

desyoo: expressing the idea 'it will probably be', it is often translated as 'I suppose; no doubt . . . will', etc.; and, in its interrogative form, as 'I wonder if . . .; do you think that . . .?'

11 **hanasimasyoo**: 'Let us speak/talk (about it)'.

12 **ikimasyoo ka**: 'Shall we go?'

13 **ii desu ga**: used as a conjunction, *ga* may vary in force from a weak 'and' to a clearly adversative 'but'. When the second clause is left unexpressed it is always adversative in feeling and implies the same as a 'but . . .' following a statement in English.

14 **datta**: the past form of *da*, both being plain forms equivalent to the *-masu* level forms *desita* and *desu* respectively.

Nagaku kakarimasu ka: a common meaning of *kakaru* is 'take (time, money, etc.)', but remember that it is intransitive, e.g. *kane ga kakaru*, 'it costs money'. It being here clearly a matter of time, the adverb *nagaku* is used alone: 'Will it take (time) to a long extent?'

16 **Sono hoo ga ii**: literally 'that direction (in the sense of "alternative") is good'; hence, 'that is/would be better'. This use of *hoo* or an equivalent (*kotira, dotira*, etc.) with an adjective or adverb is the commonest way of expressing a comparative in Japanese.

17 **ma ni au**: literally 'fit the gap', this expression covers the meanings of 'meet requirements; serve the purpose; be (good) enough' and, with reference to time, 'be in time (for)'.

年	4/5	**NEN tosi** year, age							
	ネン	ノ	ﾉ–	仁	乍	冄	年			
以	9/2	**I** -wards, -forth							
	イ	＼	ﾚ	ﾚ–	以–	以				
上	29/1	**ZYOO ue** top, part above; **nobo(ru)** *vi* climb **a(garu)** *vi* rise; **a(geru)** *vt* raise, give (dep.)							
	ジョウ	丨	卜	上						
去	32/2	**KYO, KO** past							
	キョ	一	十	土	去	去				
帰	58/7	**KI kae(ru)** *vi* return (home)							
	キ 歸	丿	刂	ﾘﾉ	ﾘｺ	ﾘﾖ	ﾘ�	ﾘ帰	帰	帰	帰
化	9/2	**KA** transform							
	カ	ノ	イ	亻ノ	化					
労	19/5	**ROO** labour							
	ロ ウ 勞	＼	＼＼	＼＼＼	＼＼＼	労	労	労		
働	9/11	**DOO hatara(ku)** *vi* work							
	ド ウ	イ	亻ノ	仁	什	佔	佰	伸	偅	働	働
党	42/7	**TOO** * party							
	ト ウ 黨	丨	ﾉ丨	ﾚﾉ丨	ﾉ丨ﾉ	业	尚	告	兴	党
支	65/0	**SI** support; branch							
	シ	一	十	方	支					

持	64/6	ZI mo(tu) *vt* hold								
	ジ	一	十	扌	扌	扌	扗	拃	拃	持	持
政	66/5	SEI administration								
	セイ	一	丁	下	正	正	玎	政	政	政	
府	53/5	HU * urban prefecture; government								
	フ	丶	宀	广	广	庁	府	府	府		
思	102/4	SI omo(u) *vt* think								
	シ	丶	冂	冂	用	田	田	思	思	思	
想	61/9	SOO imagination								
	ソウ	一	十	木	利	机	相	相	想	想	想
問	169/3	MON question								
	モン	丨	冂	冃	門	門	門	門	門	問	問
題	72/14	DAI * topic, title								
	ダイ	丶	冂	日	旦	早	旱	昆	是	題	題
注	85/5	TYUU concentrate								
	チュウ	丶	丶	氵	氵	汀	汁	注	注		
意	180/4	I mind, purpose								
	イ	丶	亠	立	立	产	音	音	意	意	意
必	3/4	HITU kanara(zu) without fail								
	ヒツ	丶	八	心	心	必					

[43]

要	146/3	**YOO**　need									
	ヨウ	一	一	一	両	両	西	覀	要	要	

標	75/11	**HYOO**　mark,　target									
	ヒョウ	一	木	杧	杆	栖	栖	標	標	標	標

準	24/11	**ZYUN**　rule,　standard									
	ジュン	丶	冫	氵	氿	沪	沪	汼	淮	淮	準

下	1/2	**KA,GE sita** bottom; **kuda(saru)** *vt* condescend; **kuda(ru)** *vi*, **kuda(su)** *vt* come (bring) down									
	カゲ	一	丁	下							

博	24/10	**HAKU**　broad,　universal									
	ハク 博	十	扩	护	恒	恒	悼	博	博	博	

光	42/3	**KOO hikari** light,　radiance; **hika(ru)** *vi* shine									
	コウ	丨	丷	屮	兴	光	光				

線	120/9	**SEN** *　line									
	セン	糸	幺	糸	糽	約	約	綧	綧	線	線

具	109/3	**GU**　equipment									
	グ 具	丨	冂	月	月	目	且	具	具		

屋	44/6	**OKU ya** premises; **(-ya)** -er, -ist (of tradesmen)									
	オク	㇕	尸	尸	尼	居	层	屋	屋		

町	102/2	**TYOO mati** town,　ward　of　town									
	チョウ	丨	冂	田	田	田	町	町			

士	33/0	**SI** gentleman, samurai
	シ	一 十 士
男	102/2	**DAN, NAN** otoko man, male
	ダ ナ ン ン	丨 冂 冂 冊 田 甼 男
仏	9/2	**BUTU** hotoke Buddha
	ブ ッ 佛	ノ イ 化 仏
教	66/7	**KYOO** osi(eru) *vt* teach
	キ ョ ウ	一 土 耂 耂 孝 孝 孝 孝 教 教
興	12/4	**KYOO** interest
	キ ョ ウ	ノ イ ƒ 们 阴 卹 卹7 卹 舅 興
味	30/5	**MI** azi taste
	ミ	丨 口 口 口＾ 叮 咪 味
宗	40/5	**SYUU** religion
	シ ュ ウ	` 丶 宀 宀 宀 宇 宗 宗
近	162/4	**KIN** tika(i) near
	キ ン 近	ノ ʃ 斤 斤 斤 近 近
約	120/3	**YAKU** promise; (as prefix to numerals) about
	ヤ ク	く 幺 幺 糸 糸 糸 紂 約 約
束	4/6	**SOKU** bind, bundle
	ソ ク	一 ㄇ 二 百 市 市 束

六

一。ダレニ手紙ヲ書イテイマスカ。英国人ノ友ダチデス。日本ニ十五年以上モ住ンデイル人デスガ、去年帰化シマシタ。労働党ヲ支持シテイタ事ガアルノデ、日本ノ政府ハ長ク帰化ヲ承知シナカッタンデス。

二。労働党ヲ支持スル人ハミナアブナイ思想ヲ持ッテイルト思ッタンデショウカ。ソウナンデショウ。

三。思想ノ問題ハモチロンヨク注意スル事ガ必要デショウガ、労働党ノ思想ガアブナイト思ウノハ変デスネ。政府ガスル事ハ何デモ標準以下デス。

四。ワタシガ働イテイル博物館ハ光線ノ具合ガ大変ワルイノデスガ、政府ハ博物館ナドニハ余リ金ヲカケマセンカラコマリマス。

ワタシノ役所ノ部屋モ非常ニクライデス。イツカ町長ト上田博士ノ長男ガ来タ事ガアリマシタガ、クラクテ書類ヲ読ム事ガ出来マセンデシタ。

五。アナタノ友ダチノ英国人ハドンナ事ヲシテイルンデスカ。

仏教ニ非常ニ興味ヲ持ッテイテ、京都デ勉強シテイマス。

六。英国ヘハ帰ラナインデスカ。

何デモイイト思ッテイマスカラ帰ラナイデショウ。

アノ人ハ英国ヨリ日本ノ方ガ

七。ソノ人ハ日本語ヲ上手ニ話スンデショウ。

エ、ソウデス。

八。日本語ハ外国人ニハムズカシイト思イマセンカ。

書ク事ハムズカシイデショウ。

読ム事ト

九。仏教ノ勉強ハホネガオレルデショウネ。

タシハ宗教ノ事ハヨク知リマセンガ。

ソウ思イマス。ワ

[47]

十。ワタシノ家ノ近所ニ住ンデイル山下サンハ八年ヨリナノニ物理学

ノ勉強ヲハジメマシタ。　　大変ナ物ヲ勉強シテイマスネ。

十一。アノ人ハ何デモナイ事ト思ッテイルカモ知レマセン。

理学ト化学トドチラガムズカシイデショウカ。

十二。化学ハ物理学ホドムズカシクナイデショウ。ヨク知リマセン

が。　　今、何時デスカ。ワタシハ時計ヲ持ッテイナイインデス。

十三。十一時デス。　　ワタシハ十二時ニ友ダチニ会ウ約束ガア夕

マスカラスグ出カケマス。

十四。ワタシモ出カケマショウ。イツモ行ク本屋ガ近イデスカラ、

ワタシハソコヘ行キマス。　　ワタシハ駅ヘ行ク電車ヲマチマス。

十五。ソウデスカ・来週ノ会ニハ来マスネ。

十六。デハ、サヨナラ・　　エ・必ズ行キマス。　　サヨナラ。

[48]

LESSON 6

ROKU

1. Dare ni tegami o kaite imasu ka. Eikokuzin no tomodati desu. Nihon ni zyuugonen izyoo mo sunde iru hito desu ga, kyonen kika simasita. Roodootoo o sizi site ita koto ga aru no de, Nihon no seihu wa nagaku kika o syooti sinakattan' desu. 2. Roodootoo o sizi suru hito wa mina abunai sisoo o motte iru to omottan' desyoo ka. Soo nan' desyoo. 3. Sisoo no mondai wa motiron yoku tyuui suru koto ga hituyoo desyoo ga, roodootoo no sisoo ga abunai to omou no wa hen desu ne. Seihu ga suru koto wa nandemo hyoozyun ika desu. 4. Watasi ga hataraite iru hakubutukan wa koosen no guai ga taihen warui no desu ga, seihu wa hakubutukan nado ni wa amari kane o kakemasen kara komarimasu. Watasi no yakusyo no heya mo hizyoo ni kurai desu. Ituka tyootyoo to Ueda-hakase no tyoonan ga kita koto ga arimasita ga, kurakute syorui o yomu koto ga dekimasen desita. 5. Anata no tomodati no Eikokuzin wa donna koto o site irun' desu ka. Bukkyoo ni hizyoo ni kyoomi o motte ite, Kyooto de benkyoo site imasu. 6. Eikoku e wa kaeranain' desu ka. Ano hito wa Eikoku yori Nihon no hoo ga nandemo ii to omotte imasu kara kaeranai desyoo. 7. Sono hito wa Nihongo o zyoozu ni hanasun' desyoo. E, soo desu. 8. Nihongo wa gaikokuzin ni wa muzukasii to omoimasen ka. Yomu koto to kaku koto wa muzukasii desyoo. 9. Bukkyoo no benkyoo wa hone ga oreru desyoo ne. Soo omoimasu. Watasi wa syuukyoo no koto wa yoku sirimasen ga. 10. Watasi no ie no kinzyo ni sunde iru Yamasita-san wa tosiyori na no ni buturigaku no benkyoo o hazimemasita. Taihen na mono o benkyoo site imasu ne. 11. Ano hito wa nandemo nai koto to omotte iru ka mo siremasen. Buturigaku to kagaku to dotira ga muzukasii desyoo ka. 12. Kagaku wa buturi-gaku hodo muzukasiku nai desyoo. Yoku sirimasen ga. Ima, nanzi desu ka. Watasi wa tokei o motte inain' desu. 13. Zyuuitizi desu. Watasi wa zyuunizi ni tomodati ni au yakusoku ga arimasu kara sugu dekakemasu. 14. Watasi mo dekakemasyoo. Itumo iku honya ga tikai desu kara, watasi wa soko e ikimasu. Watasi wa eki e iku densya o matimasu. 15. Soo desu ka. Raisyuu no kai ni wa kimasu ne. E, kanarazu ikimasu. 16. Dewa, sayonara. Sayonara.

Notes

1 **zyuugonen izyoo mo**: words beginning with this *i-* (*izyoo*, 'and above'; *ika*, 'and below', etc.) should strictly include the item to which they are attached and will do so when it really matters, e.g. *syookoo ika rokunin*, 'five men under an officer'. But they are often used to mean simply 'more than', 'less than', etc.; and in the present case it does not matter whether the translation is '15 years and more' or 'more than 15 years'.

The sense of *mo* here can be understood by thinking of it as 'even'. It implies a certain wonder or surprise at the extent mentioned in the preceding phrase—'as much as' would fit here—but translation by a separate phrase often makes too much of it in English.

sizi site ita koto ga aru no de: if *sita* had been used with *koto ga aru* instead of *site ita* the general sense would have been 'at one particular time in the past he supported'; the use of the past continuative *site ita* shows that the action, instead of having been more or less momentary, continued for some time and 'used to support' would be a reasonable translation.

No de, 'it being that', is similar to *kara* in meaning, but unlike it in that, in Japanese at the *-masu* level of politeness, it usually follows a plain (and not a *-masu*) form of the verb.

2 **Roodootoo . . . motte iru:** a subordinate clause depending on the final *to omottan' desyoo ka*, 'Would it be that (the government) thought thus (*to*): . . .?'

3 **. . . to omou no wa hen desu ne:** see n. to Lesson 4, No. 1 on this construction. *Ne* (or *nee*) is much used in Japanese, to elicit agreement, or at least some response, from the person addressed; cf. the French *n'est-ce pas?*

nandemo: used with a positive verb means 'no matter what; (in) everything'; see also No. 6 and n. to No. 11 below.

hyoozyun ika: 'below standard'.

4 **guai:** means 'state; condition', but an equivalent word is often unnecessary in translation.

nado: 'and so on; and the like'; here '(museums) and such places'.

kurakute . . . yomu koto ga dekimasen desita: on the *-te* form, see n. to Lesson 4, No. 12. The potential construction using *koto ga dekiru* (here literally 'reading was unattainable/impossible') sounds rather literary and stiff in conversation, but is easy to use. On *dekiru*, see n. to Lesson 4, No. 11.

5 **Bukkyoo ni . . . kyoomi o motte ite:** is the main part of the clause, the intervening *hizyoo ni* being merely adverbial, 'extraordinarily'.

6 **hoo ga . . . ii:** see n. to Lesson 5, No. 16.

9 **hone ga oreru:** meaning literally 'one's bones break', the expression is often used to describe difficult, laborious tasks.

sirimasen ga: this clause is added as an afterthought to limit the preceding statement. The normal order would therefore be *Sirimasen ga soo omoimasu*, and the connection between the two clauses can easily be shown in English by translating *ga* here as 'though'. See also No. 12 below.

10 **tosiyori na no ni:** 'although he is an old man; in spite of being old'. Like *no de* and the simple pronominal forms *no wa* and *no ga*, *no ni* usually follows the plain form of the verb; but when this would be *da*, *na* is used instead. (Do not forget, however, that *no ni* can also mean 'for ——ing; in ——ing' when used with most verbs, e.g. *tegami o kaku no ni pen o tukau*, 'use a pen for writing letters'.)

Taihen na mono: exclamatory expression; 'What a thing . . .!'

11 **nandemo nai koto:** 'a matter which is nothing at all'; i.e. something which is quite unimportant, trivial or, in this context, of no difficulty at all.

12 **buturigaku hodo muzukasiku nai:** 'is not difficult to the extent of (*hodo*) physics'; i.e. 'is not as difficult as physics'.

13 **au yakusoku ga arimasu:** 'there is a promise to meet', i.e. '(I) have arranged to meet'.

15 **kimasu . . . ikimasu:** Japanese is more consistently logical than English in its treatment of the ideas of 'coming' and 'going'. *Kuru* is always used of movement to a place where the speaker is or with which he identifies himself; *iku* is always used of movement away from such a place. Thus, while in English it would be possible to say, 'Yes, I'll come' in reply to the enquiry here, *ikimasu* is the only possibility in Japanese.

天	1/3	**TEN** * heaven								
	テン	一	二	于	天					
気	84/2	**KI** * spirit, vapour								
	キ	氣	ノ	仁	仁	气	気	気		
族	70/7	**ZOKU** family, group								
	ゾク	亠	方	方	方	扩	扩	扩	族	族
散	66/8	**SAN** scatter								
	サン	一	壮	壮	荓	苩	背	背	散	散
歩	77/4	**HO** aru(ku) *vi* walk								
	ホ	歩	丨	卜	止	止	牛	牛	米	歩
普	72/8	**HU** universal								
	フ	丶	丷	꾸	꾸	꾸	꾸	꾸	並	普
通	162/7	**TUU** -(ziru) *vi* be well versed; **too(ru)** *vi*, **too(su)** *vt* pass (through/by/along); **too(ri)** road, manner								
	ツウ	通	マ	マ	丹	丹	甬	甬	诵	通
同	13/4	**DOO** ona(zi) same								
	ドウ	丨	冂	冋	同	同	同			
御	60/9	**GO** (hon. pref.)								
	ゴ	ノ	彳	彳	彳	徍	徍	御	御	御
飯	184/4	**HAN** (cooked) rice								
	ハン	𠆢	今	今	今	食	食	飣	飣	飯 飯

多	36/3	**TA** oo(i) many								
	タ	ノ	ク	タ	タ	多	多			
少	4/3	**SYOO** suko(si) a little; **suku(nai)** few								
	ショウ	丨	小	小	少					
食	184/0	**SYOKU** ta(beru) *vt* eat								
	ショク	ノ	人	今	今	今	今	食	食	食
心	61/0	**SIN** kokoro heart, mind								
	シン	ノ	心	心	心					
配	164/3	**HAI** distribute								
	ハイ	一	厂	疒	两	両	酉	酉	酉	配
門	169/0	**MON** * gateway								
	モン	丨	冂	冂	門	門	門	門	門	
務	110/6	**MU** duty								
	ム 務	マ	ヱ	予	矛	矛	矛	秒	矜	務
相	75/5	**SOO** (ai) mutual. **SYOO** Minister (of State)								
	ソ ショ ウ	一	十	才	木	机	机	相	相	相
談	149/8	**DAN** talk								
	ダン	亠	言	言	言	言	言	談	談	談
分	12/2	**BU** percent, **BUN** * share; wa(karu) *vi* be clear; wa(kareru) *vi* wa(keru) *vt* separate; **HUN** minute								
	ブ フ ブン ン	ノ	八	今	分					

半	3/4	**HAN** half									
	ハン	丶	ヽ	ソ	⃛	半 半	丶				
終	120/5	**SYUU** owa(ru) *vi* & *vt* end									
	シュウ	終	ㄴ	幺	幺	糸	糸	糸′	終	終	終
点	25/7	**TEN** * spot, point									
	テン	點	l	├	┠	占	占	点	点	点	点
道	162/9	**DOO** miti road, way									
	ドウ	道	丶	ソ	⃛	爿	首	首	首	首	道
貨	154/4	**KA** goods, coin									
	カ		イ	化	化	化	貨	貨	貨	貨	貨
転	159/4	**TEN** change, turn round/over									
	テン	轉	ニ	ㄈ	冂	白	車	車	転	転	転
衝	60/12	**SYOO** impact									
	ショウ		彳	彳′	彳	衖	衏	衝	律	衝	衝
突	116/3	**TOTU** sudden; strike against									
	トツ	突	丶	⼧	宀	灾	宊	突	突		
沢	85/4	**TAKU** abundance; sawa marsh									
	タク	澤	丶	⼆	氵	沪	汀	沪	沢		
警	149/12	**KEI** warn									
	ケイ		一	﹢	⺷	艹	芍	荀	苟′	苟	敬 警

[53]

察	40/11	**SATU** investigate, conjecture									
	サツ	宀	宀	灾	灾	灾	察	突	宛	蔡	察
無	86/8	**MU, BU** without									
	ムブ	ノ	ㅗ	二	仁	無	無	無	無	無	無
仕	9/3	**SI** service									
	シ	ノ	イ	仁	什	仕					
早	72/2	**SOO** haya(i) early, quick									
	ソウ	丶	冂	日	日	旦	早				
西	146/0	**SEI, SAI** nisi west									
	セイ	二	冂	冋	丙	西	西				
洋	85/6	**YOO** ocean									
	ヨウ	丶	冫	氵	氵	沪	洋	洋	洋	洋	
音	180/0	**ON** * oto sound, noise									
	オン	丶	亠	宀	立	立	产	音	音	音	
楽	75/9	**RAKU** * comfort; **tano(simu)** vt & vi enjoy. **GAKU** music									
	ラ ガ ク ク 楽	ノ	冇	白	白	泊	泊	泊	楽		
北	21/3	**HOKU** kita north									
	ホ ク	一	十	土	北	北					
海	85/6	**KAI** umi sea									
	カ イ 海	丶	冫	氵	氵	汇	次	海	海	海	

首	185/0	**SYU** chief; **kubi** neck
	シュ	`ヽ` `ヽ'` `ニ` `ナ` `ナ` `首` `首` `首` `首`
州	2/5	**SYUU** province
	シュウ	`ヽ` `ソ` `ツ` `州` `州` `州`
地	32/3	**TI, ZI** earth, land
	チ ジ	`ー` `十` `土` `扣` `切` `地`
震	173/7	**SIN** huru(eru) *vi* shake, tremble
	シン	`一` `干` `雨` `雪` `重` `重` `震` `震` `震`
安	40/3	**AN** ease, safe; **yasu(i)** cheap
	アン	`'` `'ヽ` `宀` `安` `安` `安`
様	75/10	**YOO** * manner, appearance; **sama** Mr., Mrs., Miss (hon.)
	ヨウ	`様` `木` `栏` `栏` `样` `样` `样` `様` `様` `様`
試	149/6	**SI** test
	シ	`亠` `言` `言` `言` `訓` `試` `試` `試` `試`
験	187/8	**KEN** examine
	ケン	`験` `馬` `馬` `駅` `験` `験` `験` `験` `験`
南	24/7	**NAN** minami south
	ナン	`一` `十` `士` `市` `市` `南` `南` `南`
建	54/6	**KEN** ta(teru) *vt* build
	ケン	`フ` `ヲ` `ヨ` `聿` `聿` `聿` `津` `建`

七

きのうは日曜日でした。天気がよかったので家族の者がみなで公園へ散歩に行くつもりでした。朝おきた時間は普通の日と同じでした。けれども朝御飯がいつもより多少おくれたので、母はひるの食〜事の事を心配して、妹とうちに残りました。門を出る時に、父の事務所で働いている大山さんに出会いました。大山さんは父に相談したい事があったのでしょう。二人は話しをはじめましたから兄とわたしと弟は十五分以上もまたなければいけませんでした。

わたしたちは二時間半散歩しました。大通りを通って帰るつもりで、電車の終点に近い古道具屋の前を歩いていた時に、貨物自動車と自転車の衝突を見ました。すぐ人が沢山集まりました。だれかが警察へとどけたのでしょう。間もなく警察の人が来ました。自動車

も自転車も少しこわれましたが、人は無事だったのは仕合わせでした。

ひる御飯が終ってからラジオのニュースを聞こうと思いました。時間が少し早かったので西洋の音楽を放送していました。ニュースの放送は二時にありました。北海道へ旅行している首相の事は余り長くておもしろくありませんでした。わたしたちが心配していた九州の地震は、朝のニュースで聞いたほど大きいのでなかったので、な安心しました。九州には姉が住んでいるのです。わたしは父さえ承知すれば九州の姉の所へ行きたかったのですが、この様子では多分行く必要はないでしょう。試験の事を心配している兄はニュースを聞いてすぐ勉強をはじめました。わたしも英語の本を読みました。南洋の話しで大変おもし

c

[57]

ろいのですが少しむずかしい所がありました。兄に聞こうと思いましたが、兄は自分の勉強でいそがしくて時間がありませんでした。妹がとなりの部屋でピアノをひいているのが聞こえて、長く読んでいる事が出来ませんでした。兄は仕合わせです。部屋がはなれていますから。

30

晩には英国の東洋学校で日本語を勉強した人の放送を聞きました。日本の古い建物の事を三十分話しました。わたしたちが知らない事も非常に上手な日本語で話したのでみなおどろきました、兄が行っている大学には外人の学生が多くいて、日本語を話すのを聞いた事がありますが、この人より上手に話す人は一人もありません。この

35

人の話しはきょうもあしたもありますからまちがいなく聞くつもりです。

LESSON 7

SITI

Kinoo wa nitiyoo-bi desita. Tenki ga yokatta no de kazoku no mono ga mina de kooen e sanpo ni iku tumori desita. Asa okita zikan wa hutuu no hi to onazi desita. Keredomo asa-gohan ga itumo yori tasyoo okureta no de, haha wa hiru no syokuzi no koto o sinpai site, imooto to uti ni nokorimasita. Mon o deru toki ni, titi no zimusyo de hataraite iru Ooyama-san ni deaimasita. Ooyama-san wa titi ni soodan sitai koto ga atta no desyoo. Hutari wa hanasi o hazimemasita kara ani to watasi to otooto wa zyuugohun izyoo mo matanakereba ikemasen desita.

Watasitati wa nizikan han sanpo simasita. Oodoori o tootte kaeru tumori de, densya no syuuten ni tikai huru-dooguya no mae o aruite ita toki ni, kamotu-zidoosya to zitensya no syoototu o mimasita. Sugu hito ga takusan atumarimasita. Dareka ga keisatu e todoketa no desyoo. Mamonaku keisatu no hito ga kimasita. Zidoosya mo zitensya mo sukosi kowaremasita ga, hito wa buzi datta no wa siawase desita.

Hiru-gohan ga owatte kara razio no nyuusu o kikoo to omoimasita. Zikan ga sukosi hayakatta no de seiyoo no ongaku o hoosoo site imasita. Nyuusu no hoosoo wa nizi ni arimasita. Hokkaidoo e ryokoo site iru syusyoo no koto wa amari nagakute omosiroku arimasen desita. Watasitati ga sinpai site ita Kyuusyuu no zisin wa, asa no nyuusu de kiita hodo ookii no de nakatta no de mina ansin simasita. Kyuusyuu ni wa ane ga sunde iru no desu. Watasi wa titi sae syooti sureba Kyuusyuu no ane no tokoro e ikitakatta no desu ga, kono yoosu de wa tabun iku hituyoo wa nai desyoo.

Siken no koto o sinpai site iru ani wa nyuusu o kiite sugu benkyoo o hazimemasita. Watasi mo Eigo no hon o yomimasita. Nanyoo no hanasi de taihen omosiroi no desu ga sukosi muzukasii tokoro ga arimasita. Ani ni kikoo to omoimasita ga, ani wa zibun no benkyoo de isogasikute zikan ga arimasen desita. Imooto ga tonari no heya de piano o hiite iru no ga kikoete, nagaku yonde iru koto ga dekimasen desita. Ani wa siawase desu. Heya ga hanarete imasu kara.

Ban ni wa Eikoku no Tooyoo Gakkoo de Nihongo o benkyoo sita hito no hoosoo o kikimasita. Nihon no hurui tatemono no koto o sanzippun hanasimasita. Watasitati ga siranai koto mo hizyoo ni zyoozu na Nihongo de hanasita no de mina odorokimasita. Ani ga itte iru daigaku ni wa gaizin no gakusei ga ooku ite, Nihongo o hanasu no o kiita koto ga arimasu ga, kono hito yori zyoozu ni hanasu hito wa hitori mo arimasen. Kono hito no hanasi wa kyoo mo asita mo arimasu kara matigai naku kiku tumori desu.

Notes

2 mono: written with this character means 'person', but since it implies a certain humility, it is used only of oneself or of members of one's own circle when talking to outsiders.

no de: see n. to Lesson 6, No. 1.

mina de: 'being all', the use of *de* here giving the sense of 'all together'. *Mina* used alone would have meant simply '(They) all'.

4 itumo yori: 'than usual'. *Itumo* used alone as an adverb is normally translated as 'always' or, sometimes, 'usually' (see Lesson 6, No. 14), but when followed by *no*, *to* or *yori*, 'usual' is in most cases a more appropriate translation.

tasyoo: 'to some extent; somewhat'.

6–7 sitai: *-tai* added to the base of a verb makes a desiderative form meaning 'want to ——; would·like to ——'. Since this is an adjectival form, the object of a transitive verb should become the subject of a *-tai* form, e.g. *tegami ga kakitai desu*, 'a letter is desired-to-be-written'. Now, however, there is a strong tendency, particularly in speech, for the verbal element to predominate and to lead to the use of *o* with the noun as if it were the normal object of a verb, e.g. *tegami o kakitai desu*; but, from a strictly grammatical viewpoint, this is incorrect.

8 matanakereba ikemasen desita: 'if we had not waited, it would not have done'; one of the commonest ways of expressing the idea of 'had to (wait)'. 'We must/have to wait' would be the same phrase without *desita*.

9 Oodoori o tootte: the particle *o* is often used with normally intransitive verbs of motion (*iku, sanpo suru*, etc.) with a meaning of movement 'along' or 'about' a place, e.g. *mati o aruku*, 'walk about the town'. Cf. *huru-dooguya no mae o aruite* in l. 10 below.

15 kikoo to omoimasita: 'I thought thus (to): I will hear'; i.e. 'I thought I would hear/listen to'.

19 kiita hodo ookii no de nakatta no de: see n. to Lesson 6, No. 12 on *hodo*. Beware of the two different types of *no de* here: the second is the conjunctive use ('since, because'), but the first consists of the pronoun *no*, '(a big) one', used with the negative past form *de nakatta*, 'was not'. Cf. the two types of *no ni* mentioned in n. to Lesson 6, No. 10.

20–21 sae . . . sureba: *sae* (or *de sae*) can usually be translated as an emphatic 'even'; but when, as here, *sae* is followed by a conditional verb, it means '(if) only'. Cf. this phrase 'if only my *father* had consented' with *titi ga syooti sae sureba*, 'if only my father had *consented*'.

21 ikitakatta: past form of *ikitai* 'want to go'.

kono yoosu de wa: 'by these appearances'; thus 'from the way things seem now'.

27 Imooto ga . . . piano o hiite iru no ga kikoete: literally 'My sister's playing the piano . . . being audible', the whole of the first part down to *no ga* being the subject of the intransitive verb *kikoete*.

28–29 Heya ga hanarete imasu kara: this sentence is added as an explanation of the previous statement, and the normal order would be *Heya ga hanarete imasu kara ani wa siawase desu*. Cf. n. to Lesson 6, No. 9 *sirimasen ga*.

31–32 siranai koto mo: the object of the verb *hanasita*, the accusative particle *o* not having been used with *mo*, 'even'.

33 gakusei ga ooku ite: 'students being there in large numbers', *ooku* being the adverbial form of *ooi* used before the verb *ite* (from *iru*).

34 hitori mo arimasen: on the use of *aru* with animate subjects, see n. to Lesson 1, No. 11.

夏	1/9	KA natu summer 
	カ	一　丁　丆　万　百　百　百　頁　夏　夏
春	72/5	SYUN haru spring 
	シュン	一　二　三　丰　夫　表　春　春　春
民	1/4	MIN the people 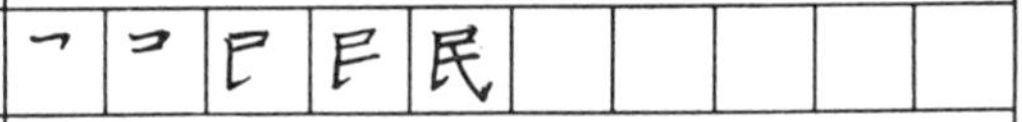
	ミン	㇆　㇖　尸　戸　民
主	8/3	SYU master, principle 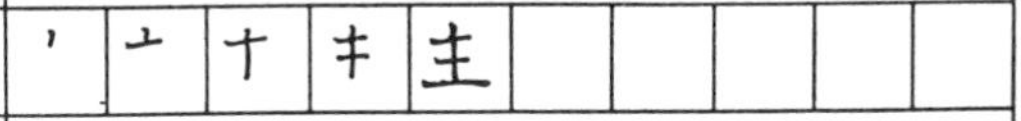
	シュ	ヽ　亠　十　主　主
義	123/7	GI righteousness, principle 
	ギ	ヽ　ソ　羊　羊　羊　羊　羊　義　義　義
切	18/2	SETU ki(ru) vt cut 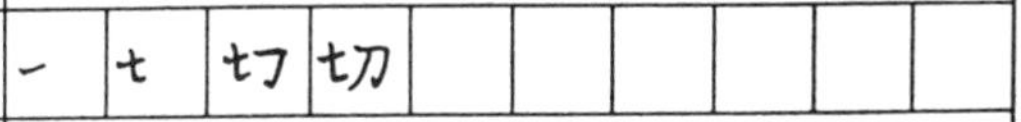
	セツ	一　七　切　切
米	119/0	BEI America. MAI, BEI kome rice 
	ベイ	ヽ　ソ　半　半　米　米
使	9/6	SI messenger; tuka(u) vt use 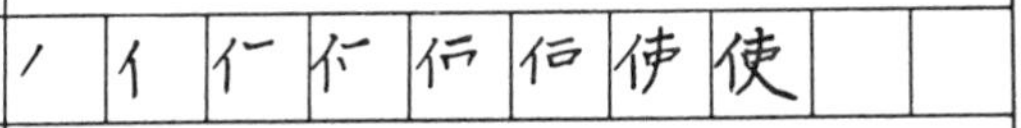
	シ	ノ　イ　仁　仁　�　侟　使　使
材	75/3	ZAI (building) material 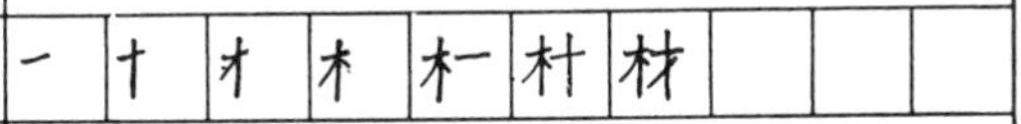
	ザイ	一　十　才　木　材　材　材
料	119/4	RYOO materials; cost 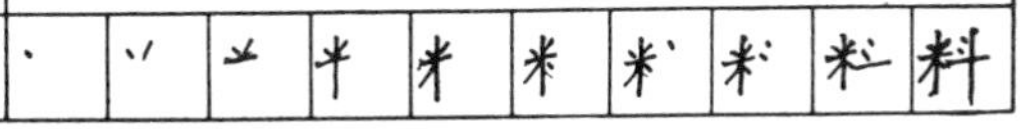
	リョウ	ヽ　ソ　ソ　半　米　米　米　料　料　料

[61]

和	115/3	**WA** harmony; Japan								
	ワ		ノ	ニ	千	禾	禾·	和	和	和
歌	76/10	**KA** uta song; uta(u) *vt* sing								
	カ		一	丁	可	可	可	哥	哥	歌 歌
言	149/0	**GEN** (koto) word; yu(u) *vt* say								
	ゲン		一	亠	三	言	言	言		
保	9/7	**HO** preserve								
	ホ		ノ	イ	伫	仔	仔	仔	保	保
険	170/8	**KEN** risk								
	ケン	険	フ	3	阝	阝	阶	阶	阶	阶 険
社	113/3	**SYA** association, Shinto shrine								
	シャ	社	丶	ク	ネ	ネ	礻	补	社	
記	149/3	**KI** record								
	キ		丶	亠	三	言	言	言	訂 訂 記	
税	115/7	**ZEI** * tax								
	ゼイ	税	ノ	ニ	千	禾	禾	利	利	稍 税
裁	24/10	**SAI** discriminate								
	サイ		土	圭	圭	幸	幸	表	裁	裁 裁
判	18/5	**HAN** * a seal; judging								
	ハン		丶	ソ	乂	三	半	判	判	

返	162/4	**HEN** kae(su) *vt* give back								
	ヘン	～	一	厂	厄	反	反	坂	返		
郵	163/8	**YUU** post, mail								
	ユウ	ノ	㇑	三	生	垂	垂	華	重	郵	郵
便	9/7	**BEN** convenience. **BIN** tayo(ri) tidings								
	ベビ ンン	ノ	イ	仁	仁	佰	佰	佰	便	便	
局	44/4	**KYOKU** office, bureau								
	キョ ク	㇐	コ	㇕	月	局	局	局			
秋	115/4	**SYÛU** aki autumn								
	シュ ウ	ノ	㇑	千	禾	禾	禾	秒	秒	秋	
県	42/6	**KEN** * prefecture								
	ケ ン	縣	㇑	冂	月	目	目	但	県	県	県
村	75/3	**SON** mura village								
	ソ ン	一	十	オ	木	村	村	村			
冗	14/2	**ZYOO** superfluous								
	ジョ ウ	ﾉ	冖	ㄣ	冗						
顔	181/9	**GAN** kao face, expression								
	ガ ン	立	产	产	彦	彦	彦	顔	顔	顔	顔
奥	4/11	**OKU** * interior, the back; wife								
	オ ク	奧	ﾉ	向	向	向	肉	角	角	奧	奥

退	162/6	**TAI** withdraw								
	タイ 退	フ	ヨ	ヨ	艮	・艮	艮	・艮	退	退
院	170/7	**IN** (an) institution								
	イン	⁷	³	⻖	⻖¹	⻖²	阝�ノ	阾	陀	陟	院
術	60/8	**ZYUTU** (an) art								
	ジュ ツ	術 術	ノ	彳	行	什	朮	休	休	術	術²	術
結	120/6	**KETU** musu(bu) *vt* tie, conclude								
	ケ ツ	結	幺	幺	糸	糸	糸¹	糸²	紅	結	結
果	2/7	**KA** result, (kuda) fruit								
	カ		ⱶ	冂	曱	日	旦	甲	果	果
胃	102/4	**I** * stomach								
	イ		⺀	冂	皿	毌	田	甲	胃	胃
健	9/9	**KEN** health								
	ケ ン		亻	亻⁷	俨	俨	伊	律	侓	健²	健
康	53/8	**KOO** ease								
	コ ウ	'	丶	一	广	庁	庐	庐	庚	庚	康
病	104/5	**BYOO** illness								
	ビョ ウ	'	亠	广	广	疒	疒	疔	病	病	病
医	22/5	**I** heal								
	イ 醫	一	匸	匡	医	医	医	医			

毒	80/4	**DOKU** * poison								
	ド ク / 毒	一	十	キ	主	丰	青	青	毒	
内	2/3	**NAI** uti inside								
	ナ イ	丨	冂	内	内					
飲	184/4	**IN** no(mu) *vt* drink								
	イ ン	ハ	ケ	今	今	食	食	食	飠	飲 飲
薬	140/13	**YAKU** kusuri medicine								
	ヤ ク / 藥	艹	艹	犬	苩	苩	苩	苩	莇	薬 薬
当	42/3	**TOO** * right, justice; the one in question; **ata(ru)** *vi* face, hit the mark								
	ト ウ / 當	丨	丷	业	严	当	当			
元	7/2	**GEN, GAN** moto origin								
	ゲ ン ガ ン	一	二	テ	元					
茶	140/6	**TYA** * tea								
	チ ャ	一	十	艹	芦	犬	芯	苯	茶	茶
休	9/4	**KYUU** yasu(mu) *vi* rest								
	キ ュ ウ	丿	亻	仁	什	付	休			
緒	120/8	**SYO** (end of) thread								
	シ ョ / 緒 緒	乚	幺	糸	糸	紵	紝	絃	絑	緒
冬	34/2	**TOO** huyu winter								
	ト ウ	丿	夂	夂	冬	冬				

八

三年前の夏の事でした。わたしはその年の春からアメリカの民主主義の事を書いていました。親切な米国大使のおかげで材料は沢山集まりましたが、論文を書くのは大変ほねがおれました。

ある日、大学の学生だった時から和歌山の方言を勉強していた友だちから手紙が来ました。自分の事はほとんど何も書いてなくて、お父さんの事を大変心配しているようでした。お父さんは大きな保険会社の社長でしたが、会社の書記によくない男がいて、税金の事で裁判所へ行かなければいけなかったのでした。

わたしはすぐ返事を書きました。切手がないので郵便局へ買いに出かけました。そこでとなりに住んでいる木下さんに出会いました。木下さんは、前には、秋田県のいなかで村長をしていた事がありま

すが、よく冗談を言う人です。所が、この日は非常にかなしそうな顔をしていました。それで、わたしは、

「木下さん、奥さんはいつ退院ですか」。

と聞きました。木下さんは、

「退院はまだなんです。手術の結果がよかったので安心していたんですが、胃の具合がわるいので秋まで入院していなければいけないんです」。

と言いました。

「それは心配ですね。奥さんはいつも大変健康そうな人ですから一週間か十日で退院出来るんだろうと思っていました」。

「わたしもそう思いました。病院の医者もそう言っていました」。

わたしは木下さんが気の毒で、これ以上会話をつづけるのをやめ

ようと思いました。けれども、木下さんはまた言いました。

「西村さん、家内は退院してからも、長い間飲食物に注意して、物を食べたあとでは必ず薬を飲まなければいけないそうです」。

木下さんは本当にいつもの元気がありませんでした。

「あそこでお茶でも飲みませんか」。

とわたしは言いました。

「そうですね。これからもう一つ行かなければいけない所があるんですが、少し休みましょうか」

と言ってわたしと一緒に郵便局を出しました。

その日はうちへ帰ってからも友だちのお父さんの事と木下さんの奥さんの事を考えていました。前の年の冬生れた子どもがおきない内にもう少し論文が書きたかったのでしたが出来ませんでした。

HATI

SANNEN mae no natu no koto desita. Watasi wa sono tosi no haru kara Amerika no minsyusyugi no koto o kaite imasita. Sinsetu na Beikoku taisi no okage de zairyoo wa takusan atumarimasita ga, ronbun o kaku no wa taihen hone ga oremasita.

Aru hi, daigaku no gakusei datta toki kara Wakayama no hoogen o benkyoo site ita tomodati kara tegami ga kimasita. Zibun no koto wa hotondo nanimo kaite nakute, otoosan no koto o taihen sinpai site iru yoo desita. Otoosan wa ooki na hoken-gaisya no syatyoo desita ga, kaisya no syoki ni yoku nai otoko ga ite, zeikin no koto de saibansyo e ikanakereba ikenakatta no desita.

Watasi wa sugu henzi o kakimasita. Kitte ga nai no de yuubinkyoku e kai ni dekakemasita. Soko de tonari ni sunde iru Kinosita-san ni deaimasita. Kinosita-san wa, mae ni wa, Akita-ken no inaka de sontyoo o site ita koto ga arimasu ga, yoku zyoodan o yuu hito desu. Tokoroga, kono hi wa hizyoo ni kanasi-soo na kao o site imasita. Sore de, watasi wa, 'Kinosita-san, okusan wa itu taiin desu ka' to kikimasita. Kinosita-san wa, 'Taiin wa mada nan' desu. Syuzyutu no kekka ga yokatta no de ansin site itan' desu ga, i no guai ga warui no de aki made nyuuin site inakereba ikenain' desu' to iimasita.

'Sore wa sinpai desu ne. Okusan wa itumo taihen kenkoo-soo na hito desu kara issyuukan ka tooka de taiin dekirun' daroo to omotte imasita.'

'Watasi mo soo omoimasita. Byooin no isya mo soo itte imasita.'

Watasi wa Kinosita-san ga kinodoku de, kore izyoo kaiwa o tuzukeru no o yameyoo to omoimasita. Keredomo, Kinosita-san wa mata iimasita: 'Nisimura-san, kanai wa taiin site kara mo, nagai aida insyokubutu ni tyuui site, mono o tabeta ato de wa kanarazu kusuri o nomanakereba ikenai soo desu.' Kinosita-san wa hontoo ni itumo no genki ga arimasen desita.

'Asoko de o-tya de mo nomimasen ka' to watasi wa iimasita.

'Soo desu ne. Kore kara moo hitotu ikanakereba ikenai tokoro ga arun' desu ga, sukosi yasumimasyoo ka' to itte watasi to issyo ni yuubinkyoku o demasita.

Sono hi wa uti e kaette kara mo tomodati no otoosan no koto to Kinosita-san no okusan no koto o kangaete imasita. Mae no tosi no huyu umareta kodomo ga okinai uti ni moo sukosi ronbun ga kakitakatta no desita ga dekimasen desita.

Notes

3 (. . . no) o-kage de: or, in a more polite form, *o-kage-sama de*, means 'thanks to (you, etc.)'.

5 daigaku no . . . site ita: all qualifies the noun *tomodati*.

6 kaite nakute: negative -*te* form of *kaite aru*. The -*te aru* form is a kind of passive used with transitive verbs and indicates a state resulting from someone's action. Thus, here, '(nothing) was/had been written'. (See also n. to Lesson 13, l. 12.)

7 sinpai site iru yoo desita: 'he seemed to be worried'. The use of *yoo (desu)* after a final form of the verb or adjective refers to a general view of the situation in the light of all one knows about it, and is translatable as 'appearances are that; it seems that', etc.

8 syoki ni yoku nai otoko ga ite: 'there being a bad man for/as secretary'.

9 ikanakereba ikenakatta: see n. to Lesson 7, l. 8.

10–11 kai ni dekakemasita: 'went out to buy'. When the main verb is a verb of motion *ni* can be used with the base of another verb to express purpose: '(go, come, etc.) in order to . . .'

11 Kinosita: family name. In some names the syllables *no* or *ga* are not shown in the writing.

12 sontyoo o site ita: certain nouns indicating an occupation (e.g. *sensei*) are used with *o suru* to mean 'is (working as)'. On *site ita*, see n. to Lesson 6, No. 1 *sizi site ita*.

13 yuu: this romanization represents the pronunciation more closely than the literal transcription *iu*, but the latter shows how other forms of the verb are derived.

13–14 kanasi-soo na kao o site: the suffix -*soo* added to the base of verbs and Japanese -*i* adjectives, or straight on to many words used with *na* as '*na* adjectives', gives the meaning '——looking'; e.g. *naki-soo (desu)*, '(is) weepy-looking, looks as if he will cry'; *omosiro-soo*, 'interesting-looking'; *zyoobu-soo*, 'strong-looking'. Such words are used with forms of *desu*, or with a linking *na* when they qualify a following noun, as here. Thus 'having an expression (*kao o site*) which is (*na*) sad-looking (*kanasi-soo*)'.

17 mada nan' desu: abbreviated form of *mada na no desu*, which is itself more emphatic than *mada desu* '(it is) not yet'.

24 kore izyoo kaiwa o tuzukeru no o: is all the object of *yameyoo*. This, in turn, depends on the final *to omoimasita*. Thus 'I thought that I would stop the continuation. . . .'

27 soo desu: is used in the same way as *yoo desu* (see n. to l. 7 above), but is more specific in referring only to spoken (or written) information and is equivalent to something like 'I hear; they say'. Thus, here: 'They tell me that (even after my wife . . .)'. Do not confuse this use of *soo (desu)* with the suffix -*soo* explained above.

29 o-tya de mo nomimasen ka: 'won't you have a drink, be it even tea?', i.e. 'won't you have a cup of tea or something?' The *de mo* shows that *o-tya* is just one of a number of possibilities.

31 Soo desu ne: a common phrase which can be anything from a firm expression of agreement to an almost meaningless phrase, as here, used to gain time for thought.

Kore kara: refers to time; 'from here on; after this'.

35–36 okinai uti ni: literally 'while (he) is not up'. This construction of a negative verb with *uti ni* is similar in meaning to *(okiru) mae ni*, 'before (getting up)', but usually implies also a feeling of urgency or speed.

36 ronbun ga kakitakatta: see n. to Lesson 7, ll. 6–7.

横	75/11	**OO** yoko side								
	オウ 横	木	杧	杧	杧	杧	桪	桪	桪	横	横
浜	85/7	**HIN** hama beach								
	ヒン 濱	`	` `	` ` `	氵	汀	汴	沂	浜	浜	浜
百	1/5	**HYAKU** * hundred								
	ヒャク	一	丆	亓	石	有	百				
軒	159/3	**KEN** (unit for counting buildings)								
	ケン	一	ㄏ	而	百	自	車	車	車	軒	軒
口	30/0	**KOO** kuti mouth								
	コウ	＼	冂	口							
千	4/2	**SEN** * thousand								
	セン	ノ	二	千							
第	118/5	**DAI** (prefix: " -th " etc. with numbers)								
	ダイ 弟	ノ	㇄	㇀	怍	竹	竺	笒	笃	第	第
等	118/6	**TOO** class								
	トウ	ノ	㇀	怍	竹	竹	竺	笁	筆	等	等
数	66/9	**SUU** * kazu number; kazo(eru) vt count								
	スウ 數	`	ヽ	半	米	米	娄	娄	数	数	数
神	113/5	**SIN, ZIN** kami god								
	シジ ン 神	`	フ	オ	礻	礻	和	秬	神		

背	130/5	**HAI** se stature, back (of body)									
	ハイ	一	㇉	孑	北	北	背	背	背	背	
頭	151/9	**TOO, ZU** atama head									
	トゥ ズ	一	口	戸	豆	豆	豆	豆丁	�	頭	頭
脳	130/7	**NOO** brain									
	ノゥ 腦	)	几	月	月	朋	朋	朋	脳	脳	脳
森	75/8	**SIN** mori wood									
	シン	一	十	オ	木	杰	森	森	森	森	森
声	32/4	**SEI** koe voice									
	セイ 聲	一	十	士	声	声	声	声			
肺	130/4	**HAI*** lung									
	ハイ	)	月	月	月	月'	肝	肝	肺	肺	○
白	106/0	**HAKU** siro, siro(i) white									
	ハク	'	⺊	白	白	白					
女	38/0	**ZYO** onna woman									
	ジョ	く	女	女							
世	2/4	**SE** yo world; **SEI** age									
	セイ	一	十	廿	廿	世					
掃	64/8	**SOO** sweep									
	ソゥ	一	扌	扌	扫	扫	扫	掃	掃	掃	掃

[72]

除	170/7	**ZYO, ZI** put away, exclude									
	ジョ ジ	ˋ	３	ß	ßˊ	ßゝ	阶	阶	阶	除	除
洗	85/6	**SEN** ara(u) *vt* wash									
	セン	ˋ	ˋ冫	氵	氵	汋	汫	洗	洗	洗	
式	56/3	**SIKI** * ceremony; style									
	シ キ	一	二	于	王	式	式				
客	40/6	**KYAKU** * guest, client									
	キャ ク	ˋ	ˊˋ	宀	宀	灾	灾	灾	客	客	
室	40/6	**SITU** compartment, room									
	シ ツ	ˋ	ˊˋ	宀	宀	宏	宏	宏	室	室	
寝	40/10	**SIN** ne(ru) *vi* sleep; ne(kasu) *vt* put to sleep									
	シ ン	寝	宀	宀	宀	宍	宍	宍	寍	寢	寝
哲	30/7	**TETU** wisdom									
	テ ツ	一	十	才	扩	扩	扩	折	折	哲	哲
広	53/2	**KOO** hiro(i) wide, spacious									
	コ ウ	廣	ˋ	亠	广	広	広				
告	30/4	**KOKU** inform									
	コ ク	ˊ	一	牛	生	牛	告	告			
毎	80/2	**MAI** every									
	マ イ	毎	ˊ	一	仁	勺	毎	毎			

[73]

林	75/4	**RIN** hayasi forest									
	リン		一	十	才	木	朾	村	材	林	
池	85/3	**TI** ike pond									
	チ		丶	冫	氵	汋	汕	池			
葉	140/9	**YOO** ha leaf									
	ヨウ		一	艹	艹	芏	芏	莘	苹	苹	葉
寺	32/3	**ZI** tera Buddhist temple									
	ジ		一	十	土	士	寺	寺			
青	174/0	**SEI** immaturity; **ao, ao(i)** blue, green									
	セイ	青	一	十	主	主	丰	青	青	青	
畳	102/7	**ZYOO** (unit for area of room); **tatami** mat									
	ジョウ	疊	丶	冂	田	田	冊	畍	畍	胃	骨	畳
毛	82/0	**MOO** ke hair, wool									
	モウ		ノ	二	三	毛					
立	117/0	**RITU** ta(tu) vi stand (up), depart, elapse; ta(teru) vt set up									
	リツ		丶	一	立	立	立				
派	85/6	**HA** * sect, faction									
	ハ		丶	冫	氵	汀	沪	沪	沂	沂	派
絵	120/6	**KAI, E** * picture									
	カイ エ	絵 繪	く	幺	幸	糸	糹	糸	给	絵	絵

着	123/6	**TYAKU** ki(ru)*vt* wear, put on; **ki(seru)** *vt* dress (another) in; **tu(ku)** *vi* arrive									
	チャ ク	`	ソ	ᅩ	ナ	ヰ	芏	羊	羊	芐	着

運	162/9	**UN** * fortune; transporting									
	ウ ン	運	`	一	口	尸	吕	旦	軍	軍	渾	運

場	32/9	**ZYOO** ba site; situation									
	ジョ ウ	塲	一	十	土	圵	坦	坍	堝	場	場	場

正	1/4	**SEI, SYOO** tada(sii) right, correct								
	セ シ ョ イ ウ	一	丁	下	正	正				

戸	63/0	**KO** to door								
	コ	户	一	ヨ	ᄀ	戸				

代	9/3	**DAI** *repayment, yo generation; **kawa(ru)** *vi* be a substitute								
	ダ イ	ノ	亻	仁	代	代				

留	102/5	**RYUU, RU** stay, detain									
	リ ュ ル ウ	ノ	⺃	ム	幻	卯	幻	纫	畄	留

守	40/3	**SYU, SU** mamo(ru) *vt* guard								
	シュ ス	`	⺍	宀	宀	宁	守			

関	169/6	**KAN** connection									
	カ ン	關	丨	阝	戸	門	門	閂	閂	関	関	関

係	9/7	**KEI** concern (in); **kaka(ri)** (person in) charge								
	ケ イ	ノ	亻	仁	代	侄	係	伻	係	

九

ワタシノ住ンデイル所ハ横浜ト金沢トノ間ニアッテ、家ハ三百軒、人口ハ千七百アリマス。ココニハ様子ガ変ナ人ガ三人イマス。

第一ハ横浜ニアル高等学校ノ数学ノ先生デス。コノ人ハ大通リノ西ニアル神社ノソバノ古イ家ニ一人デ住ンデイマス。年ハマダワカイヨウデスガ、背ガ高ク、アゴニハ長イヒゲガアリマス。大変イイ頭脳ヲ持ッテイルソウデスガ、ココノ人人ト話シタ事ガアリマセン。朝早ク自転車デ出カケテ行ッテ、晩オソク帰ッテ来マス。日曜日ニハ神社ノウラニアル森ノ中ヘ入ッテ大キナ声デ歌ヲ歌イマスガ、ヤカマシクテ近所ノ人ハマドヲシメナケレバイケナイホドデス。肺ガワルイノデ森ノ中デ歌ウノダロウト言ウ人モアリマス。

第二ハ教会ノトナリニ住ンデイル白人デス。ドコデ生レタ人カダ

[76]

レモ知リマセン。日本人ノ女中ガ食事トカ掃除トカ洗濯クナドノ世

話ヲシテイマス。コノ白人ノ家ハ半分日本式デ半分西洋式デス。客

15 室ト寝室ト便所ガ西洋式ダソウデス。人人ハコノ人ハ哲学者ダト言

ッテイマス。イツカ新聞ニコノ人ガ書イタ本ノ広告ガ出テイタソウ

デスが、何ノ本ダカワタシハ知リマセン。毎日近所ノ林ノ中ヘ散歩

ニ行キマス。林ノ中ニハ小サナ池ガアリマスガ、ソノ池ノソバニ長

イ間トマッテイテ、ダレモ分カラナイ言葉デ何カ言ッテイマス。

20 第三ハ東光寺ニ住ンデイル青年デス。寺ノ中ノ六畳ノ部屋ヲ使ッ

テイマス。頭ノ毛ガ長クテ首ニトドキソウデス。カタノハバが広ク

テ立派ナカラダヲ持ッテイマス。絵書キダト言イマスが、ダレモコ

ノ人ノ絵ヲ見タ事ガアリマセンカラ本当デナイカモ知レマセン。外

ヘ出ル時ハイツモ日本ノ着物ヲ着テハカマヲハイテイマス。天気ノ

[77]

25 イ日ニハ必ズ小学校ノ運動場ノ横デ子ドモタチガアソンデイル

ヲボンヤリトナガメテイマス。

ワタシタチガココニウツッテ来タ時ハ正月デ、戸主ノ兄ガ家族ノ

者ヲ代表シテコノ人タチノ所ヘモ新年ノアイサツニ行キマシタ。数

学ノ先生ノ所デハ何モ返事ガアリマセンデシタ。白人ノウチデハ女

30 中ガ出テ来テ、「ダンナ様ハオ留守デス」ト言イマシタ。青年ノ所デ

ハ、戸ヲアケテ兄ノ顔ヲ見テ、スグマタシメテシマイマシタ。兄ハ

オコッテイイノカ、ワラッテイイノカ分カラナカッタソウデス。

コノ三人ノ人タチハミナ宗教ト関係ガアル建物ノソバニ住ンデイ

マスガ、ミナ宗教トハ少シモ関係ガナイ変ナ人タチナノハ大変オモ

35 シロイ事デス。ココノ人ガコノ人タチノ事ヲ話サナイ日ハ一日モ

アリマセン。

LESSON 9

KU

WATASI no sunde iru tokoro wa Yokohama to Kanazawa to no aida ni atte, ie wa sanbyakken, zinkoo wa sen-nanahyaku arimasu. Koko ni wa yoosu ga hen na hito ga sannin imasu.

Daiiti wa Yokohama ni aru kootoo-gakkoo no suugaku no sensei desu. Kono hito wa oodoori no nisi ni aru zinzya no soba no hurui ie ni hitori de sunde imasu. Tosi wa mada wakai yoo desu ga, se ga takaku, ago ni wa nagai hige ga arimasu. Taihen ii zunoo o motte iru soo desu ga, koko no hitobito to hanasi o sita koto ga arimasen. Asa hayaku zitensya de dekakete itte, ban osoku kaette kimasu. Nitiyoo-bi ni wa zinzya no ura ni aru mori no naka e haitte, ooki na koe de uta o utaimasu ga, yakamasikute kinzyo no hito wa mado o simenakereba ikenai hodo desu. Hai ga warui no de mori no naka de utau no daroo to yuu hito mo arimasu.

Daini wa kyookai no tonari ni sunde iru hakuzin desu. Doko de umareta hito ka daremo sirimasen. Nihonzin no zyotyuu ga syokuzi toka soozi toka sentaku nado no sewa o site imasu. Kono hakuzin no ie wa hanbun Nihon-siki de hanbun seiyoo-siki desu. Kyakusitu to sinsitu to benzyo ga seiyoo-siki da soo desu. Hitobito wa kono hito wa tetugakusya da to itte imasu. Ituka sinbun ni kono hito ga kaita hon no kookoku ga dete ita soo desu ga, nan no hon da ka watasi wa sirimasen. Mainiti kinzyo no hayasi no naka e sanpo ni ikimasu. Hayasi no naka ni wa tiisa na ike ga arimasu ga, sono ike no soba ni nagai aida tomatte ite, daremo wakaranai kotoba de nanika itte imasu.

Daisan wa Tookoo-zi ni sunde iru seinen desu. Tera no naka no rokuzyoo no heya o tukatte imasu. Atama no ke ga nagakute kubi ni todoki-soo desu. Kata no haba ga hirokute rippa na karada o motte imasu. Ekaki da to iimasu ga, daremo kono hito no e o mita koto ga arimasen kara hontoo de nai ka mo siremasen. Soto e deru toki wa itumo Nihon no kimono o kite hakama o haite imasu. Tenki no ii hi ni wa kanarazu syoogakkoo no undoozyoo no yoko de kodomotati ga asonde iru no o bonyari to nagamete imasu.

Watasitati ga koko ni utuette kita toki wa syoogatu de, kosyu no ani ga kazoku no mono o daihyoo site kono hitotati no tokoro e mo sinnen no aisatu ni ikimasita. Suugaku no sensei no tokoro de wa nanimo henzi ga arimasen desita. Hakuzin no uti de wa zyotyuu ga dete kite, 'Danna-sama wa o-rusu desu' to iimasita. Seinen no tokoro de wa, to o akete ani no kao o mite, sugu mata simete simaimasita. Ani wa okotte ii no ka, waratte ii no ka wakaranakatta soo desu.

Kono sannin no hitotati wa mina syuukyoo to kankei ga aru tatemono no soba ni sunde imasu ga, mina syuukyoo to wa sukosi mo kankei ga nai hen na hitotati na no wa taihen omosiroi koto desu.

Koko no hitobito ga kono hitotati no koto o hanasanai hi wa itiniti mo arimasen.

Notes

2 Yokohama to Kanazawa to no aida ni: 'in (the space) between Yokohama and Kanazawa'. The second *to* in such a phrase is sometimes omitted. Vowel changes such as that from *kane* to *kana-* in Kanazawa are not uncommon.

3 yoosu ga hen na hito ga sannin imasu: *hito* is the subject of the main verb *imasu* and is preceded by an attributive phrase with its own subject (*yoosu*) and 'quasi-verb' (*na*). In such a phrase the *ga* used with the subject can be replaced by *no* (see n. to Lesson 4, No. 18). Grammatically, *sannin* is adverbial: '(people . . . are present) to the extent of three'.

5–6 wakai yoo desu: see n. to Lesson 8, l. 7.

6 se ga takaku, . . . hige ga arimasu: *takaku* is here used as a 'suspensive', i.e. a form used at the end of a complete clause in which the tense element is 'suspended' until determined by the verb in a later parallel clause (here *arimasu*). The use of this form avoids having two separate parallel sentences, which, in this case, would have been: *Se ga takai desu. Hige ga arimasu.*

The suspensive of *-i* adjectives (including *nai* and *-tai*) is the same as the adverbial *-ku* form (e.g. *yoku*); that of '*na* adjectives' is the same as their *-te* form, i.e. the relevant word plus *de*, the suspensive form of *desu* (e.g. *kenkoo de*); and that of verbs is the base (e.g. *iki, tabe*). The suspensive is essentially a literary form and is usually replaced in speech by the *-te* form, where this is different—hence the often weak connection in meaning between a *-te* form and the following verb (see n. to Lesson 4, No. 12). On the suspensive, see also n. to Lesson 12, l. 8 *nakunari*.

12–13 Doko de umareta hito ka . . . sirimasen: the verb *da*, which would be needed to make the first part grammatically complete, is often omitted in such subordinate clauses. See n. to Lesson 4, No. 7 on this, and l. 17 below for an example of *da* being used in such a clause.

21 kubi ni todoki-soo desu: by a slight extension of its basic meaning of '——looking', the construction of *-soo* (*desu*) added to the base of a verb (see n. to Lesson 8, ll. 13–14) is used to cover the idea of 'ready to——; almost——ing', etc. E.g. *hukuro ga yabure-soo desu*, 'the bag looks as if it will burst; —— is ready to burst; —— is nearly bursting'.

22–23 daremo kono hito no e o mita koto ga arimasen: grammatically, *daremo* is the subject of *mita* and the sentence can be interpreted literally as 'there is no case (*koto ga arimasen*) of anyone having seen. . . .'

24 hakama o haite imasu: *hakama* is a kind of divided skirt or wide trousers which formed part of the formal dress of Japanese men; *haku* is the verb used for 'wearing' anything on the legs or feet (cf. *haitte* from *hairu vi*, 'enter').

28 kono hitotati no tokoro e mo: *mo* can be taken here as 'also', the meaning being that he went to other houses and 'to theirs too'.

30 Danna-sama: 'the master; sir'; a term used by servants, shop-keepers, etc.

32 okotte ii no ka: 'is getting angry all right/better?' There are three main interrogative particles: *ka, no,* and *no ka. Ka* is the commonest, but sounds abrupt and rude with plain forms of verbs and adjectives; *no* is much softer and more friendly in feeling; *no ka* comes between the two and is often used, as here, mainly for euphony.

34 hitotati na no wa: 'the fact that they are people', *na* being the equivalent of *da* used before the pronoun *no*; see n. to Lesson 6, No. 10.

LESSON 10

石	112/0	**SEKI·** **isi** stone								
	セキ	一	厂	石	石	石				
油	85/5	**YU** **abura** oil								
	ユ	'	冫	氵	汁	汩	油	油	油	
昭	72/5	**SYOO** brilliance								
	ショウ	丨	冂	日	日	日	昭	昭	昭	昭
重	4/8	**ZYUU** **omo(i)** heavy; **kasa(naru)** *vi*, **kasa(neru)** *vt* pile up								
	ジュウ	'	二	仁	台	台	盲	車	軍	重
目	109/0	**MOKU** **me** eye								
	モク	丨	冂	月	月	目				
的	106/3	**TEKI** target, (adjectival suffix)								
	テキ	'	冂	白	白	白	的	的		
急	61/5	**KYUU** * suddenness **iso(gu)** *vi* hurry								
	キュウ	'	ク	ヲ	刍	刍	刍	急	急	急
飛	183/0	**HI** **to(bu)** *vi* fly, jump								
	ヒ	飞	飞	飞	飛	飛	飛	飛	飛	飛
次	15/4	**ZI** **tugi** next								
	ジ	'	冫	刁	冷	汐	次			
経	120/5	**KEI** pass through; **KYOO** * Buddhist sutra								
	ケイ キョウ	経 經	乄	纟	纟	糸	糸	糸	経	経	経

[81]

済	85/8	**SAI** save, settle								
	サイ 済	`	:	�:;	:;	:氵	汁	汶	済	済	済

明	72/4	**MEI, MYOO** aka(rui) bright; a(ku) vi, a(keru) vt open							
	メイ ミョウ	丨	冂	月	日	刖	明	明	明

治	85/5	**ZI, TI** govern, soothe							
	ジチ	`	:	:;	汁	治	治	治	治

紹	120/5	**SYOO** link								
	ショウ 紹	く	幺	乡	糸	糸	糸	紹	紹	紹

介	9/2	**KAI** be between				
	カイ	ノ	人	介	介	

昨	72/5	**SAKU** yester-							
	サク	丨	冂	月	日	日'	旷	昨	昨

図	31/4	**ZU *, TO** plan, illustration						
	ズト 圖	丨	冂	冂	冈	図	図	

交	8/4	**KOO** intercourse, exchange					
	コウ	`	亠	广	六	亦	交

換	64/9	**KAN** ka(eru) vt exchange								
	カン	一	扌	扩	护	护	护	掐	換	換

番	165/5	**BAN *** one's turn, watch; number								
	バン	ノ	亠	兴	厶	平	釆	釆	釆	番

号	30/3	**GOO** number							
	ゴ ウ 號	`	口	口	口	号			
玄	95/0	**GEN** dark							
	ゲ ン	`	亠	亠	玄	玄			
作	9/5	**SAKU** * a work; **tuku(ru)** *vt* make, cultivate							
	サ ク	ノ	イ	伊	竹	竹	作	作	
太	37/1	**TAI**, **TA** large; **huto(i)** thick; **huto(ru)** grow fat							
	タ イ タ	一	大	大	太				
郎	163/6	**ROO** man, (ending in male personal names)							
	ロ ウ 郞	`	丬	彐	彐	自	良	良	郞	郎
階	170/9	**KAI** * storey, a level							
	カ イ	フ	３	阝	阝	阯	阰	阰	陼	階	階
段	79/5	**DAN** * step, grade							
	ダ ン	`	イ	千	乍	耳	臣	段	段	段
左	48/2	**SA** hidari left(-hand side)							
	サ	一	ナ	左	左	左			
右	30/2	**YUU** migi right(-hand side)							
	ユ ウ	一	ナ	ナ	右	右			
側	9/9	**SOKU** kawa side							
	ソ ク	イ	們	們	俱	側	側	側	側	側	側

向	2/5	**KOO mu(koo)** opposite side; **mu(kau)** *vi* **mu(ku)** *vi* & *vt* face; **mu(keru)** *vt* turn towards								
	コウ	′	⌐	竹	向	向	向			
付	9/3	**HU tu(keru)** *vt* fix, put on								
	フ	′	イ	仁	付	付				
秒	115/4	**BYOO** * second (of time)								
	ビョウ	′	⸀	千	禾	禾	利	利	秒	秒
特	93/6	**TOKU** * special								
	トク	′	⸀	牛	牛	牛	牜	牪	牪	特 特
冊	2/4	**SATU** (unit for counting books)								
	サツ 冊	l	冂	冊	冊	冊				
井	4/3	**SEI, ZYOO (i)** a well								
	セイ ジョウ	一	二	井	井					
灯	86/2	**TOO** light, lamp								
	トウ 燈	′	′′	火	火	灯	灯			
蚊	142/4	**ka** mosquito								
		′	口	口	中	虫	虫	虫	蚁	蚉 蚊
匹	22/2	**HIKI** (unit for counting animals)								
	ヒキ	一	丆	兀	匹					
箱	118/9	**hako** box								
		′	⸀	片	竹	竺	笎	筣	筘	箱 箱

万	1/2	**MAN** 10,000									
	マ ン	萬	一	丂	万						
封	41/6	**HUU** seal, close									
	フ ウ	二	十	土	圭	丰	圭	封	封	封	
筒	118/6	**TOO** tube									
	ト ウ	ノ	⺮	⺮	竹	竹	竹	筒	筒	筒	筒
谷	150/0	**KOKU** tani valley									
	コ ク	ノ	八	夕	父	公	谷	谷			
川	47/0	**SEN** kawa river									
	セ ン	ノ	川	川							
区	22/2	**KU** * urban district									
	ク	區	一	丆	又	区					
丁	1/1	**TYOO** division of town ward; **TYOO. TEI** exactness									
	テ ョ イ ウ	一	丁								
愛	87/9	**AI** * (-suru) *vt* love									
	ア イ	ノ	⺈	四	𤔦	爫	夵	愛	愛	愛	
郡	163/7	**GUN** * rural district, sub-prefecture									
	ゲ ン	丁	ヨ	ヨ	尹	尹	君	君	君⻏	君⻏	郡
用	101/0	**YOO** * business; use									
	ョ ウ	ノ	刀	月	月	用					

十

長野さんはある石油会社に関係している人ですが、昭和二十八年ごろから外国へ行っていました。この間、重役と相談する目的で急に飛行機で帰って来ました。わたしのおじは長野さんの古い友だちで、おじの次男と長野さんの長男とは同じ大学で経済学を勉強しています。長野さんはおじより一つ年下ですが、おじは父より少し年上ですから長野さんが生れたのは明治四十三年ごろでしょう。父は大正元年に生れました。

おじの紹介でわたしは昨晩長野さんがとまっている旅館へ行きました。旅館は図書館と交換局との間にありました。部屋の番号を知りませんでしたから玄関でおじいさんに、

「長野作太郎さんのお部屋は何号ですか」。

[86]

と聞きました。親切そうなおじいさんは、

「二十六号です。あの階段を上って左へおまがりなさい。次に右へ行ってまた左へおまがりなさい。二十六号は右側の三番目です」と教えてくれました。教えてもらった通りに二階へ上がって行きましたが方向がよく分かりませんでした。掃除をしている女中さんに聞いてやっと二十六号が見付かりました。長野さんは電話をかけていました。わたしを見て、

「ちょっとまって下さい。すぐ終ります」

と言って三十秒ばかり電話で話しをつづけました。終ってからわたしの方を向いて、

「あなたは急ぎますか。手紙が少し書きたいんですが、まってくれますか。十分ぐらいしかかかりません」。

と言いました。わたしは

「特に急ぎませんからどうぞ」

と言って、持って来た本を一冊明けて読みました。天井の電灯は明

るいのですが、わたしがすわっていた所は少しくらくて蚊が一匹飛

んで来ました。長野さんは立派な箱の中から万年筆とレターペーパ

ーと封筒を出して手紙を二つ書きました。

「谷さんと大川さんの住所を知っていますか」

「谷さんの住所を知っていますか」

「谷さんのは東京都中野区野方町一丁目二百五十九番地です。大川

さんのは愛知県ですが郡と村の名はわすれました」

「あとでだれかに聞きましょう。それであなたの用事は・・・・」

「あなたの経験のお話しが聞きたいのです」

長野さんは一時間ばかり外国での経験を話してくれました。

LESSON 10

ZYUU

NAGANO-SAN wa aru sekiyu-gaisya ni kankei site iru hito desu ga, Syoowa nizyuuhatinen-goro kara gaikoku e itte imasita. Kono aida, zyuuyaku to soodan suru mokuteki de kyuu ni hikooki de kaette kimasita. Watasi no ozi wa Nagano-san no hurui tomodati de, ozi no zinan to Nagano-san no tyoonan to wa onazi daigaku de keizaigaku o benkyoo site imasu. Nagano-san wa ozi yori hitotu tosisita desu ga, ozi wa titi yori sukosi tosiue desu kara Nagano-san ga umareta no wa Meizi yonzyuusannen-goro desyoo. Titi wa Taisyoo gannen ni umaremasita.

Ozi no syookai de watasi wa sakuban Nagano-san ga tomatte iru ryokan e ikimasita. Ryokan wa tosyokan to kookankyoku to no aida ni arimasita. Heya no bangoo o sirimasen desita kara genkan de oziisan ni, 'Nagano Sakutaroo-san no o-heya wa nangoo desu ka' to kikimasita. Sinsetu-soo na oziisan wa, 'Nizyuuroku-goo desu. Ano kaidan o nobotte hidari e o-magari nasai. Tugi ni migi e itte mata hidari e o-magari nasai. Nizyuuroku-goo wa migigawa no sanbanme desu' to osiete kuremasita. Osiete moratta toori ni nikai e agatte ikimasita ga hookoo ga yoku wakarimasen desita. Soozi o site iru zyotyuu-san ni kiite yatto nizyuuroku-goo ga mitukarimasita. Nagano-san wa denwa o kakete imasita. Watasi o mite, 'Tyotto matte kudasai. Sugu owarimasu' to itte sanzyuubyoo bakari denwa de hanasi o tuzuke-masita. Owatte kara watasi no hoo o muite, 'Anata wa isogimasu ka. Tegami ga sukosi kakitain' desu ga, matte kuremasu ka. Zippun-gurai sika kakarimasen' to iimasita. Watasi wa, 'Toku ni isogimasen kara doozo' to itte, motte kita hon o issatu akete yomimasita. Tenzyoo no dentoo wa akarui no desu ga, watasi ga suwatte ita tokoro wa sukosi kurakute ka ga ippiki tonde kimasita. Nagano-san wa rippa na hako no naka kara mannenhitu to retaa-peepaa to huutoo o dasite tegami o hutatu kakimasita.

'Tani-san to Ookawa-san no zyuusyo o sitte imasu ka.'

'Tani-san no wa Tookyoo-to Nakano-ku Nogata-tyoo ittyoome nihyakugozyuuku-banti desu. Ookawa-san no wa Aiti-ken desu ga gun to mura no na wa wasuremasita.'

'Ato de dareka ni kikimasyoo. Sore de anata no yoozi wa. . . .'

'Anata no keiken no o-hanasi ga kikitai no desu.'

Nagano-san wa itizikan bakari gaikoku de no keiken o hanasite kuremasita.

Notes

2 Syoowa nizyuuhatinen: the traditional Japanese way of referring to a particular year is to say what year of the reign period of the emperor it was. The corresponding Christian year can be found by adding the number of the reign year to the year (by the Western calendar) before the reign began. 1926 was the first year of the present reign, which is known as Syoowa, and its twenty-eighth year was therefore 1953. The two preceding reign periods were Taisyoo and Meizi, the first years (*gannen*) of which were 1912 and 1868 respectively.

6 ozi yori hitotu tosisita desu: literally 'is younger-in-years by one than my uncle'.

12 o-heya: the honorific prefix *o-* is used to show respect to the person concerned, in this case Mr. Nagano. See also *o-hanasi* in l. 35 below.

14 kaidan o nobotte: both *o* and *ni* can be used with *noboru*, but —— *o noboru* refers to progress up the whole length of something and —— *ni noboru* to an ascent on to the top. Thus *yama o noboru* means 'climb (up the side of) a mountain' and *yama ni noboru*, 'climb (the summit of) a mountain'. Cf. the n. to Lesson 7, l. 9 on the use of *o* with verbs of motion.

o-magari nasai: a common polite imperative form consisting of the base of the verb preceded by the honorific *o-*, and the imperative of the honorific verb *nasaru*, 'do'. Hence: 'Be so good as to do (*nasai*) a turning (*o-magari*)'.

16 osiete kuremasita: *kureru* and *kudasaru* both mean 'give' and are used with both direct objects and with the *-te* forms of verbs. In the latter construction they convey the idea of 'condescend by ——ing', and hence 'be good/kind enough to ——'. It is seldom necessary to express this idea in translation when *kureru* is used, however, because it does not show as much respect for the 'giver' as *kudasaru*.

osiete moratta toori ni: 'in the way that I had (him) tell me', i.e. 'as directed'. The *-te morau* construction means 'receive a ——ing', i.e. have someone do something for one. *Itadaku*, 'receive (with reverence)', is used in exactly the same way as *morau* but, being a very humble verb, is much more respectful to the person performing the action. When this person, the agent, is expressed in Japanese, by the way, it is followed by the particle *ni*, e.g. *sensei ni yonde moraimasita* (*itadakimasita*), 'I received a reading by my teacher', i.e. 'I had my teacher (kindly) read it'.

20 matte kudasai: the *-te* form of a verb (or the base preceded by *o-* as in *o-mati*) before *kudasai* is the most common form of polite imperative.

21 sanzyuubyoo bakari: with numerals *bakari* means 'thereabouts; or so'. It is only with other words that it can be translated as 'only'.

21–22 watasi no hoo o muite: *o muku* is only used after words involving direction, e.g. *hidari, sita.*

23 tegami ga . . . kakitai: see n. to Lesson 7, ll. 6–7.

24 sika kakarimasen: *sika* (or, more emphatically, *bakari sika* or *dake sika*) with a negative verb means 'only' or, more literally, 'not . . . but'. Thus, here: 'it will not take but (ten minutes or so)'.

26 doozo: softens a following imperative, here left unexpressed.

27–28 akarui no desu: in describing past events, Japanese often uses an historic present tense, which is usually best translated into English by a plain past.

36 gaikoku de no keiken: *no* is used to make the phrase *gaikoku de* attributive to the noun *keiken*. Literally, then '(his) in-foreign-countries experiences'.

竹	118/0	**TIKU take** bamboo									
	ナ ケ	ノ	ﾉ	⺮	⺮	竹	竹				
両	1/5	**RYOO** both									
	リ ョ ウ 両	一	一	一	丙	両	両				
貧	12/9	**BIN** poverty									
	ビ ン	ノ	八	今	分	仒	分	斧	貧	貧	貧
乏	4/2	**BOO** deficiency									
	ホ ウ	ノ	㇉	乏	乏						
育	8/6	**IKU** education									
	イ ク	`	亠	云	云	云	育	育	育		
農	161/6	**NOO** farming									
	ノ ウ	口	曲	曲	曲	曲	農	農	農	農	農
死	78/2	**SI** * death; **si(nu)** *vi* die									
	シ	一	丆	歹	歹	歹	死				
責	154/4	**SEKI** duty									
	セ キ	一	十	丰	主	丰	青	青	青	責	責
任	9/4	**NIN** responsibility; appointment (to office)									
	ニ ン	ノ	イ	仁	仁	仟	任				
調	149/8	**TYOO** tune; **sira(beru)** *vt* investigate, search									
	チ ョ ウ	`	言	言	言	訂	訂	訂	調	調	調

過	162/9	**KA** su(giru) *vi*, su(gosu) *vt* pass; -su(giru), *v. suff.* —to excess
	カ 過	丨 冂 冂 冊 冎 冎 咼 咼 咼 過 過
損	64/10	**SON** * loss
	ソン	一 十 扌 扌 扩 护 捐 捐 損 損
例	9/6	**REI** * example; tato(eba) for example
	レイ	丿 亻 仁 伢 佇 例 例 例
婚	38/8	**KON** marriage
	コン	く 女 女 妒 妒 妒 婚 婚 婚 婚
糸	120/0	**SI** ito thread
	シ 絲	幺 幺 幺 千 弁 糸
誕	149/8	**TAN** birth
	タン	亠 言 言 言 訂 訂 誕 誕 誕 誕
夫	4/3	**HU** man; otto husband
	フ	一 二 夫 夫
妻	38/5	**SAI** * tuma wife
	サイ	一 彐 彐 彐 圭 妻 妻 妻
乗	4/8	**ZYOO** no(ru) *vi* ride; no(seru) *vt* give ride to, put on (vehicle etc.)
	ジョウ 乘	丿 乀 二 乑 乑 乑 乖 乖 乗
汽	85/4	**KI** steam
	キ	丶 丶 氵 汽 汽 汽 汽

鉄	167/5	**TETU** * iron									
	テ ツ	鐵	ノ	ノ	年	牟	金	釗	釒	鉌	鉢	鉄
橋	75/12	**KYOO** hasi bridge									
	キョ ウ		木	栌	栌	栌	林	枯	棒	橋	橋	橋
工	48/0	**KOO, KU** work									
	コ ウ		一	丁	工							
速	162/7	**SOKU** speed									
	ソ ク	速	一	一	一	日	申	束	束	凍	涑	速
力	19/0	**RYOKU, RIKI** tikara power, strength									
	リョ ク キ		フ	力								
熱	86/11	**NETU** * heat, fever; **atu(i)** hot									
	ネ ツ		土	夫	坴	坴ノ	埶	埶	熱	熱	熱	熱
然	86/8	**ZEN** " -ness " etc.									
	ゼ ン		ノ	ク	タ	タ	タ-	タ大	外	然	然	然
戦	62/9	**SEN** battle									
	セ ン	戰	ツ	ヅ	沖	当	旦	単	単	戦	戦	戦
争	4/5	**SOO** fighting									
	ソ ウ	争	ノ	ク	ヨ	乌	乌	争				
祭	113/6	**SAI** maturi festival									
	サ イ		ノ	タ	タ	タフ	癶	祭	祭	祭	祭	祭

不	1/3	**HU** not								
	フ	一	ア	不	不					

苦	140/5	**KU*** suffering; **kuru(simu)** *vi* suffer; **kuru(sii)** painful; **niga(i)** bitter								
	ク	一	ヰ	サ	艹	芓	芒	苦	苦	

失	4/4	**SITU** loss, error								
	シツ	ノ	亡	乍	失	失				

礼	113/1	**REI *** politeness, thanks								
	レイ	禮	丶	ラ	ネ	ネ	礼			

遠	162/10	**EN too(i)** far								
	エン	遠	一	圭	吉	吉	专	専	袁	袁	遠

慮	141/9	**RYO** consider								
	リョ	丨	上	上	广	虍	虍	虘	虜	慮	慮

億	9/13	**OKU** hundred million								
	オク	亻	亻	仁	位	位	倍	億	億	億	億

円	13/2	**EN *** yen; **maru(i)** round								
	エン	圓	丨	冂	冂	円				

財	154/3	**ZAI** wealth								
	ザイ	丨	冂	月	月	目	貝	貝	財	財	財

産	117/6	**SAN u(mu)** *vt* produce, give birth to								
	サン	産	丶	亠	六	立	产	产	産	産	産

活	85/6	**KATU** living, activity									
	ガ ツ	`	:	シ	シ	汁	汗	汗	活	活	
願	4/18	**GAN** nega(u) *vt* request									
	ガ ン	一	厂	厂	居	原	原	原	顆	願	願
符	118/5	**HU** tally, token									
	フ	ノ	ト	片	片	竹	竹	竹	竹	符	符
枚	75/4	**MAI** (unit for counting 'sheets' etc.)									
	マ イ	一	十	才	木	朴	朴	枚	枚		
芝	140/2	**siba** turf									
		一	ヤ	サ	サ	芝	芝				
居	44/5	**KYO** i(ru) *vi*, o(ru) *vi* (*def.*) be									
	キ ョ	フ	コ	尸	尸	尼	居	居	居		
零	173/5	**REI** * zero									
	レ イ	一	二	乛	币	雨	雫	雫	零	零	零
業	3/12	**GYOO** industry									
	ギ ョ ウ	｜	｜｜	｜｜	｜｜	业	芣	芣	業	業	業
成	62/2	**SEI** na(ru) *vi* become, reach completion									
	セ イ	ノ	厂	厉	成	成	成				
功	48/2	**KOO** achievement									
	コ ウ	一	エ	エ	功	功					

[95]

十一

竹田さんは、両親が貧乏でしたから、義務教育が終るとすぐ北海道の農場へ行って働かなければいけませんでした。五年ばかり前に、農場の主人が死んで竹田さんがその責任者になりました。はじめは調子がよかったのですが、過去三年間は損をしているそうです。竹田さんは何か新しい計画を立てる目的で、日本のばかりでなく外国の農場の例も調べています。

竹田さんは去年結婚しました。先週の水曜日に奥さんの糸子さんと一緒に東京へ出て来ました。その日はわたしの誕生日でしたから竹田さん夫妻を晩御飯によびました。竹田さんたちが乗っていた汽車は鉄橋の工事のため速力をゆるめたので、上野駅へ着いたのは八時過ぎでした。食事が終ってわたしたちは農場の事を話しました。

[96]

竹田さんは普通は言葉の少ない人ですが、農場の問題では会話に熱中します。

「農場の仕事はなかなか楽じゃありません。わたしたちの仕事は自然を相手とする戦争です。日曜日も祭日も休まないで働いても、天気がわるい年は大きな損をするのです。そしてお金の事で不必要な苦心をします。もう少しお金があればと思う事がどのくらいあるか分かりません」。

「失礼ですがお金の事は御遠慮なくわたしに相談して下さい。わたしは父が死んだ時、一億円ばかりの財産が手に入りました。わたしは親の残した財産を使って、何も社会の役に立たない生活をするのはきらいです。それでわたしはお金の事であなたを助けて上げたいと思うんです」。

「どうもありがとうございます。わたしはどんなに苦しくても出来るだけ自分の力でして行こうと思います。けれども、どうにもならない事があるかも知れませんから、その時にはどうぞよろしくお願いします」。

竹田さん夫妻はきのうまで東京で過ごしました。きのうの晩には切符を三枚もらいましたから、三人で芝居を見に行きました。そして二人は零時二十五分の汽車で神戸へ立って行きました。竹田さんのいとこは神戸の大学で農業経済の先生をしているので、この人に会いに行くのだと言っていました。

竹田さんは今苦しんでいますが、まだわかいのですからいつか必ず成功するでしょう。奥さんも立派な妻として、夫の竹田さんを助けて行くと思います。

LESSON 11

ZYUUITI

TAKEDA-SAN wa, ryoosin ga binboo desita kara, gimu-kyooiku ga owaru to sugu Hokkaidoo no noozyoo e itte hatarakanakereba ikemasen desita. Gonen bakari mae ni, noozyoo no syuzin ga sinde Takeda-san ga sono sekininsya ni narimasita. Hazime wa tyoosi ga yokatta no desu ga, kako sannenkan wa son o site iru soo desu. Takeda-san wa nanika atarasii keikaku o tateru mokuteki de, Nihon no bakari de naku gaikoku no noozyoo no rei mo sirabete imasu.

Takeda-san wa kyonen kekkon simasita. Sensyuu no suiyoo-bi ni okusan no Itoko-san to issyo ni Tookyoo e dete kimasita. Sono hi wa watasi no tanzyoo-bi desita kara Takeda-san husai o ban-gohan ni yobimasita. Takeda-san tati ga notte ita kisya wa tekkyoo no koozi no tame sokuryoku o yurumeta no de, Ueno-eki e tuita no wa hatizi sugi desita. Syokuzi ga owatte watasitati wa noozyoo no koto o hanasimasita. Takeda-san wa hutuu wa kotoba no sukunai hito desu ga, noozyoo no mondai de wa kaiwa ni nettyuu simasu.

'Noozyoo no sigoto wa nakanaka raku d'ya arimasen. Watasitati no sigoto wa sizen o aite to suru sensoo desu. Nitiyoo-bi mo saizitu mo yasumanai de hataraite mo, tenki ga warui tosi wa ooki na son o suru no desu. Sosite o-kane no koto de huhituyoo na kusin o simasu. Moo sukosi o-kane ga areba to omou koto ga dono kurai aru ka wakarimasen.'

'Siturei desu ga o-kane no koto wa go-enryo naku watasi ni soodan site kudasai. Watasi wa titi ga sinda toki, itiokuen bakari no zaisan ga te ni hairimasita. Watasi wa oya no nokosita zaisan o tukatte, nanimo syakai no yaku ni tatanai seikatu o suru no wa kirai desu. Sore de watasi wa o-kane no koto de anata o tasukete agetai to omoun' desu.'

'Doomo arigatoo gozaimasu. Watasi wa donna ni kurusikute mo dekiru dake zibun no tikara de site ikoo to omoimasu. Keredomo, doo ni mo naranai koto ga aru ka mo siremasen kara, sono toki ni wa doozo yorosiku o-negai simasu.'

Takeda-san husai wa kinoo made Tookyoo de sugosimasita. Kinoo no ban ni wa kippu o sanmai moraimasita kara, sannin de sibai o mi ni ikimasita. Sosite hutari wa reizi-nizyuugohun no kisya de Koobe e tatte ikimasita. Takeda-san no itoko wa Koobe no daigaku de noogyoo keizai no sensei o site iru no de, kono hito ni ai ni iku no da to itte imasita.

Takeda-san wa ima kurusinde imasu ga, mada wakai no desu kara ituka kanarazu seikoo suru desyoo. Okusan mo rippa na tuma to site, otto no Takeda-san o tasukete iku to omoimasu.

Notes

2 owatu to: *to* added to the plain 'dictionary' form of a verb means 'if' or 'when'. Note that this can become either a present or, as here, a past tense in English, depending on the tense of the main verb in the Japanese sentence.

5 tyoosi: the basic meaning of 'tune; tone' is extended, as in English, to refer to the 'condition' of the body, engines, the market, etc.

6 nanika: makes a following noun less definite; '—— or something; some —— or other'.

6–7 . . . bakari de naku . . . mo: 'not only (Japanese) but also (foreign examples)'.

11 tame: a noun meaning 'purpose, benefit, sake', it is used with verbs and other nouns to mean: (i) 'on account of', as here, and (ii) 'in order to', e.g. *hon o kau tame (ni)*, 'in order to buy a book'.

12 noozyoo no koto o hanasimasita: 'we talked farm matters', i.e. '—— about farming'. *Koto* is often equivalent to the English 'about'; see, e.g., l. 17 below *o-kane no koto de*, 'on matters of/about money'.

15–16 sizen o aite to suru sensoo: 'a war which makes Nature as (*to*) the opponent'; *aite* means 'opposite number, partner' in the sense of 'companion' or 'opponent'.

16 yasumanai de: 'without rest(ing)'; *de* following the plain negative of a verb is often used in place of the regular negative -*te* form -*nakute*.

hataraite mo: 'even working; even though (we) work'.

18 moo sukosi o-kane ga areba to omou: 'I think, "If I had a little more money . . ."'

18–19 . . . koto ga dono kurai aru ka wakarimasen: 'I don't know to what extent it happens that . . .'; i.e. 'I can't tell you how often I . . .'

20 go-enryo naku: 'without reserve'; a phrase much used to encourage people to make themselves at home, not stand on ceremony, etc.

21 te ni hairimasita: 'came into (my) hands'; *te ni hairu* is a common expression for 'obtain'.

22 nanimo: makes the following negative expression more emphatic: '(be of no service) whatever; (be) quite (useless)'.

23 Sore de: 'It being that', i.e. 'That being so; So . . .'.

anata o tasukete agetai: 'I want/would like to help you'; -*te ageru* and, less respectfully, -*te yaru* mean literally 'offer up/give a (do)ing' and are used when the speaker or some such 'inferior' does something for someone else. Cf. n. to Lesson 10, l. 16 on the parallel uses of -*te kudasaru* and -*te kureru* for 'giving' *to* an inferior.

25 donna ni kurusikute mo: 'even if it is painful in whatever way'; i.e. 'however hard it may be'. An interrogative word followed by -*te mo* can usually be rendered by an '——ever' in English, e.g. *doko e itte mo*, 'wherever (he) goes'.

26 site ikoo to omoimasu: 'I think/feel that I shall go along doing (things) . . .' Cf. *tasukete iku*, ll. 35–36 below.

26–27 doo ni mo naranai koto: 'something which does not turn out any way at all'; i.e. 'something which comes to nothing' or, as here, 'something which cannot be resolved; an impasse'.

27 doozo yorosiku: 'please (do) well (by me, etc.)'. This phrase, with or without *o-negai simasu*, 'I humbly request', is used to commend someone to the good offices of the person addressed.

30 mi ni ikimasita: see n. to Lesson 8, ll. 10–11.

35 rippa na tuma to site: '(in her capacity) as a good wife'.

景	72/8	**KEI, KE** scenery, appearance									
	ケイ ケ		丶	冂	日	甲	旦	早	昴	昌	景	景
色	139/0	**SYOKU, SIKI** iro colour									
	ショク シキ		⁄	⁊	占	占	毎	色			
展	44/7	**TEN** unroll, exhibit									
	テン		丆	𠃍	尸	尸	屈	屈	屉	展	展
覧	147/9	**RAN** look									
	ラン 覧		丨	丆	丆	臣	臣	臣	臤	監	覧
陸	170/8	**RIKU** * land (as opposed to 'sea')									
	リ ク		𠃌	阝	阝	阝⁻	阝⁺	阹	陸	陸	陸
軍	14/7	**GUN** army									
	グ ン		⁄	冖	冖	写	屌	吾	冒	宣	軍
平	1/4	**HEI, HYOO** tai(ra na), hira(tai) flat, even									
	ヘヒ イウ ョ		一	丆	丆	立	平				
耳	128/0	**ZI** mimi ear									
	ジ		一	丅	打	斤	耳	耳			
適	162/11	**TEKI** suitable									
	テ キ	適	丶	亠	古	啇	产	商	商	啇	適
職	128/12	**SYOKU** occupation, work									
	ショ ク		耳	耵	耴	耶	聊	耺	睢	職	職	職

殺	79/6	**SATU** **koro(su)** *vt* kill
	サツ	ノ ㄨ 三 手 ⺶ ⺶ 杀 杀 杀 殺
炭	46/6	**TAN** coal; **sumi** charcoal
	タン	丨 山 山 ⺊ ⺊ 岸 炭 炭 炭
鉱	167/5	**KOO** mineral
	コウ	鑛 ノ ㇒ ⺍ ⾦ ⾦ 金 金' 釒 鉱 鉱
満	85/9	**MAN** full
	マン	満 氵 汀 汀 汁 満 洪 満 満 満 満
足	157/0	**SOKU** **asi** foot, leg; **ta(riru)** *vi* suffice
	ソク	丶 ㅁ 口 早 足 足 足
艦	137/14	**KAN** warship
	カン	丿 舟 舟 舮 舻 舻 艦 艦 艦 艦
敵	66/11	**TEKI** * enemy
	テキ	丶 ㇒ ⺇ 啇 啇 啇 敵 敵 敵
島	4/9	**TOO** **sima** island
	トウ	ノ 亻 ⼾ ⼾ 白 白 鳥 鳥 島 島
刀	18/0	**TOO** **katana** sword
	トウ	フ 刀
将	90/7	**SYOO** officer; future
	ショウ	将 丨 ⺕ 扌 护 护 护 护 将 将 将

兵	4/6	**HEI** soldier									
	ヘイ		ノ	丷	仁	斤	丘	乒	兵			
隊	170/9	**TAI** * (military) unit									
	タイ		阝	阝	阝	阼	陼	防	防	隊	隊	隊
臣	131/0	**SIN** subject, retainer									
	シン		丨	匚	匸	臣	臣	臣	臣			
信	9/7	**SIN** (-ziru) *vt* believe in									
	シン		ノ	イ	仁	仨	仨	信	信	信	信	
団	31/3	**DAN** group									
	ダン	團	丨	冂	冃	用	団	団				
体	9/5	**TAI** karada body									
	タイ	體	ノ	イ	仁	什	休	休	体			
庭	53/7	**TEI** niwa garden									
	テイ		丶	亠	广	广	庁	庄	庭	庭	庭	
性	61/5	**SEI** * sex; nature									
	セイ		丨	忄	忄	忄	忄	忤	性	性		
質	154/8	**SITU** * quality; **SITI** * pawn, pledge									
	シ シ ツ チ		ノ	厂	斤	斤	竹	竹	竹	質	質	質
連	162/7	**REN** connection; tu(reru) *vt* take (someone) along									
	レン	連	一	亓	亓	亓	亘	車	車	連	連	

| 絡 | 120/6 | **RAKU** bind together | | | | | | | | | |
| | ラ ク／絡 | く | 纟 | 幺 | 纟 | 糸 | 糸 | 紅 | 紋 | 終 | 絡 |

| 偶 | 9/9 | **GŪU** chance | | | | | | | | | |
| | グ ウ | イ | 们 | 们 | 俱 | 偅 | 偶 | 偶 | 偶 | 偶 | |

| 芸 | 140/4 | **GEI** * artistic accomplishment | | | | | | | | | |
| | ケ イ／藝 | 一 | 十 | 艹 | 艹 | 芒 | 芸 | 芸 | | | |

| 短 | 111/7 | **TAN mizika(i)** short | | | | | | | | | |
| | タ ン | ノ | 上 | 午 | 矢 | 知 | 知 | 短 | 短 | | |

| 徒 | 60/7 | **TO** follower | | | | | | | | | |
| | ト | ノ | ク | 彳 | 彳 | 徉 | 华 | 徍 | 徉 | 徒 | |

| 馬 | 187/0 | **BA uma** horse | | | | | | | | | |
| | バ | 1 | 厂 | 厂 | 厈 | 馬 | 馬 | 馬 | 馬 | 馬 | 馬 |

| 牛 | 93/0 | **GYŪU usi** ox, cow, bull | | | | | | | | | |
| | ギュウ | ノ | ヒ | 二 | 牛 | | | | | | |

| 肉 | 130/0 | **NIKU** * meat, flesh | | | | | | | | | |
| | ニ ク | 1 | 冂 | 内 | 内 | 肉 | 肉 | | | | |

| 酒 | 85/7 | **SYU sake** rice-wine, (alcoholic) drink | | | | | | | | | |
| | シュ | 丶 | 二 | シ | 汀 | 汀 | 沂 | 洒 | 洒 | 酒 | |

| 杯 | 75/4 | **HAI** vesselful | | | | | | | | | |
| | ハ イ | 一 | 十 | 才 | 木 | 朾 | 杯 | 杯 | 杯 | | |

全	9/4	**ZEN** **matta(ku)** completely								
	ゼン	ノ	入	仝	仐	仐	全			
決	85/4	**KETU** ki(maru) *vi* be decided, **ki(meru)** *vt* decide; **kes(site)** with neg.: by no means, never								
	ケツ	丶	冫	氵	沪	沪	汢	決		
覚	147/5	**KAKU** obo(eru) *vt* remember, learn								
	カク	覺	丶	丷	丷	丷	炏	炒	炒	覚	覚
悟	61/7	**GO** perception								
	ゴ	丨	忄	忄	忄	忆	忏	悟	悟	悟
乱	135/1	**RAN** disorder								
	ラン	亂	ノ	二	千	舌	舌	舌	乱	
暴	72/11	**BOO** violence								
	ボウ	日	旦	早	昇	昗	昇	異	异	暴	暴
棒	75/8	**BOO** * stick, pole, bar								
	ボウ	一	木	朾	朾	栏	栱	栱	栱	棒	棒
巡	162/3	**ZYUN** make the rounds								
	ジュン	巡	く	巜	巛	巛	巡	巡		
査	75/5	**SA** investigate								
	サ	査	一	十	才	木	杏	杏	杳	査
署	122/8	**SYO** (government) office; signing								
	ショ	署	丶	冖	罒	罒	罒	罘	罘	罘	署

十二

秋山さんはわかい絵書きです。特に景色の絵が大変上手です。毎年秋の終りか冬のはじめにある展覧会へ絵を送りますが、まだ成功した事がありません。

秋山さんのお父さんは陸軍の軍人でした。戦争が終って平和になった時、耳がよく聞こえないために適当な職業が見付からない事を心配して自殺してしまいました。長い間苦しい生活をしたお母さんは夫に死なれて生きて行く力がなくなり、一年もたたない内に死にました。両親をなくした秋山さんはしばらく石炭の鉱業会社で働いていましたが、満足出来る仕事ではありませんでした。

秋山さんにはことし七十八になるおじいさんがあります。むかしは海軍の軍人でした。わかい時 小さい軍艦に乗って敵のいる島に

上陸して刀で敵の将校とか兵隊を十人ばかり切り殺したという話しです。大臣とけんかして海軍をやめてから神道をふかく信じるようになりました。何か宗教的な団体に入った事もあります。今では海に近い小さな村でしずかにくらしています。

秋山さんはこういう軍人の家庭に生れた人とは思われない性質を持っています。わたしは四国へ行く連絡船の上で偶然会ってから、秋山さんは芸術家としては立派な人だと思っています。けれども秋山さんには一つ大きな短所があります。秋山さんがまだ小学校の生徒だった時、ある日おじいさんが馬車で秋山さんのうちへ来ました。おじいさんとお母さんが牛肉の料理をしてみなで食事をしました。お父さんは少し日本酒を飲みましたが、秋山さんはだれも見ていない時、お酒を茶わんに一杯入れて全部飲んでしまいました。あとで

25秋山さんは非常に苦しんで、お酒は決して飲まない覚悟をしました

が、それは長くつづきませんでした。

今では秋山さんは酒とタバコとコーヒーがなくては生きて行けな

いそうです。秋山さんの短所と言うのは酒を飲んで乱暴をする事で

す。こないだも友だちと二人で料理屋へ行った時、お酒を飲んだ秋

30山さんは棒か何かで友だちの頭を強くうちました。そばにいた人が

とめようとしましたが、秋山さんはその人の足をけりました。料理

屋の主人が巡査をよんで来て、秋山さんは警察署へ連れられて行き

ました。頭をうたれた友だちはまだ入院しています。

秋山さんはこの晩に何をしたか少しも覚えていないそうです。い

35なかで、牛とか馬とかぶたなどの動物をかっているおじいさんは、

こまったまごだと思っているでしょう。

LESSON 12

ZYUUNI

AKIYAMA-SAN wa wakai ekaki desu. Toku ni kesiki no e ga taihen zyoozu desu. Mainen aki no owari ka huyu no hazime ni aru tenrankai e e o okurimasu ga, mada seikoo sita koto ga arimasen. Akiyama-san no otoosan wa rikugun no gunzin desita. Sensoo ga owatte heiwa ni natta toki, mimi ga yoku kikoenai tame ni tekitoo na syokugyoo ga mitukaranai koto o sinpai site zisatu site simaimasita. Nagai aida kurusii seikatu o sita okaasan wa otto ni sinarete ikite iku tikara ga nakunari, itinen mo tatanai uti ni sinimasita. Ryoosin o nakusita Akiyama-san wa sibaraku sekitan no koogyoo-gaisya de hataraite imasita ga, manzoku dekiru sigoto de wa arimasen desita.

Akiyama-san ni wa kotosi sitizyuuhati ni naru oziisan ga arimasu. Mukasi wa kaigun no gunzin desita. Wakai toki, tiisai gunkan ni notte teki no iru sima ni zyooriku site katana de teki no syookoo toka heitai o zyuunin bakari kirikorosita to yuu hanasi desu. Daizin to kenka site kaigun o yamete kara Sintoo o hukaku sin-ziru yoo ni narimasita. Nanika syuukyoo-teki na dantai ni haitta koto mo arimasu. Ima de wa umi ni tikai tiisa na mura de sizuka ni kurasite imasu.

Akiyama-san wa koo yuu gunzin no katei ni umareta hito to wa omowarenai seisitu o motte imasu. Watasi wa Sikoku e iku renrakusen no ue de guuzen atte kara, Akiyama-san wa geizyutuka to site wa rippa na hito da to omotte imasu. Keredomo Akiyama-san ni wa hitotu ooki na tansyo ga arimasu. Akiyama-san ga mada syoogakkoo no seito datta toki, aru hi oziisan ga basya de Akiyama-san no ie e kimasita. Okaasan ga gyuuniku no ryoori o site mina de syokuzi o simasita. Oziisan to otoosan wa sukosi Nihonsyu o nomimasita ga, Akiyama-san wa daremo mite inai toki, o-sake o tyawan ni ippai irete zenbu nonde simaimasita. Ato de Akiyama-san wa hizyoo ni kurusinde, o-sake wa kessite nomanai kakugo o simasita ga, sore wa nagaku tuzukimasen desita.

Ima de wa Akiyama-san wa sake to tabako to koohii ga nakute wa ikite ikenai soo desu. Akiyama-san no tansyo to yuu no wa sake o nonde ranboo o suru koto desu. Konaida mo tomodati to hutari de ryooriya e itta toki, o-sake o nonda Akiyama-san wa boo ka nanika de tomodati no atama o tuyoku utimasita. Soba ni ita hito ga tomeyoo to simasita ga, Akiyama-san wa sono hito no asi o kerimasita. Ryooriya no syuzin ga zyunsa o yonde kite, Akiyama-san wa keisatusyo e turerarete ikimasita. Atama o utareta tomodati wa mada nyuuin site imasu.

Akiyama-san wa kono ban ni nani o sita ka sukosi mo oboete inai soo desu. Inaka de, usi toka uma toka buta nado no doobutu o katte iru oziisan wa, komatta mago da to omotte iru desyoo.

LESSON 12

Notes

3 ka: between nouns means 'or'. Beware, however: *A ka B desu ka* means only 'Is it A-or-B?', i.e. is it either of them? To ask 'is it A or (is it) B?', two parallel sentences must be used: *A desu ka. B desu ka.*

6 kikoenai: usually 'cannot be heard' (see n. to Lesson 7, l. 27), but with *mimi* as the subject it means 'cannot hear'.

7 -te simaimasita: following a -te form, *simau* gives a sense of finality. See l. 24 below: *nonde simaimasita*, 'drank it right down'.

8 otto ni sinarete: the passive forms of verbs (both *vi* and *vt*) can be used with *ni* following the agent responsible for the action of the verb (and *o* following the object as usual, if there is one) to convey the feeling 'be caused trouble by someone -ing'. This is sometimes called an 'indirect' passive, and here expresses the idea 'she suffered the dying-by-her-husband'.

nakunari: suspensive form of *nakunaru*, here parallel to *sinimasita*; see n. to Lesson 9, l. 6.

A verb in the suspensive form may sometimes depend on a following verbal form, not only for its tense, but also for its mood and construction. That is, in a sentence such as *Gaikoku no dokuritu o sontyoo si, kozin no ziyuu o syooti sinakereba naranai*, 'One must respect the independence of foreign countries and acknowledge the freedom of the individual', (*sontyoo*) *si* is parallel to (*syooti*) *sinakereba*, and consequently shares the same negative conditional form and the same *-nakereba naranai*, 'must', construction; but such cases are usually clear enough from the context.

itinen mo tatanai uti ni: see n. to Lesson 8, ll. 35–36.

14–15 sin-ziru yoo ni narimasita: 'it turned out (in such a way) that he believed', i.e. 'he came to believe'. (*Sin-ziru*) *koto ni naru* has a very similar meaning.

16 tiisa na: alternative for *tiisai*. Similarly, *ooki na* (see l. 20 below) for *ookii*.

17 koo yuu: equivalent to *konna*, 'this kind of'.

... hito ni wa omowarenai seisitu: 'a character which is not thought of as (that of) a person ...'

19 to site wa: 'as, in (his) capacity as'.

24 o-sake: here refers to *Nihonsyu*, 'rice-wine', but is used below in its other meaning of 'alcoholic drink' in general.

27–28 ikite ikenai soo desu: '(he) says that he could not go on living'. In the context, this *soo desu* (see n. to Lesson 8, l. 27) is better taken as referring to what Akiyama himself says. *Ikenai* is the negative of *ikeru*, potential of *iku*.

28 to yuu no wa: literally 'what (I) call', but this phrase has little force in Japanese. It often serves only to set off a noun or phrase to be explained, and here 'this (shortcoming)' would be enough for it.

31 tomeyoo to simasita: the *-oo* form of a verb plus *to suru* covers two main meanings: (i) try to ——; (ii) be about to ——. Cf. the English 'make as if to ——' and the more or less literal 'he acted thus: he would stop him'.

32 syuzin ga zyunsa o yonde kite: 'the proprietor came along, having called a policeman, and ...' or, according to the English way of thinking, '—— went and called ——'.

32–33 turerarete ikimasita: passive form of *turete iku* 'lead/take away'. *Turete ikaremasita* is an alternative.

33 atama o utareta tomodati: 'the friend who was hit on the head', *utareta* being an 'indirect' passive (see n. to l. 8 above).

[110]

植	75/8	**SYOKU**　u(eru)　*vt*　plant									
	ショク	一	木	朾	朾	村	枦	枯	椬	桔	植
識	149/12	**SIKI**　understand									
	シキ	言	言	訁	謸	詳	諳	諳	識	識	識
虫	142/0	**TYUU**　musi.　insect,　grub									
	チュウ	蟲	丶	冂	口	中	虫	虫			
害	40/7	**GAI** *　harm									
	ガイ	丶	宀	宀	宀	宝	宝	宝	害	害	害
法	85/5	**HOO** *　law,　rule									
	ホウ	丶	冫	氵	汀	汁	汢	法	法		
発	105/4	**HATU**　issue forth									
	ハッ	發	フ	ヌ	癶	癶	癶	癶	卆	発	
界	102/4	**KAI**　boundary									
	カイ	丶	冂	冂	田	田	甲	界	界	界	
形	59/4	**KEI,**　**GYOO**　katati　form									
	ケイ ギョウ	一	二	干	开	形	形	形			
実	40/5	**ZITU** *　truth;　**mi**　fruit, nut									
	ジッ	實	丶	宀	宀	宀	宁	宇	実		
際	170/11	**SAI** *　occasion;　limit									
	ナイ	阝	阝	阡	阡	阼	阼	隆	陝	際	際

由	2/4 ユ ウ	**YUU** reason	丨	冂	巾	由	由			
央	2/4 オ ウ	**OO** centre	丶	冂	央	史	央			
丸	4/2 ガ ン	**GAN** ball; **-maru** (suffix added to names of ships); **maru(i)** round	ノ	九	丸					
貝	154/0	kai shell	丨	冂	月	月	目	貝	貝	
草	140/6 ソ ウ	**SOO** kusa grass, vegetation	一	十	サ	艹	芦	芇	芑	苜 草
花	140/4 カ	**KA** hana flower	一	十	サ	艹	疒	花	花	
赤	155/0 セ キ	**SEKI** aka, aka(i) red	一	十	土	亍	赤	赤	赤	
菜	140/8 サ イ	**SAI** vegetable	一	艹	艹	艹	芇	苧	苹 芣	菜 菜
鳥	196/0 チョ ウ	**TYOO** tori bird	ノ	亻	广	白	自	鸟	鸟	鳥 鳥 鳥
鳴	30/11 メ イ	**MEI na(ku)** vi sing(of birds, insects etc.); **na(ru)** vi sound, ring (of bells etc.)	丶	冂	口	叮	叨	吖	咆	鳴 鳴 鳴

球	96/7	**KYUU** **tama** ball									
	キュウ	一	丁	干	王	玌	玎	玗	玝	球	球
種	115/9	**SYU** sort; **tane** seed									
	シュ	ノ	千	禾	禾	秆	秆	秆	稆	種	種
可	1/4	**KA** possibility, permission									
	カ	一	丁	戸	戸	可					
能	22/8	**NOO** * Nō (drama); ability									
	ノ ウ	ム	ム	自	肖	肖	自	能	能	能	
件	9/4	**KEN** matter									
	ケン	ノ	亻	亻	仁	仵	件				
現	96/7	**GEN** appear, present									
	ゲン	一	丁	干	王	珇	玑	玥	珇	現	現
在	32/3	**ZAI** be present									
	ザイ	一	ナ	才	木	在	在				
倍	9/8	**BAI** * double; —times									
	バイ	ノ	亻	亻	仁	代	俗	位	倅	倍	倍
坂	32/4	**HAN** **saka** slope									
	ハン	一	十	土	圹	圻	坂	坂			
置	122/8	**TI** o(ku) *vt* put, place									
	チ	丶	一	罒	罒	甲	甼	罘	罢	署	置

[113]

片	91/0	**HEN** (kata) one side, one (of two)								
	ヘン	ノ	バ	广	片					

美	123/3	**BI** * beauty; **utuku(sii)** beautiful								
	ビ	丶	ヽ	丷	꾸	羊	羊	美	美	美

原	27/8	**GEN** origin; **hara** moorland								
	ケン	一	厂	厂	尸	厈	所	盾	厚	原 原

因	31/3	**IN** origin, cause								
	イン	丨	冂	冃	冈	因	因			

賛	154/8	**SAN** approval								
	サン 賛	一	二	夫	夫	扶	梺	梺	替	賛

反	27/2	**HAN** opposition, anti-								
	ハン	一	厂	万	反					

対	67/3	**TAI** confront								
	タイ 對	丶	亠	ナ	疒	文	対	対		

議	149/13	**GI** discussion								
	ギ	言	訝	詳	詳	詳	詳	議	議	議

辺	162/2	**HEN** * locality								
	ヘン 邊	フ	刀	刃	切	辺				

構	75/10	**KOO** structure; **kama(u)** *vi* care about; **kama(eru)** *vt* set up (as)								
	コウ	木	杧	栌	椲	椲	槹	構	構	構

| 組 | 120/5 | **SO** **kumi** group, class, team |
| | ソ 組 | ⺖ ⺀ ⺀ ⺀ 糸 糸 糸 糸 糸 組 |

| 織 | 120/12 | **SIKI,** **SYOKU** **o(ru)** *vt* weave |
| | シキ/ショク 織 | 糸 糸 糸 糸 糸 糸 織 織 織 |

| 選 | 162/12 | **SEN** **era(bu)** *vt* choose |
| | セン 選 | ⺆ ⺕ 己 己 己 己 巽 巽 巽 選 |

| 挙 | 64/6 | **KYO** raise |
| | キョ 挙 | ⺀ ⺀ ⺀ ⺌ ⺌ 兴 兴 挙 挙 挙 |

| 簡 | 118/12 | **KAN** simple |
| | カン 簡 | ⺮ ⺮ ⺮ ⺮ ⺮ 節 節 簡 簡 簡 |

| 単 | 3/8 | **TAN** unit, simple |
| | タン 単 | ⺀ ⺀ ⺀ ⺀ ⺌ 当 当 単 単 |

| 態 | 61/10 | **TAI** form, manner |
| | タイ 態 | ⺀ ⺀ 肖 角 能 能 能 態 態 態 |

| 個 | 9/8 | **KO,** **KA** individual |
| | コ カ | ノ 亻 们 们 佣 佣 佣 個 個 |

| 直 | 24/6 | **TYOKU,** **ZIKI** direct; **ZIKI** * immediate; **nao(su)** *vt* put right, mend |
| | チョク/ジキ | 一 十 十 古 古 直 直 |

| 接 | 64/8 | **SETU** contact |
| | セツ | 一 十 扌 扩 拉 拉 拉 接 接 接 |

十三

ワタシノ家ノ近所ニ大キナ植物園ガアリマス。ムカシハ大名ノ庭

デシタガ、早川博士ノオカゲデ立派ナ植物園ニナリマシタ。早川博

士ハ有名ナ植物学者デスガ、化学ノ知識モフカク、毛虫ノ損害ヲ少ナ

クスル方法ヲ発見シタ人トシテ世界ニ知ラレテイマス。コノ植物園

ハ形式的ニハ大学デ植物学ヲ勉強スル学生ノタメノモノデスガ、実

際ハグレデモ自由ニ入レマス。ムカシノ大名ノ家ハコワレテ今ハア

リマセンガ庭ノ一部分ハソノママニ残ッテイテ、日本式ノ庭ノ一番

イイ例ノ一ツニナッテイマス。

植物園ノ中央ニハ丸イ池ガアッテ、水ノ中デサカナガオヨイデイ

ルノガ見エマス。池ノマワリニハ大キナ石ガアリマスガ、ソノ外側

ニハ色々ナ形ノ貝ガナラベテアッテ、石ト貝トノ間ニハイツモキレ

イナ草花ガサイテイマス。赤道ニ近イ所カラ来タメズラシイ木トカ花トカガ植エテアル建物モアリマス。大キナ野菜ノハタケモアリマス。オイシソウナ実ガ出来ル果物ノ木モ沢山アリマス。一部分ハ高クテ太イ木ガ多イ森ニナッテイテ、何万トイウ鳥ガ朝カラ晩マデ鳴イテイマス。コノ植物園デハ地球ノ上ノホトンド全部ノ種類ノ植物ガ見ラレルソウデス。

所ガ、今、植物園ニ関係シテ大キナ政治問題ニナル可能性ガアル事件ガオコッテイマス。元ノ大名ノ庭ハ現在ノ植物園ノ二倍以上ノ大キサデシタ。明治時代ノ終リニ、庭ノ東側ノ一部分ヲ売ッテ、小サナ家ヲ沢山建テマシタ。今、電車トカ自動車ナドガ通ッテイル道ハ植物園ノ西側ニアリマスガ、コレハセマクテ急ナ坂ガアルノデ交通ニ不便デス。東側ハ小サイ家ガジャマニナッテ新シイ道ヲ作ルノ

二ハ不適当デス。ソレデ植物園ヲ南カラ北ヘ半分ニ切ッテ、西ノ半

分ハ今マデノヨウニ植物園トシテ残シテ置キ、東ノ半分ノ中央ニ新

シイ道ヲ作ッテ、ソノ片側ニハ美術館ト病院トヲ建テ、片側ニハ商

店トカアパートナドヲ作ル計画ガアルノデス。コノ計画ガ原因ニナ

ッテ、賛成スル人ト反対スル人トガ議論ヲシテ、コノ辺ニ住ンデイ

ル人バカリデナク、議会トカ新聞ナドデモ問題ニナッテイマス。賛

成スル人ハ「大変結構ナ事ダ」ト言ッテイマスが、反対スル人ハ「ユ

ルス事ガ出来ナイツミダ」ト言ッテ反対運動ヲ組織ショウトシテイ

マス。選挙ガ近イノデ政府ハ簡単ニ態度ヲ決メル事ガ出来ナイヨウ

デス。ワタシハコノ問題ニハ直接ニ関係ガアリマセンカラ将来ドウ

ナッテモ構イマセンが、個人トシテハ有名ナ植物園ガ小サクナルノ

ハ残念ナ事ダト思ッテイマス。

ZYUUSAN

WATASI no ie no kinzyo ni ooki na syokubutuen ga arimasu. Mukasi wa daimyoo no niwa desita ga, Hayakawa-hakase no o-kage de rippa na syokubutuen ni narimasita. Hayakawa-hakase wa yuumei na syokubutugakusya desu ga, kagaku no tisiki mo hukaku, kemusi no songai o sukunaku suru hoohoo o hakken sita hito to site sekai ni sirarete imasu. Kono syokubutuen wa keisiki-teki ni wa daigaku de syokubutugaku o benkyoo suru gakusei no tame no mono desu ga, zissai wa daredemo ziyuu ni hairemasu. Mukasi no daimyoo no ie wa kowarete ima wa arimasen ga niwa no itibubun wa sono mama ni nokotte ite, Nihon-siki no niwa no itiban ii rei no hitotu ni natte imasu.

Syokubutuen no tyuuoo ni wa marui ike ga atte, mizu no naka de sakana ga oyoide iru no ga miemasu. Ike no mawari ni wa ooki na isi ga arimasu ga, sono sotogawa ni wa iroiro na katati no kai ga narabete atte, isi to kai to no aida ni wa itumo kirei na kusabana ga saite imasu. Sekidoo ni tikai tokoro kara kita mezurasii ki toka hana toka ga uete aru tatemono mo arimasu. Ooki na yasai no hatake mo arimasu. Oisi-soo na mi ga dekiru kudamono no ki mo takusan arimasu. Itibubun wa takakute hutoi ki ga ooi mori ni natte ite, nanman to yuu tori ga asa kara ban made naite imasu. Kono syokubutuen de wa tikyuu no ue no hotondo zenbu no syurui no syokubutu ga mirareru soo desu.

Tokoroga, ima, syokubutuen ni kankei site ooki na seizi mondai ni naru kanoosei ga aru ziken ga okotte imasu. Moto no daimyoo no niwa wa genzai no syokubutuen no nibai izyoo no ookisa desita. Meizi zidai no owari ni, niwa no higasigawa no itibubun o utte, tiisa na ie o takusan tatemasita. Ima, densya toka zidoosya nado ga tootte iru miti wa syokubutuen no nisigawa ni arimasu ga, kore wa semakute kyuu na saka ga aru no de kootuu ni huben desu. Higasigawa wa tiisai ie ga zyama ni natte atarasii miti o tukuru no ni wa hutekitoo desu. Sore de syokubutuen o minami kara kita e hanbun ni kitte, nisi no hanbun wa ima made no yoo ni syokubutuen to site nokosite oki, higasi no hanbun no tyuuoo ni atarasii miti o tukutte, sono katagawa ni wa bizyutukan to byooin to o tate, katagawa ni wa syooten toka apaato nado o tukuru keikaku ga aru no desu. Kono keikaku ga gen-in ni natte, sansei suru hito to hantai suru hito to ga giron o site, kono hen ni sunde iru hito bakari de naku, gikai toka sinbun nado de mo mondai ni natte imasu. Sansei suru hito wa 'Taihen kekkoo na koto da' to itte imasu ga, hantai suru hito wa 'Yurusu koto ga dekinai tumi da' to itte hantai undoo o sosiki siyoo to site imasu. Senkyo ga tikai no de seihu wa kantan ni taido o kimeru koto ga dekinai yoo desu.

Watasi wa kono mondai ni wa tyokusetu ni kankei ga arimasen kara syoorai doo natte mo kamaimasen ga, kozin to site wa yuumei na syokubutuen ga tiisaku naru no wa zannen na koto da to omotte imasu.

Notes

4 hukaku: the suspensive form of *hukai* (see n. to Lesson 9, l. 6). Here the parallel verb which gives *hukaku* its tense is (*sirarete*) *imasu.*

4-5 songai o sukunaku suru: Japanese often uses *sukunai* and *ooi* of things which, in English, are regarded quantitatively and described by such words as 'small, little' and 'big, much', e.g. *hookyuu ga sukunai*, 'the salary is small'; *ame ga ookatta*, 'there was much rain'.

7 hairemasu: potential form from *hairu.*

8 mama: a noun meaning 'unchanged state', hence 'just as it is/was', etc.; e.g. *sono mama ni oite kudasai*, 'please leave it as it is'; *kono mama de ii desu*, 'it is all right like this'.

12 kai ga narabete atte: 'shells having been set out in a row'. The *-te aru* form is a type of passive used with transitive verbs which imply in some way a change of position, and it describes a state resulting from someone's action. The subject of the *-te aru* form would be the object of the ordinary active verb (*kai o naraberu*, 'line up shells'). E.g. *hon ni namae o kaku*, 'write one's name in the book'; *hon ni namae ga kaite aru*, 'the name exists by (someone) writing it—i.e. is written—in the book'. See also l. 14 below.

15 Oisi-soo na mi ga dekiru ... ki: 'trees which produce delicious-looking fruit'. On the *-soo*, see n. to Lesson 8, ll. 13–14.

16 nanman to yuu tori: 'birds in their (tens of) thousands'.

18 mirareru: this regularly formed potential/passive of *miru* means 'can be seen', i.e. it is possible to see (something because one makes efforts to do so). It has some common ground with *mieru*, although this means rather 'be visible before the eyes' whether one does anything in order to see it or not; see, e.g., l. 11 above.

24-25 tukuru no ni wa hutekitoo: 'unsuitable for building'. See n. to Lesson 6, No. 10 on the two types of *no ni*, although the use of *wa* here shows that it can only be the pronoun and particle and not the conjunction.

25-28 ... hanbun ni kitte, ... nokosite oki, ... miti o tukutte, ... tate, ... tukuru keikaku ga aru no desu: the construction of the sentence is as follows: (i) *keikaku* is governed by the whole of the preceding part: 'There is a plan which ...'; (ii) the preceding part is in two halves, each introduced by a *-te* form going closely with the main verb or verbs that follow: *nokosite oki* in the first half, and *tate* and *tukuru* in the second; (iii) *oki* and *tate* are suspensive forms and depend on the parallel verb *tukuru* for their tense. Thus: 'There is a plan which, by cutting in half ... will leave ...; and, by making a road ... will put up ... and make ...'

The *-te oku* construction means 'do and leave (for future use)', e.g. *oite oite kudasai*, 'please put it down and leave it (for later)'. It is thus quite different in sense from the absolute finality of the *-te simau* construction (see n. to Lesson 12, l. 7).

32-33 sosiki siyoo to site imasu: 'are trying to organize'; see n. to Lesson 12, l. 31.

包	4/4	**HOO tutu(mu)** *vt* wrap; **tutu(mi)** parcel
	ホ ウ	ノ ｜ ク ｜ 勹 ｜ 匀 ｜ 包				
服	130/4	**HUKU** * clothes
	フ ク	ノ ｜ 月 ｜ 月 ｜ 月 ｜ 用 ｜ 那 ｜ 朋 ｜ 服
私	115/2	**SI** private; **watakusi, watasi** I
	シ	ノ ｜ 二 ｜ 千 ｜ 千 ｜ 禾 ｜ 秂 ｜ 私
印	2/5	**IN** imprint
	イ ン	ノ ｜ イ ｜ F ｜ E ｜ 臼 ｜ 印
刷	4/7	**SATU** printing
	サ ツ	⁊ ｜ ⁊ ｜ ⼫ ｜ ⼫ ｜ 局 ｜ 刷 ｜ 刷
械	75/7	**KAI** machine
	カ イ	一 ｜ 十 ｜ 才 ｜ 朽 ｜ 杠 ｜ 杚 ｜ 栃 ｜ 械 ｜ 械 ｜ 械
罰	122/9	**BATU** * punishment
	バ ツ	丶 ｜ 冂 ｜ 罒 ｜ 罒 ｜ 罜 ｜ 罰 ｜ 罰 ｜ 罰 ｜ 罰 ｜ 罰
払	64/2	**HUTU hara(u)** *vt* pay off, wipe off
	フ ツ 拂	一 ｜ 十 ｜ 扌 ｜ 払 ｜ 払
免	10/6	**MEN** permit, pardon
	メ ン	ノ ｜ 勹 ｜ 刍 ｜ 刍 ｜ 孕 ｜ 岛 ｜ 免
状	90/4	**ZYOO** condition, letter
	ジ ョ ウ 狀	丨 ｜ 丬 ｜ 爿 ｜ 扩 ｜ 状 ｜ 状 ｜ 状

取	128/2	**SYU** **to(ru)** *vt* take								
	シュ	一	丆	丌	耳	耳	耳	取	取	
歯	211/0	**SI** **ha** tooth								
	シ 歯	丨	上	止	止	步	步	毕	柴	茜 歯
達	162/9	**TATU** reach, accomplish								
	タ ツ 達	一	土	去	去	幸	幸	查	幸 幸	達
器	30/12	**KI** utensil, talent								
	キ 器	丶	𠮛	口	吅	吅	哭	哭	哭	器 器
引	57/1	**IN** **hi(ku)** *vt* pull								
	イ ン	𬺰	コ	弓	引					
受	87/4	**ZYU** **u(keru)** *vt* receive								
	ジュ	丿	𠂉	𤓅	𤓷	𤓷	爫	受	受	
進	162/8	**SIN** **susu(mu)** *vi* progress								
	シ ン 進	丿	亻	彳	彳	什	隹	隹	隹	隹 進
技	64/4	**GI** expert								
	ギ	一	十	才	扌	扌	technique 技	技		
利	115/2	**RI** * advantage, profit								
	リ	丿	二	千	禾	禾	利	利		
他	9/3	**TA** * **hoka** other								
	タ	丿	亻	伫	㐾	他				

給	120/6	**KYUU** bestow, salary									
	ケフ 給	く	ㇵ	ㇰ	糸	糸	糽	給	給	給	給
得	60/8	**TOKU** * gain									
	トク	ノ	ㇵ	彳	彳	彳日	彳日	復	得	得	得
習	124/5	**SYUU** nara(u) *vt* learn									
	シ ュウ	フ	ㇰ	ㇱ	㓞㓞	㋣㋣	㓞㓞	㓞㓞	習	習	習
慣	61/11	**KAN** na(reru) *vi* become used (to)									
	カン	ノ	ㇵ	忄	忄	忄口	忄口	忄毌	愲	慣	慣
欲	150/4	**YOKU** * greed, desire									
	ヨ ク	ノ	ㇵ	分	谷	谷	谷	谷	欲	欲	欲
銭	167/6	**SEN** 'sen' (100th of a yen)									
	セ ン 銭	ノ	ㇵ	仝	金	金	金	鈝	銭	銭	銭
勘	19/9	**KAN** account									
	カ ン	一	十	卄	甘	甚	其	甚	甚	甚フ	勘
定	40/5	**TEI, ZYOO** be fixed									
	テジ イョ ウ	㇑	ㇰ	宀	宁	宁	定	定		
煙	86/9	**EN** kemuri smoke									
	エ ン	丶	ㇵ	火	火	炉	炉	煙	煙	煙	
空	116/3	**KUU** sora sky									
	ク ウ	㇑	ㇰ	宀	宀	穴	空	空	空		

爆	86/15	**BAKU** burst									
	バク		゛	火	炉	炉	炉	煜	焊	爆	爆	爆

貸	154/5	**TAI** ka(su) *vt* lend									
	タイ		ノ	イ	仁	代	代	代	伐	貸	貸	貸

条	34/4	**ZYOO** item							
	ジョウ	條	ノ	ク	タ	冬	圣	条	条

借	9/8	**SYAKU** ka(riru) *vt* borrow								
	シャク		ノ	イ	仁	仕	借	供	伴	借	借	借

夜	8/6	**YA** yoru night						
	ヤ		゛	亠	广	存	夜	夜	夜

面	176/0	**MEN** omote face, surface							
	メン		一	ア	ア	石	而	而	而	面

漁	85/11	**GYO** fishing								
	ギョ		冫	汀	沪	浐	汋	漁	漁	漁	漁	漁

感	61/9	**KAN** (-ziru) *vt* feel; (-zi) feeling							
	カン		ノ	厂	厂	后	咸	咸	咸	感	感

情	61/8	**ZYOO** emotions; state							
	ジョウ	情	゛	八	忄	忙	忕	忓	情	情	情

秘	115/5	**HI** conceal							
	ヒ		ノ	二	千	千	千	秆	秋	秋	秘

密	40/8	**MITU** secrecy									
	ミ ツ	'	'	宀	宀	穴	宓	宓	宓	密	密
影	59/12	**EI** kage shadow									
	エ イ	日	甲	旦	昌	景	景	景	景	影	影
響	180/10	**KYOO** reverberate									
	キョ ウ	響	'	纟	彳	幻	纟	纪	組	郷	響 響
共	12/4	**KYOO** -tomo both, all; tomo (ni) together									
	キョ ウ	一	十	卄	卅	共	共				
命	9/6	**MEI** command; inoti life									
	メ イ	ノ	人	个	合	合	合	命	命		
令	9/3	**REI** order									
	レ イ	令	ノ	人	人	今	令				
温	85/9	**ON** warm									
	オ ン	温	氵	汀	氵	沪	沪	湢	渭	渭	温
泉	106/4	**SEN** spring (of water)									
	セ ン	'	勹	白	白	白	皁	身	身	泉	
像	9/12	**ZOO** * image, statue									
	ゾ ウ	亻	俨	俨	伊	伊	侉	像	傷	像	
途	162/7	**TO** road(way)									
	ト	途	ノ	人	人	会	今	余	余	途	途

[125]

十四

けさ、広島のおばから小包がとどきました。明けてみると、おじ
の古い服が入っていました。わたしは私立の工業学校で印刷機械の
使い方を教えていますから着物が油で非常によごれます。それでお
5 ばは仕事をする時に着たらいいと思って送ってくれたのでしょう。
服を包んだ広島の新聞に横山さんが自動車にひかれて死んだ事が出
ていました。自動車の運転手は罰金を払わされただけでなく、免状
も取られたそうです。

横山さんはわたしの家を建てている時働いていた大工です。もう
10 六十以上で歯はほとんどありませんでしたが、からだは達者なよう
でした。大変器用な人で、どんな仕事でもいやな顔をしないで、引
き受けてくれました。家を建てる進歩した材料とか技術の事もかな

りよく知っていたので、わたしは大変便利な人だと思いました。し

かし、横山さんには、他人よりずっとよく仕事が出来るのに、同じ

15 給料しかもらえないので、他人は得をして自分は損をしていると考

える習慣があったようです。他の人は、欲がふかくて一銭のまちが

いもないようにお金の勘定ばかりしている人間ではないかとうたが

っていました。

わたしが新しい家へうつってから三個月たった時、横山さんのむ

20 すめさんが電話をかけて来ました。横山さんは、どこかの工場で煙

突を直していた時、エンジンに空気が入って爆発したため目にけが

をして入院している、それでお金が足りないから少し貸してもらい

たいとの事でした。わたしは六個月たって返してもらえるのなら貸

してもいいと言いましたら、その条件で借りたいとの返事でした。

あれからもう五年になります。横山さんからは何の便りもありま
せんでした。去年の秋、夜おそく横山さんのむすこという男が面会
に来て、「父はとうとうめくらになりました。わたしは遠くの漁業会
社で働いていますから世話が出来ません。妹に世話させようとしま
すが、父は感情的になるだけで承知しません。」などと言っていまし
た。この男は表面はよさそうな人間でしたが、何か秘密を持ってい
るように感じさせられました。横山さんはいつかむすこは友だちの
影響で共産主義者になっていると話した事があります。
わたしは医者の命令で毎年夏には温泉へ行きますが、ことしは九
州の温泉へ行くつもりでした。めくらの横山さんが自動車にひかれ
た様子を想像しながら、何かさびしい気持になったわたしは、九
州へ行く途中広島へよる事に決めました。

LESSON 14

ZYUUSI

KESA, Hirosima no oba kara kozutumi ga todokimasita. Akete miru to, ozi no hurui huku ga haitte imasita. Watasi wa siritu no koogyoo-gakkoo de insatu-kikai no tukaikata o osiete imasu kara kimono ga abura de hizyoo ni yogoremasu. Sore de oba wa sigoto o suru toki ni kitara ii to omotte okutte kureta no desyoo. Huku o tutunda Hirosima no sinbun ni Yokoyama-san ga zidoosya ni hikarete sinda koto ga dete imasita. Zidoosya no untensyu wa bakkin o harawasareta dake de naku, menzyoo mo torareta soo desu.

Yokoyama-san wa watasi no ie o tatete iru toki hataraite ita daiku desu. Moo rokuzyuu izyoo de ha wa hotondo arimasen desita ga, karada wa tassya na yoo desita. Taihen kiyoo na hito de, donna sigoto de mo iya na kao o sinai de, hikiukete kuremasita. Ie o tateru sinpo sita zairyoo toka gizyutu no koto mo kanari yoku sitte ita no de, watasi wa taihen benri na hito da to omoimasita. Sikasi, Yokoyama-san ni wa, tanin yori zutto yoku sigoto ga dekiru no ni, onazi kyuuryoo sika moraenai no de, tanin wa toku o site zibun wa son o site iru to kangaeru syuukan ga atta yoo desu. Hoka no hito wa, yoku ga huka-kute issen no matigai mo nai yoo ni o-kane no kanzyoo bakari site iru ningen de wa nai ka to utagatte imasita.

Watasi ga atarasii ie e ututte kara sankagetu tatta toki, Yokoyama-san no musume-san ga denwa o kakete kimasita. Yokoyama-san wa, dokoka no koozyoo de entotu o naosite ita toki, enzin ni kuuki ga haitte bakuhatu sita tame me ni kega o site nyuuin site iru, sore de o-kane ga tarinai kara sukosi kasite moraitai to no koto desita. Watasi wa rokkagetu tatte kaesite moraeru no nara kasite mo ii to iimasitara, sono zyooken de karitai to no henzi desita.

Are kara moo gonen ni narimasu. Yokoyama-san kara wa nan no tayori mo arimasen desita. Kyonen no aki, yoru osoku Yokoyama-san no musuko to yuu otoko ga menkai ni kite, 'Titi wa tootoo mekura ni narimasita. Watasi wa tooku no gyogyoo-gaisya de hataraite imasu kara sewa ga dekimasen. Imooto ni sewa saseyoo to simasu ga, titi wa kanzyoo-teki ni naru dake de syooti simasen' nado to itte imasita. Kono otoko wa hyoomen wa yosasoo na ningen desita ga, nanika himitu o motte iru yoo ni kanzi saseraremasita. Yokoyama-san wa ituka musuko wa tomodati no eikyoo de kyoosansyugisya ni natte iru to hanasita koto ga arimasu.

Watasi wa isya no meirei de mainen natu ni wa onsen e ikimasu ga, kotosi wa Kyuusyuu no onsen e iku tumori desita. Mekura no Yoko-yama-san ga zidoosya ni hikareta yoosu o soozoo si-nagara, nanika sabisii kimoti ni natta watasi wa, Kyuusyuu e iku totyuu Hirosima e yoru koto ni kimemasita.

Notes

2 akete miru to: after a *-te* form *miru* may mean literally '(open and) see/look', as here, or it may mean 'see (what happens)'; e.g. *kiite mimasyoo*, 'let's ask him and see; let's try asking him'.

4 tukaikata: *-kata* added to the base of a verb gives the meaning 'way (of doing)'; e.g. *arukikata*, 'way of walking; gait'.

5 kitara: 'if I were to wear it'; one of the three basic 'conditionals' used for 'if' and 'when' (the others being *kiru to* and *kireba* for this verb). It is formed by adding *-ra* to the past form of the verb, either to the plain past, as here, or sometimes to *-masita*.

  okutte kureta: see n. to Lesson 10, l. 16.

7–8 bakkin o harawasareta . . . menzyoo mo torareta: 'was made to pay a fine . . . had his licence taken away'. Both verbs are 'indirect' passives (see n. to Lesson 12, l. 8), the former being the passive of the causative **harawaseru**, 'cause to pay', from *harau*.

11 sinai de: see n. to Lesson 11, l. 16.

14–16 Yokoyama-san ni wa . . . syuukan ga atta yoo desu: 'Mr. Yokoyama seemed to have the habit . . .'.

14 zutto: an adverb having a basic meaning of 'right through; to the limit', it can here be translated as something like 'far and away (better than . . .)'.

15 sika moraenai: 'can only receive'; see n. to Lesson 10, l. 24.

17–18 (ningen) de wa nai ka to utagatte: 'suspecting thus: "Is he not (a person who . . .)" '. The question is strongly rhetorical and implies 'surely he is'; and since it is in common use with *to omou*, etc., it is important to distinguish it from an ordinary negative.

20 denwa o kakete kimasita: 'came by telephoning', i.e. 'came on the phone'.

20–23 Yokoyama-san wa . . . to no koto desita: the last phrase 'It was a matter of' or, here, 'She told me that', governs the whole of the preceding part. Grammatically *site iru* in l. 22 is the end of a complete sentence, but it is in the plain form because it is part of what she is quoted as saying.
  On the *-te morau* form, see n. to Lesson 10, l. 16. Note that in reported speech the speaker usually reduces to a more 'neutral' level the polite forms that had been addressed to him; here, for example, the girl doubtless used *itadakitai* and not *moraitai* as reported.

23 kaesite moraeru no nara: since *nara* serves as a conditional equivalent of *desu*, *no nara* is a conditional equivalent of *no desu*; 'if (it is that) I can have you return it'.

23–24 kasite mo ii: see n. to Lesson 5, No. 7 *Mite mo ii desu ka.*

24 iimasitara: see n. to l. 5 above.

25 Are kara: cf. n. on *Kore kara* Lesson 8, l. 31.

28 Imooto ni sewa saseyoo to simasu: 'I try to cause a looking-after (him) by my young sister', i.e. 'I try to have my sister take care of him'. For *sewa* 'care, assistance', cf. uses in previous sentence and Lesson 9, ll. 13–14.

30 yosasoo: *ii* (*yoi*) and *nai* are irregular when used with the *-soo* suffix (see n. to Lesson 8, ll. 13–14) in that they become *yosasoo* and *nasasoo* respectively.

31 kanzi saseraremasita: 'I was made to feel', i.e. 'I could not help feeling'.

35 si-nagara: *-nagara* added to the base of a verb means 'while ——ing', and can be used when the action (or, here, the state) described by the main verb of the sentence is felt to be, not momentary, but continuing for some time.

| 黒 | 203/0 | KOKU kuro, kuro(i) black | | | | | | | | |
| | コク | ` | 冖 | 冖 | 曰 | 甲 | 甲 | 里 | 里 | 黒 黒 |

| 板 | 75/4 | HAN, BAN ita board | | | | | | | | |
| | ハン バン | 一 | 十 | 才 | 木 | 朾 | 扏 | 板 | 板 | |

| 競 | 117/15 | KYOO compete | | | | | | | | |
| | キョウ | ` | 丄 | 立 | 並 | 竒 | 竞 | 竞 | 竞 | 競 |

| 走 | 156/0 | SOO hasi(ru) *vi* run | | | | | | | | |
| | ソウ | 一 | 十 | 土 | 半 | 牛 | 走 | 走 | | |

| 距 | 157/5 | KYO distant from | | | | | | | | |
| | キョ | ` | 口 | 叴 | 足 | 足 | 趴 | 趴 | 距 | 距 |

| 離 | 172/11 | RI hana(reru) *vi*, hana(su) *vt* separate | | | | | | | | |
| | リ | ` | 亣 | 卤 | 卤 | 卤 | 离 | 斉 | 斳 | 離 |

| 順 | 47/9 | ZYUN * regularity | | | | | | | | |
| | ジュン | 丿 | 刂 | 川 | 川 | 川 | 川 | 順 | 順 | 順 |

| 序 | 53/4 | ZYO order, arrangement | | | | | | | | |
| | ジョ | ` | 亠 | 广 | 庐 | 庐 | 庍 | 序 | | |

| 風 | 182/0 | HUU * manner; kaze wind | | | | | | | | |
| | フウ | 丿 | 几 | 几 | 凡 | 凩 | 凬 | 風 | 風 | |

| 流 | 87/7 | RYUU naga(reru) *vi* flow; naga(su) *vt* pour, set adrift | | | | | | | | |
| | リュウ | ` | ` | 氵 | 汸 | 汁 | 泙 | 泱 | 浐 | 流 流 |

[131]

LESSON 15

| 勝 | 130/8 | **SYOO ka(tu)** *vi* win |
| | シ ョ ウ | 丿 | 月 | 月 | 月 | 月' | 胖 | 肸 | 朕 | 勝 | 勝 |

| 負 | 154/2 | **HU ma(keru)** *vi* be defeated |
| | フ | ' | 𠂉 | 𠂆 | 角 | 角 | 負 | 負 | 負 | 負 |

| 練 | 120/8 | **REN** practise |
| | レ ン | 練 | 乀 | 乡 | 幺 | 牟 | 糸 | 糽 | 糺 | 綀 | 紳 | 練 |

| 丈 | 4/2 | **ZYOO** stature |
| | ジ ョ ウ | 一 | ナ | 丈 |

| 予 | 6/3 | **YO** previous |
| | ヨ | 豫 | 乛 | マ | 予 | 予 |

| 報 | 32/9 | **HOO** report |
| | ホ ウ | 一 | 十 | 土 | 查 | 幸 | 幸 | 幸 | 韩 | 執 | 報 |

| 雨 | 173/0 | **U ame** rain |
| | ウ | 一 | 厂 | 门 | 雨 | 雨 | 雨 | 雨 | 雨 |

| 均 | 32/4 | **KIN** equal |
| | キ ン | 一 | 十 | 土 | 圵 | 均 | 均 | 均 |

| 別 | 18/5 | **BETU** *different; **waka(reru)** *vi* part (from) |
| | ベ ツ | 丶 | 冖 | 口 | 尸 | 号 | 別 | 別 |

| 星 | 72/5 | **SEI hosi** star |
| | セ イ | 丶 | 冂 | 口 | 日 | 尸 | 星 | 早 | 里 | 星 |

[132]

玉	96/0	**GYOKU** tama jewel								
	ギョク	一	丁	干	王	玉				
科	115/4	**KA** category, section								
	カ	ノ	ニ	千	千	禾	禾	科	科	科
再	1/5	**SAI** (SA) twice								
	サイ	一	厂	冂	丙	再	再			
官	40/5	**KAN** official								
	カン	丶	丷	宀	宁	宁	官	官	官	
級	120/4	**KYUU** class, grade								
	キュウ	級	∠	幺	幺	牟	糸	糸	級	級
漢	85/10	**KAN** * China, Han (dynasty)								
	カン	氵	汁	汁	汁	汫	洪	浩	漢	漢
字	40/3	**ZI** * written sign								
	ジ	丶	丷	宀	宁	字	字			
程	115/7	**TEI** hodo extent, degree								
	テイ	ノ	ニ	千	禾	禾	和	和	和	程
雲	173/4	**UN** kumo cloud								
	ウン	一	厂	雨	雨	雨	雪	雪	雲	雲
雪	173/3	**SETU** yuki snow								
	セツ	雪	一	厂	雨	雨	雨	雪	雪	雪

寒	40/9	**KAN** samu(i) cold									
	カン	、	宀	宀	宁	宁	审	宝	実	実	寒
暖	72/9	**DAN** atata(kai) warm									
	ゲン	丨	日	日	日′	日′	旷	旷	昨	晖	暖
君	30/4	**KUN** ruler, Mr.; **kimi** you									
	クン	コ	ヲ	ヨ	尹	尹	君	君			
候	9/8	**KOO** weather									
	コウ	ノ	イ	亻	亻′	仁	�037	候	候	候	
案	40/7 (75/6)	**AN** * proposal									
	アン	、	丷	宀	宀	安	安	安	安	案	案
菓	140/8	**KA** fruit									
	カ	一	十	艹	艹	甼	苩	苴	草	菓	菓
荷	140/7	**KA** ni baggage, cargo									
	カ	一	十	艹	艻	芢	莅	荷	荷	荷	
弁	28/3	**BEN** discriminate, explain									
	ベン 辨 辯	ム	ム	厶	千	弁					
黄	201/0	**KOO, OO (ki)** yellow									
	コオ ウ	一	一	廿	世	芒	苩	苦	苗	苗	黄
孝	24/5	**KOO** filial piety									
	コ ウ	一	十	土	少	老	考	孝			

律	60/6	**RITU** law
	リ ツ	ノ ク 彳 行 行 伊 律 律 律
専	41/6	**SEN** exclusive
	セ ン 専	一 𠃌 亡 亡 盲 甫 重 専 専
抵	64/5	**TEI** reach, resist
	テ イ	一 十 扌 扌 扩 扺 抵 抵
複	145/9	**HUKU** repetition, complexity
	フ ク	丶 ナ 衤 礻 礻 衤 衤 栢 複 複
傾	9/11	**KEI** slant
	ケ イ	ノ 亻 仁 化 化 化 侗 倾 傾 傾
氏	83/0	**SI** * Mr.
	シ	ノ 𠂆 𠃜 氏
尊	12/10	**SON** esteem
	ソ ン	丶 丷 丷 兯 肖 酋 酋 酋 尊 尊
敬	66/8	**KEI** respect
	ケ イ	一 艹 艹 芍 芍 苟 苟 苟 敬 敬
規	147/4	**KI** regulation
	キ	一 二 丰 夫 利 㓝 规 相 規 規
則	154/2	**SOKU** a rule
	ソ ク	丨 冂 月 月 目 貝 貝 則 則

十五

先週の金曜日に井口さんと一緒に村役場の前を通っていた時、門の横にある黒板に次のような事が書いてあるのに気が付きました。

「今度ノ日曜日（三月五日）ニ自転車ノ競走ヲシマス。コノ村ニ住ン
5 デ十六以上ノ者ハダレデモ出ル事が出来マス。黒板ニハッテアル地図ニ道
ノ順序ノシルシが付ケテアリマス。距離ハ二十キロ
デ午前十時ニ小学校ノ運動場ヲ出マス。」

わたしは井口さんに言いました。

「こんな風な自転車の競走が流行しているようですね。あなたはも
10 ちろん出るんでしょう。」

「え、出るつもりです。勝負は問題にしませんが……。」

「あなたはいつも勝っていたんでしょう。」

[136]

「え、仕合せにもまだ負けた事がありませんが、今度は大丈夫とは言えません。このごろ余り練習していませんから……」。

土曜日の晩の天気予報は、「朝ハクモッテ午後雨ニナル。カナリ強イ西北ノ風ガフイテ、温度ハ平均ヨリ二三度ヒクイ」、というのでした。その晩わたしは川村さんと大石さんの送別会に出て、夜おそく帰って来ました。空はすっかりはれていて星が玉のように光っています。

川村さんは科学者で再来週ドイツへ行く事になっています。大石さんは外交官で来月インドへ行きます。二人共この村で生れました。わたしは、ちがった階級の人の漢字の知識の程度を調べるため四個月前からこの村へ来ています。

日曜日の朝は、真っ黒な雲が出ていて、雪になるのではないかと思いました。寒暖計を見ると平均よりも十度もひくいのです。寒い

[137]

風がふいていて、競走には適当な日ではありませんでした。助手の大野君が競走を見に行きたがっていましたから、わたしは気候がわるい事の不平を言いながら、大野君を道案内にして出かけました。大野君は果物とか菓子などを持って行きましたが、わたしの荷物は小さな弁当の包だけでした。

黄色のシャツを着た井口さんは三番だったのでわたしはがっかりしました。あとで井口さんはかたこしがいたくなって途中でやめようかと思ったと言っていました。大野君は親友が勝ったのでよろこんでいました。大野君は親孝行な青年で、大学へ入ったら法律を専門にしたいと言っています。大抵の仕事はよくしますが少し複雑な事になるとすぐなげ出す傾向があります。法律家の長島正次氏を尊敬していますが、長島氏の不規則な生活は知らないようです。

LESSON 15

ZYUUGO

SENSYUU no kinyoo-bi ni Iguti-san to issyo ni mura-yakuba no mae o tootte ita toki, mon no yoko ni aru kokuban ni tugi no yoo na koto ga kaite aru no ni ki ga tukimasita.

'Kondo no nitiyoo-bi (sangatu ituka) ni zitensya no kyoosoo o simasu. Kono mura ni sunde iru zyuuroku izyoo no mono wa dare-demo deru koto ga dekimasu. Kyori wa nizikkiro de gozen zyuuzi ni syoogakkoo no undoozyoo o demasu. Kokuban ni hatte aru tizu ni miti no zyunzyo no sirusi ga tukete arimasu.'

Watasi wa Iguti-san ni iimasita: 'Konna huu na zitensya no kyoosoo ga ryuukoo site iru yoo desu ne. Anata wa motiron derun' desyoo.'

'E, deru tumori desu. Syoobu wa mondai ni simasen ga . . .'

'Anata wa itumo katte itan' desyoo.'

'E, siawase ni mo mada maketa koto ga arimasen ga, kondo wa daizyoobu to wa iemasen. Konogoro amari rensyuu site imasen kara. . . .'

Doyoo-bi no ban no tenki-yohoo wa, 'Asa wa kumotte gogo ame ni naru. Kanari tuyoi seihoku no kaze ga huite, ondo wa heikin yori nisando hikui' to yuu no desita. Sono ban watasi wa Kawamura-san to Ooisi-san no soobetukai ni dete, yoru osoku kaette kimasita. Sora wa sukkari harete ite hosi ga tama no yoo ni hikatte imasita. Kawamura-san wa kagakusya de saraisyuu Doitu e iku koto ni natte imasu. Ooisi-san wa gaikookan de raigetu Indo e ikimasu. Hutaritomo kono mura de umaremasita. Watasi wa, tigatta kaikyuu no hito no kanzi no tisiki no teido o siraberu tame yonkagetu mae kara kono mura e kite imasu.

Nitiyoo-bi no asa wa, makkuro na kumo ga dete ite, yuki ni naru no de wa nai ka to omoimasita. Kandankei o miru to heikin yori mo zyuudo mo hikui no desu. Samui kaze ga huite ite, kyoosoo ni wa tekitoo na hi de wa arimasen desita. Zyosyu no Oono-kun ga kyoosoo o mi ni ikitagatte imasita kara, watasi wa kikoo ga warui koto no huhei o ii-nagara, Oono-kun o miti-annai ni site dekakemasita. Oono-kun wa kudamono toka kasi nado o motte ikimasita ga, watasi no nimotu wa tiisa na bentoo no tutumi dake desita.

Ki-iro no syatu o kita Iguti-san wa sanban datta no de watasi wa gakkari simasita. Ato de Iguti-san wa kata to kosi ga itaku natte totyuu de yameyoo ka to omotta to itte imasita. Oono-kun wa sinyuu ga katta no de yorokonde imasita. Oono-kun wa oya-kookoo na seinen de, daigaku e haittara hooritu o senmon ni sitai to itte imasu. Taitei no sigoto wa yoku simasu ga sukosi hukuzatu na koto ni naru to sugu nagedasu keikoo ga arimasu. Hoorituka no Nagasima Seizi-si o sonkei site imasu ga, Nagasima-si no hu-kisoku na seikatu wa siranai yoo desu.

[139]

LESSON 15

Notes

3 **tugi no yoo na koto**: 'something like the following'; *tugi no koto*, 'the following', would have been used if the actual words were quoted.

kaite aru no ni: on *-te aru*, see n. to Lesson 13, l. 12; on this combination of *no* and *ni*, see n. to Lesson 13, ll. 24–25.

5 **zyuuroku izyoo**: see n. to Lesson 6, No. 1.

deru koto ga dekimasu: see n. to Lesson 6, No. 4.

11 **mondai ni simasen ga**: see n. to Lesson 6, No. 9 on this use of *ga*.

13 **siawase ni mo**: 'luckily'; an emphatic *mo* is often used in such 'emotional' expressions, e.g. *zannen ni mo*, 'unfortunately'.

14 **iemasen**: from *ieru*, potential form of *yuu*. (The passive form is *iwareru*.)

rensyuu site imasen kara: this clause is added as an afterthought to explain the previous statement. The normal order would therefore be: . . . *site imasen kara kondo wa* . . . Cf. the clause ending in *ga* in l. 11 above.

19 **iku koto ni natte imasu**: 'it has turned out that he will go', i.e. 'he is due to go'; see n. to Lesson 12, ll. 14–15.

22 **. . . mae kara . . . kite imasu**: 'I am (having come) here since . . .', i.e. 'I have been here since . . .'

23 **naru no de wa nai ka to**: see n. to Lesson 14, ll. 17–18.

26 **-kun**: 'Mr.'; a term used by men of another man to whom they do not need to show any particular respect and in talking to whom they would probably use plain forms of speech.

ikitagatte imasita: from *ikitagaru*, the *-garu* form of *ikitai*, 'want to go'. In making definite statements about the feelings of other people, the Japanese use an 'objective' verbal ending *-garu* with a number of adjectives describing personal sensations. It is added, for example, to the stem of *atu(i)*, *hosi(i)*, *ita(i)*, *kowa(i)*, *samu(i)* and the *-ta(i)* endings, and directly on to *kinodoku*, *iya*, and *zannen*. Any deviation from a plain, direct statement (e.g. by using *desyoo*, *yoo desu*, etc.), however, makes its use unnecessary; see, e.g., l. 34 below.

27 **ii-nagara**: see n. to Lesson 14, l. 35.

31–32 **yameyoo ka to omotta**: 'he thought: "Shall I give up" ', i.e. 'he wondered whether to . . .'

35 **-si**: 'Mr.'; a literary, formal term of address.

暑	72/8	**SYO** atu(i) hot
	シ ョ 暑	` 冂 日 目 甲 里 昇 昇 暑 暑
蓄	140/10	**TIKU** storage
	チ ク	一 艹 艹 壬 芋 茔 芎 莟 莟 蓄
席	53/7	**SEKI** * seat
	セ キ	` 亠 广 广 庐 庐 庐 庐 席 席
輪	159/8	**RIN** wa ring, wheel
	リ ン	一 ㄇ 三 車 軩 軩 輪 輪 輪 輪
波	85/5	**HA** nami wave
	ハ	` 氵 氵 氵 汀 沙 波 波
位	9/5	**I** kurai rank
	イ	ノ イ 亻 仁 位 位 位
権	75/11	**KEN** authority, power
	ケ ン 権	一 十 木 杧 柠 栌 栌 栐 椎 権
列	78/2	**RETU** * row, line
	レ ッ	一 丆 歹 歹 列 列
袋	145/5	**TAI** hukuro bag, sack
	タ イ	イ 亻 代 代 代 岱 岱 袋 袋 袋
房	63/4	**BOO** room
	ボ ウ	一 ㄱ ㅋ 戸 戸 戻 房 房

堂	42/8	**DOO** hall									
	ド ウ		丶	⺌	⺌	⺌	屵	峃	峃	峃	峇	堂
角	148/0	**KAKU** * angle; **tuno** horn									
	カ ク		ノ	⺈	⺈	角	角	角	角		
綿	120/8	**MEN** **wata** cotton (-wool)									
	ノ ン	綿	幺	幺	糸	糸	糸	糽	綢	綿	綿
婦	38/8	**HU** woman, wife									
	フ		く	乆	女	女コ	女ヨ	女ヨ	女ヨ	婦コ	婦	婦
召	18/3	**SYOO** **me(su)** *vt* summon, eat, drink, wear etc. (*hon.*)									
	ショ ウ		刀	刀	刀	召	召			
銅	167/6	**DOO** * copper									
	ド ウ		人	牟	牟	牟	金	釻	釦	銅	銅	銅
台	28/3	**DAI** * platform, stand; (unit for counting vehicles)									
	ダ イ	臺	亻	ム	ム	台	台			
血	143/0	**KETU** **ti** blood									
	ケ ツ		ノ	亻	句	血	血	血		
刃	18/1	**ZIN** **ha** blade									
	ジ ン		刀	刀	刃					
根	75/6	**KON** **ne** root									
	コ ン		一	十	才	木	杧	杧	桿	柊	根	根

砂	112/4	SA, SYA suna sand								
	サ シ	一	ア	石	石	石	砂	砂	砂	
糖	119/10	TOO sugar								
	ト ウ	⸰	⸰	米	籵	籵	籵	糟	糖	糖
皮	107/0	HI kawa skin, leather, fur, bark								
	ヒ	ノ	厂	广	皮	皮				
湯	85/9	TOO yu hot water								
	ト ウ	⸰	氵	氵	汨	沔	渭	渭	湯	湯
蒸	140/10	ZYOO steam								
	ジ ウ	一	艹	艼	芋	芴	蒸	蒸	蒸	蒸
燃	86/12	NEN burn								
	ネ ン	⸰	⸰	火	灯	灯	炒	燃	燃	燃
勢	19/11	SEI energy, influence								
	セ イ	一	土	去	幸	埶	刳	埶	勢	勢
統	120/6	TOO unify, govern								
	ト ウ	統	么	幺	糸	糸	糸	紵	結	統
港	85/9	KOO minato harbour								
	コ ウ	⸰	氵	汁	汫	港	洪	港	港	港
皇	106/4	KOO, OO emperor, imperial								
	コオ ウウ	・	ノ	亇	白	白	自	皁	皇	

后	4/5	**KOO** empress								
	コ ウ		ノ	ノ	仁	仁	后	后			
帆	50/3	**HAN** ho sail								
	ハ ン		丶	冂	巾	帄	帆	帆			
章	180/2	**SYOO** chapter, badge								
	シ ョ ウ		丶	亠	立	立	立	产	音	音	音	章
完	40/4	**KAN** complete								
	カ ン		丶	宀	宀	宀	完	完	完		
訳	149/4	**YAKU** * translation; **wake** meaning, reason								
	ヤ ク	譯	丶	亠	二	言	言	言	訂	訳	訳	訳
王	96/0	**OO** * king								
	オ ウ		一	丁	王	王					
祖	113/5	**SO** ancestor								
	ソ		丶	ラ	才	ネ	礻	初	柤	祖	祖	
歴	27/12	**REKI** successive								
	レ キ	歷	一	厂	厂	厈	床	麻	厤	厤	歴	歴
史	2/4	**SI** annals, history								
	シ		丶	冂	口	史	史				
帳	50/8	**TYOO** note-book								
	チ ョ ウ		丶	冂	巾	帄	帄	帳	帳	帳	帳	帳

帝	8/7	**TEI** emperor								
	テ イ・	`	一	十	productive 立	亠	产	产	帝	

申	2/4	**SIN** moo(su) *vt* say (*def.*)								
	シ ン	`	冂	日	日	申				

参	28/6	**SAN** mai(ru) *vi* go, come (*def.*)								
	サ ン	参	`	ム	亠	仐	糸	糸	参	参

存	39/3	**SON, ZON** exist; **ZON** (-ziru) *vt* think, know								
	ソ ン ゾ ン		一	ナ	才	存	存	存		

品	30/6	**HIN** * refinement; **sina** article								
	ヒ ン	品	`	冂	口	口	吕	吕	品	品

床	53/4	**SYOO** yuka floor, **toko** bed								
	シ ョ ウ		`	亠	广	庐	床	床	床	

拝	64/5	**HAI** worship								
	ハ イ	拝	一	十	才	扌	扩	扩	拝	拝

致	133/4	**TI** ita(su) *vt* do (*depr.*)								
	チ	`	一	工	五	至	至	至	到	致	致

臓	130/14	**ZOO** internal organ								
	ゾ ウ	臓	月	月	肝	肝	肝	脏	臓	臓	臓

精	119/8	**SEI** fine, detailed; spirit								
	セ イ	精	`	`	二	半	米	米	料	粘	精	精

十六

夏の暑い日でした。となりでやかましい蓄音器をかけているので
わたしは自分の席を立ってまどをしめに行きました。その時、平山
さんが美しい花輪を持って入って来ました。電波の事とか波長の単
5 位の事などを書かなくてはならないから助けてもらいたいと言うの
です。平山さんは、他人がどんなにいそがしくても、自分が聞きた
い事はすぐ聞く権利があると思っている人です。わたしは名古屋行
きの列車に乗りおくれるのではないかと心配しながら一時間ばかり
話しました。平山さんはわたしのテーブルの上から大きな紙の袋を
10 取って、それに花輪を入れて出て行きました。

平山さんは新聞記者で色色おもしろい事を経験するようです。あ
る時、平山さんは文房具を買ってからデパートの食堂で食事をして

[146]

いました。四角なテーブルの片側に木綿の着物を着た年よりの夫婦がいました。給仕が「何を召し上がりますか」と聞くと、おじいさんは「何かおいしいものが食べたい」と言うだけで何を注文していいのか分からない様子でした。気が付くと平山さんが食べている御飯の中から古い銅貨が出て来ました。前に平山さんの友だちがこの食堂の台所では血がついた刃物を使う事、大根に大きな虫がいる事、砂糖の中にいもの皮が入っている事、湯がわいて蒸気を出しながらこぼれているので燃料のガスがいやなにおいをしている事などを話した事を思い出して銅貨の事と一緒に書こうと思いました。

次は余り勢力がない小さな国の大統領が来た時の事です。平山さんは大統領が乗っている船が横浜の港に入ってから東京で天皇と皇右に会う時までの事を書けとの命令を受けました。平山さんは帆か

船を借りて船の上から見える横浜の景色を見に行ったり、東京と
横浜の間を自動車で行ったり来たりして大統領の目に付くような物
をすっかり見て置きました。新聞に出た平山さんの文章は完全なも
のでした。非常によく出来ていたので外国語に訳されて外国の新聞
にも出たそうです。

あるアジアの古い国の王様だった人が来た時には、その人の祖先
とかその国の歴史とかを知るために、大学の先生に会いに行こうと
思いました。大学へ電話をかけましたが先生はいませんでした。電
話帳でうちの方の番号を調べて電話をかけました。

「井上先生でいらっしゃいますか。私は帝国新聞の平山と申す者で
ございます。少しおうかがいしたい事がございまして、これからそ
ちらへ参りたいと存じますが……」

「だめです。いそがしいからまた他の日に来て下さい」。

「実は先生にお目にかけしたい品がございますんですが……」。

「何ですか」。

「古いシナの絵でございます。東洋美術に非常に興味を持って居られる外国人の方が大変めずらしい品をお買いになったのでございます。前に先生が床の間にかけていらっしゃった絵を拝見させていただいたので、お礼の意味で先生にお目にかけしたいと申されて居ります」。

「それは見たいですね。今すぐ来れますか」。

「は、参れます。おいそがしい所を大変失礼致しました」。

平山さんが聞きたがっていた事がすっかり開けたのはもちろんです。

こんな風に「心臓が強い」のが新聞記者の精神だそうです。

[149]

ZYUUROKU

Natu no atui hi desita. Tonari de yakamasii tikuonki o kakete iru no de watasi wa zibun no seki o tatte mado o sime ni ikimasita. Sono toki, Hirayama-san ga utukusii hanawa o motte haitte kimasita. Denpa no koto toka hatyoo no tan-i no koto nado o kakanakute wa naranai kara tasukete moraitai to yuu no desu. Hirayama-san wa, tanin ga donna ni isogasikute mo, zibun ga kikitai koto wa sugu kiku kenri ga aru to omotte iru hito desu. Watasi wa Nagoya-yuki no ressya ni noriokureru no de wa nai ka to sinpai si-nagara itizikan bakari hana-simasita. Hirayama-san wa watasi no teeburu no ue kara ooki na kami no hukuro o totte, sore ni hanawa o irete dete ikimasita.

Hirayama-san wa sinbun-kisya de iroiro omosiroi koto o keiken suru yoo desu. Aru toki, Hirayama-san wa bunboogu o katte kara depaato no syokudoo de syokuzi o site imasita. Sikaku na teeburu no katagawa ni momen no kimono o kita tosiyori no huuhu ga imasita. Kyuuzi ga 'Nani o mesiagarimasu ka' to kiku to, oziisan wa 'Nanika oisii mono ga tabetai' to yuu dake de nani o tyuumon site ii no ka wakaranai yoosu desita. Ki ga tuku to Hirayama-san ga tabete iru gohan no naka kara hurui dooka ga dete kimasita. Mae ni Hirayama-san no tomodati ga kono syokudoo no daidokoro de wa ti ga tuita hamono o tukau koto, daikon ni ooki na musi ga iru koto, satoo no naka ni imo no kawa ga haitte iru koto, yu ga waite zyooki o dasi-nagara koborete iru no de nenryoo no gasu ga iya na nioi o site iru koto nado o hanasita koto o omoidasite dooka no koto to issyo ni kakoo to omoimasita.

Tugi wa amari seiryokų ga nai tiisa na kuni no daitooryoo ga kita toki no koto desu. Hirayama-san wa daitooryoo ga notte iru hune ga Yokohama no minato ni haitte kara Tookyoo de tennoo to koogoo ni au toki made no koto o kake to no meirei o ukemasita. Hirayama-san wa hokakebune o karite hune no ue kara mieru Yokohama no kesiki o mi ni ittari, Tookyoo to Yokohama no aida o zidoosya de ittari kitari site daitooryoo no me ni tuku yoo na mono o sukkari mite okimasita. Sinbun ni deta Hirayama-san no bunsyoo wa kanzen na mono desita. Hizyoo ni yoku dekite ita no de gaikokugo ni yaku sarete gaikoku no sinbun ni mo deta soo desu.

Aru Azia no hurui kuni no oosama datta hito ga kita toki ni wa, sono hito no sosen toka sono kuni no rekisi toka o siru tame ni, daigaku no sensei ni ai ni ikoo to omoimasita. Daigaku e denwa o kakemasita ga sensei wa imasen desita. Denwatyoo de uti no hoo no bangoo o sirabete denwa o kakemasita.

'Inoue-sensei de irassyaimasu ka. Watakusi wa Teikoku Sinbun no Hirayama to moosu mono de gozaimasu. Sukosi o-ukagai sitai

koto ga gozaimasite, kore kara sotira e mairitai to zonzimasu
ga. . . .
'Dame desu. Isogasii kara mata hoka no hi ni kite kudasai.'
'Zitu wa sensei ni o-me ni o-kake sitai sina ga gozaimasun' desu
ga. . . .'
'Nan desu ka.'
'Hurui Sina no e de gozaimasu. Tooyoo bizyutu ni hizyoo ni
kyoomi o motte orareru gaikokuzin no kata ga taihen mezurasii sina o
o-kai ni natta no de gozaimasu. Mae ni sensei ga tokonoma ni kakete
irassyatta e o haiken sasete itadaita no de, o-rei no imi de sensei ni
o-me ni o-kake sitai to moosarete orimasu.'
'Sore wa mitai desu ne. Ima sugu koremasu ka.'
'Ha, mairemasu. O-isogasii tokoro o taihen siturei itasimasita.'
Hirayama-san ga kikitagatte ita koto ga sukkari kiketa no wa
motiron desu. Konna huu ni 'sinzoo ga tuyoi' no ga sinbun-kisya no
seisin da soo desu.

Notes

5 **kakanakute wa naranai**: 'not writing will not do', i.e. 'must write'. The idea
of 'must, should' is most commonly expressed by *-nakute wa* or *-nakereba* (and
'must not' by *-te wa* or *-eba*) followed by some form of *naranai* or *ikenai*; see
n. to Lesson 7, l. 8.
6 **donna ni isogasikute mo**: see n. to Lesson 11, l. 25.
14 **mesiagarimasu**: *mesiagaru*, like *o-agari ni naru* or *o-agari nasaru*, is an honorific
equivalent for *taberu* or *nomu*.
15-16 **nani o tyuumon site ii no ka**: see n. to Lesson 9, l. 32.
17-21 **Mae ni Hirayama-san no tomodati ga [kono syokudoo no daidokoro
de wa (a) koto, (b) koto, (c) koto, (d) koto nado o] hanasita koto o omoidasite**: *omoidasite* has a subject—Mr. Hirayama—which is not expressed and an
object, *hanasita koto*; *hanasita* in turn has an adverbial phrase *mae ni*, a subject
H-san no tomodati ga, and for an object the long part shown within brackets.
Thus: 'Hirayama, recalling that previously his friend had talked about (a),
(b), (c), (d) and so on happening in the kitchen . . .'
20 **gasu ga . . . nioi o site iru**: *nioi ga suru* is the usual expression, but this means
simply 'there is a smell; (something) smells'. Here the preceding *gasu ga*
requires the use of *o* instead of *ga* with *nioi* to give the meaning 'the gas makes a
smell' exactly as in English.
23-24 **(daitooryoo ga . . . au toki made no) koto o kake**: *kake* is the plain or
brusque imperative from *kaku*, and the part within the brackets all qualifies
koto. Thus: 'write about things from . . . up to the time . . .'
24-27 **Hirayama-san wa . . . mi ni ittari . . . ittari kitari site . . . mite okimasita**: on *-te oku*, see n. to Lesson 13, ll. 25-28. The *-tari* form of verbs is
made by adding *-ri* to the plain past forms, and usually two or more followed
by some form of *suru* are used to express such ideas as 'keeps on ——ing and
——ing; does (first) this and (then) that; sometimes does this and sometimes

that.' Thus, here: 'Mr. H took a preparatory look . . . by going to see . . . and by going to and fro . . .'

33 uti no hoo: the use of *hoo* here implies '(his home) as opposed to (the university)'.

34 sensei: a term of respect widely applied to teachers, of whatever description and rank, and sometimes to doctors. There is no English equivalent, but, when used loosely, 'Professor' corresponds to some extent.

watakusi: a formal 'I', usually shortened to *watasi*. *Watakusi* is the only reading officially recognized for the character, but, in fact, it is widely used to write *watasi*.

34–36 Hirayama is here addressing the teacher with great esteem, using a wide range of respect language. This language is of three main types:

(1) **True Honorifics**: certain verbs which show respect towards their subjects (here, e.g., *de irassyaimasu*); and words which show respect to the persons of whom they are used (e.g. *-sama, kata*).

(2) **Depreciatories (Negative Honorifics)**: certain verbs which, by depreciating the status of their subjects, show proportionate respect for someone else who is in some way involved in the action; here, e.g., *o-ukagai sitai*, 'I should like to ask *you* (or, in another context, *some other respected person*)'. The combination of *o* + base + *suru* is a standard depreciatory form for verbs which do not use a special word for this function.

When, as in the text, the other person involved in the action of the verb and the person addressed are one and the same, these verbs will be in a *-masu* form when used as final verbs; when they are not the same, however, a *-masu* form will only be used when the speaker also wants to show respect to the person addressed.

(3) **Deferentials**: certain verbs (here, e.g., *moosu, de gozaimasu, gozaimasite*, and *zon-zimasu*), all the *-masu* endings, and words such as the formal *watakusi* and the *mono* 'person' used here, which show respect only to the person addressed.

In practice, therefore, deferential verbs will invariably be in a *-masu* form when used as final verbs. They can, in fact, be regarded as a group of depreciatory verbs, (2) above, of limited application.

A table of verbs used in respect language and a fuller account of their use is given after the notes to Lesson 20.

A normal *-masu* level version of the lines in question would be: *Inoue sensei desu ka. Watasi wa Teikoku Sinbun no Hirayama to yuu mono/hito desu. Sukosi kikitai koto ga atte, kore kara sotira e ikitai to omoimasu ga . . .*

Cf. the unctuous language of the reporter with the brusqueness of the replies.

38 o-me ni o-kake sitai: depreciatory (negative honorific) form from *o-me ni kakeru*, itself a depreciatory equivalent for *miseru*.

gozaimasun' desu ga: or, alternatively, with the same meaning: *arun' de gozaimasu ga*.

40–41 motte orareru: the passive forms of verbs are sometimes used as honorifics, without any corresponding change in grammatical structure; this is an honorific equivalent for *motte iru*.

41 o-kai ni natta: a standard honorific form for verbs which do not use a special word for this function is *o* + base + *ni naru* (or *nasaru*); thus, this is an honorific equivalent for *katta*.

42 kakete irassyatta: honorific equivalent for *kakete ita*.

42-43 haiken sasete itadaita: 'I humbly received a being-allowed-to-see', i.e. 'I was allowed to see'; 'I was shown'; thus, a depreciatory equivalent for *misete moratta*.

43-44 moosarate orimasu: respect is here being shown (i) to Inoue, the person addressed, by the use of the deferential verbs *moosu* and *oru* (see n. to ll. 34-36, sec. (3) above), and (ii) to the foreigner, the subject of the verb, by the use of the passive form as an honorific (see n. to ll. 40-41 above). Thus, it is equivalent to *itte imasu*.

46 mairemasu: from *maireru*, potential of *mairu*, itself the deferential for *iku* (or *kuru*).

    O-isogasii tokoro o: a standard form of apology, often used alone, for taking up another's time.

    itasimasita: from *itasu*, depreciatory for *suru*.

47 kikitagatte ita koto: see n. to Lesson 15, l. 26.

48 Konna huu ni: 'In such a way as this'.

INTRODUCTION TO LESSONS 17–20

To show different kinds of Japanese text, all these lessons have been prepared in printed form and one, Lesson 20, in semi-cursive hand-written form. Lessons 17 and 18 also use the old, full forms of the characters introduced in Lessons 1–16 and the traditional forms of *kana* spelling, and introduce a few more new miscellaneous signs.

Kana Spelling

It has been seen already that, although two or more *kana* must sometimes be read together to form a diphthong, the same diphthong or long vowel is now written in only one, or at the most two, ways. Before the post-war simplification of the writing system, however, there were many possible combinations of *kana*, most of them involving *u* or *hu* as the final element. They may be summarized as follows:

-i + *ya, yu* or *yo* = *-ya, -yu* or *-yo* (e.g. キ ヤ = *kya*, シ ュ = *syu*, ヂ ョ = *zyo*)

ku + *wa* = *ka* (e.g. グ ワ = *ga*, ク ワ イ = *kai*)

wa or *wo* + *u* or *hu* = *oo* (e.g. ワ ウ = *oo*)

-a or *-o* + *u* or *hu* = *-oo* (e.g. シ ヤ ウ = *sya* + ウ = *syoo*, ト フ = *too*)

e (or *-e*) + *u* or *hu* = *yoo* (or *-yoo*) (e.g. セ ウ = *syoo*, デ フ = *zyoo*)

i (or *-i*) + *u* or *hu* = *yuu* (or *-yuu*) (e.g. キ ウ = *kyuu*, ニ フ = *nyuu*)

With a few exceptions (e.g. *desyoo* written で せ う), the above combinations were found only in the ON readings of Chinese characters, but there are also some native Japanese words which traditionally have unusual *kana* spellings. In nearly all cases these involve the *kana* signs for sounds beginning with *h* or *w*, and take the form either of the sign は (or, of course, ハ) being pronounced *wa*, as is still the case with the particle *wa*; or of an *h* or *w* consonant having disappeared in the modern pronunciation, as in the case of the particles へ (*h*)*e* and を (*w*)*o*. (Such words as *taoreru* and *moosu*, traditionally written たふれる and まをす, were exceptional in showing a vowel change as well as the disappearance of a consonant.)

The following are words occurring in Lesson 17 which show typical variations between spelling and pronunciation:

いふ *yuu* きらひ *kirai* さへ *sae*
ゐます *imasu* くはしく *kuwasiku* やう *yoo*

Less unusually, the sounds *zi* and *zu* were in many words traditionally written ぢ and づ, instead of じ and ず as nearly always in the modern spelling (e.g. みづ 'water', now みず).

Miscellaneous Signs

(1)　(2)　(3)

ま　た　と　所
ゝ　び　こ　々
　　　　ろ
　　〳　〵
　　〴　〵

(1) *mama*, showing the sign used to repeat a single *kana*.

(2) *tabitabi* and *tokorodokoro*, showing the sign used, with *nigori* where necessary, to repeat two or more *kana*.

(3) *tokorodokoro*, showing the sign used to repeat a Chinese character.

十七

安田さんと橋本さんは子どもの時からわたしと同じ學校へ行きました。今は安田さんは政府の役人で橋本さんは會社員です。大學を出てからしばらく會ふ機會がありませんでしたが、間接には色々な事を聞いてゐました。

今年の正月元日、偶然に橋本さんに出會ひました。これから安田さんのうちへ行く所だと言ふので、わたしも一緒に行きました。安田さんは死んだ親が住んでゐた大きな家に召使と二人で氣樂にくらしてゐます。三人で長い時間むかしの事を話し合ひましたが、橋本さんは近く結婚するので、貸家をさがすのが大變な仕事である事、安い給料で生活しなければならないのが心配な事など話しました。

橋本さんは頭腦がよく學問がすきな人ですが少し短氣な所があり

ます。大學にゐた時には友だちはみな學者になるのだと思つてゐました。自分もそのつもりでゐたやうでした。ある時、勞働組合の事で先生に質問をしてから大學に殘る考へをすててしまひました。橋本さんはどちらかと言へば社會主義的な考へを持つてゐる人ですから、先生の保守主義に滿足出來なかつたのでせう。

わたしの父はゐなかの小さな町で米屋をしてゐます。父の弟であるをぢはとなりで酒屋をしてゐます。それで兄は商人になりましたが、わたしは商業はきらひで歷史に興味を持つてゐました。父はわたしに經濟學を勉強させたかつたのですが、わたしは安田さんと橋本さんと同じやうに法律を勉強しました。今、白狀すればなぜ法律をえらんだのだか分かりませんが、適當な職業が見付けやすいといふ話しを信じたからでせう。法律の事は餘り勉強しないで、ある有

名なむかしの將軍と藝人のやうな家來との關係をくはしく調べまし

た。將來本にするつもりでした。

大學を出たわたしは電信局で働いてゐたいとこの紹介で放送局へ

面會に行きましたがだめでした。それで、ある政治運動に熱中して

ゐる友だちが新しい政黨を組織するのを助けてもらひたいといふの

30で、人のい、わたしはしばらくその人の書記の仕事をしました。毎

日、何千枚といふ葉書を書いたり、電報をうつたり、電話をかけた

りしました。この友だちは利口な男ですが、國民の心理をはっきり

つかむ事が出來ませんでしたから、新しい政黨の組織は無理でした。

強情なこの男はそれでも運動をつゞけましたが、とう〴〵不成功に

35なつてしまひました。この友だちは、わたしがほとんど給料を取ら

ないで働いたのを氣の毒がって、國際問題を專門にする雜誌の編集

長に紹介してくれました。そこでわたしはヨーロッパの國の植民地で文化の程度のひくい土人をどんなに教育してゐるかといふ事を調べて、論文を少し書きました。もちろん材料は外國の本とか雑誌で

40 すが、語學が余り達者でないわたしにはかなりむづかしい仕事でした。この仕事をしてゐる間に土人の習慣とか宗教とかに興味を持つやうになりました。大學では法律を勉強しましたから、習慣の問題は全然關係のない事ではありませんでした。例へば土人が考へてゐ

45 る「神」といふものと、わるい事をした場合の罰との關係はわたしが一番おもしろいと思つた事でした。そしてもっとふかく調べたいと思ひました。それには外國語の知識が必要である事を感じました。わたしは外國語は英語とフランス語を少しばかりしか知りませんでしたから、何とかしてドイツ語が習ひたいと思ひました。

わたしが橋本さんと安田さんに會つたのは丁度この時でした。そ

50 れでわたしの考へを二人に話しました。そしたら安田さんが、い、

先生を知つてゐるから紹介して上げる、前に安田さんのお父さんが

世話した人だから、何もお禮はしないでい、と言つてくれました。

それからわたしは毎日この人の所へ行つてドイツ語を習つてゐま

す。この人は日本人とドイツ人との合の子で、ドイツ語はもちろん

55 達者ですが、日本語も語學的に調べてわたしの文法は標準語のでな

いから直さなければいけないと言った事もあります。わたしはドイ

ツ語が讀めさへすればい、と思つてゐますが、この人は話す事も出

來なければいけないと言つて、毎日會話の練習をさせられます。い

つドイツ語が字引を使ふだけで讀めるやうになるか分かりませんが

60 とにかく出來るだけの事をしてゐます。

[160]

LESSON 17

ZYUUSITI

YASUDA-SAN to Hasimoto-san wa kodomo no toki kara watasi to onazi gakkoo e ikimasita. Ima wa Yasuda-san wa seihu no yakunin de Hasimoto-san wa kaisyain desu. Daigaku o dete kara sibaraku au kikai ga arimasen desita ga, kansetu ni wa iroiro na koto o kiite imasita. Kotosi no syoogatu ganzitu, guuzen ni Hasimoto-san ni deaimasita. Kore kara Yasuda-san no uti e iku tokoro da to yuu no de, watasi mo issyo ni ikimasita. Yasuda-san wa sinda oya ga sunde ita ooki na ie ni mesitukai to hutari de kiraku ni kurasite imasu. Sannin de nagai zikan, mukasi no koto o hanasiaimasita ga, Hasimoto-san wa tikaku kekkon suru no de, kasiya o sagasu no ga taihen na sigoto de aru koto, yasui kyuuryoo de seikatu sinakereba naranai no ga sinpai na koto nado hanasimasita.

Hasimoto-san wa zunoo ga yoku gakumon ga suki na hito desu ga sukosi tanki na tokoro ga arimasu. Daigaku ni ita toki ni wa tomodati wa mina gakusya ni naru no da to omotte imasita. Zibun mo sono tumori de ita yoo desita. Aru toki, roodoo-kumiai no koto de sensei ni situmon o site kara daigaku ni nokoru kangae o sutete simaimasita. Hasimoto-san wa dotiraka to ieba syakaisyugi-teki na kangae o motte iru hito desu kara, sensei no hosyusyugi ni manzoku dekinakatta no desyoo.

Watasi no titi wa inaka no tiisa na mati de komeya o site imasu. Titi no otooto de aru ozi wa tonari de sakaya o site imasu. Sore de ani wa syoonin ni narimasita ga, watasi wa syoogyoo wa kirai de rekisi ni kyoomi o motte imasita. Titi wa watasi ni keizaigaku o benkyoo sasetakatta no desu ga, watasi wa Yasuda-san to Hasimoto-san to onazi yoo ni hooritu o benkyoo simasita. Ima, hakuzyoo sureba naze hooritu o eranda no da ka wakarimasen ga, tekitoo na syokugyoo ga mitukeyasui to yuu hanasi o sin-zita kara desyoo. Hooritu no koto wa amari benkyoo sinai de, aru yuumei na mukasi no syoogun to geinin no yoo na kerai to no kankei o kuwasiku sirabemasita. Syoorai hon ni suru tumori desita.

Daigaku o deta watasi wa densinkyoku de hataraite ita itoko no syoo-kai de hoosookyoku e menkai ni ikimasita ga, dame desita. Sore de aru seizi undoo ni nettyuu site iru tomodati ga atarasii seitoo o sosiki suru no o tasukete moraitai to yuu no de, hito no ii watasi wa sibaraku sono hito no syoki no sigoto o simasita. Mainiti, nanzenmai to yuu hagaki o kaitari, denpoo o uttari, denwa o kaketari simasita. Kono tomodati wa rikoo na otoko desu ga, kokumin no sinri o hakkiri tukamu koto ga dekimasen desita kara, atarasii seitoo no sosiki wa muri desita. Goozyoo na kono otoko wa sore de mo undoo o tuzukemasita ga, tootoo huseikoo ni natte simaimasita. Kono tomodati wa, watasi ga hotondo kyuuryoo o toranai de hataraita no o kinodoku-gatte, kokusai-mondai o senmon ni suru zassi no hensyuutyoo ni syookai site kuremasita. Soko de watasi wa Yooroppa no kuni no syokuminti de bunka no teido no hikui dozin o donna ni kyooiku site iru ka to yuu koto o sirabete, ronbun o sukosi kakimasita. Motiron zairyoo wa gaikoku no hon toka zassi desu ga, gogaku ga amari tassya de nai watasi ni wa kanari muzukasii sigoto desita. Kono sigoto o site iru aida ni dozin no syuukan toka syuukyoo toka ni kyoomi o motu yoo ni narimasita. Daigaku de wa hooritu o benkyoo simasita kara, syuukan no mondai wa zenzen kankei no nai koto de wa arimasen desita. Tatoeba dozin ga kangaete iru 'kami' to yuu mono to, warui koto o sita baai no batu to no kankei wa watasi ga itiban omosiroi to omotta koto desita. Sosite motto hukaku sirabetai to omoimasita. Sore ni wa gaikokugo no tisiki ga hituyoo de aru koto o kan-zimasita. Watasi wa gaikokugo wa Eigo to Huransugo o sukosi bakari sika sirimasen desita kara, nantoka site Doitugo ga naraitai to omoimasita.

Watasi ga Hasimoto-san to Yasuda-san ni atta no wa tyoodo kono toki desita. Sore de watasi no kangae o hutari ni hanasimasita. Sositara Yasuda-san ga, ii sensei o sitte iru kara syookai site ageru, mae ni Yasuda-san no otoosan ga sewa sita hito da kara, nanimo o-rei wa sinai de ii to itte kuremasita.

Sore kara watasi wa mainiti kono hito no tokoro e itte Doitugo o naratte imasu. Kono hito wa Nihonzin to Doituzin to no ainoko de, Doitugo wa motiron tassya desu ga, Nihongo mo gogaku-teki ni sirabete watasi no bunpoo wa hyoozyungo no de nai kara naosana-kereba ikenai to itta koto mo arimasu. Watasi wa Doitugo ga yome sae sureba ii to omotte imasu ga, kono hito wa hanasu koto mo dekina-kereba ikenai to itte, mainiti kaiwa no rensyuu o saseraremasu. Itu Doitugo ga zibiki o tukau dake de yomeru yoo ni naru ka wakarimasen ga, tonikaku dekiru dake no koto o site imasu.

Notes

7 **iku tokoro da**: 'is on the point of going; is just about to go'. As well as 'place' and 'time, moment', as here, *tokoro* is also used to mean 'point/aspect of character'; see, e.g., l. 12 below.

8 **mesitukai to hutari de**: 'two with a servant', i.e. himself and *one* servant.

9 **hanasiaimasita**: 'talked together'; as the second half of a compound verb, -*au* means 'with one another, mutually'.

10 **tikaku**: here refers to time; 'in the near future'.

de aru: a plain form of *desu*, sometimes used before *koto* in reported speech (*da* and *desu* are not used in such relative clauses before nouns).

12 **yoku**: suspensive form, parallel to (*suki*) *na*.

16 dotiraka to ieba: 'if one says the one or the other; of the two (alternatives)'; hence 'rather (more) —— (than the opposite)'.

18 komeya o site imasu: see n. to Lesson 8, l. 12.

19 sakaya: see n. to Lesson 9, l. 2.

20-21 watasi ni ... benkyoo sasetakatta: 'wanted to cause a studying ... by me', i.e. 'wanted to make me study'. The use of a -*garu* ending (see n. to Lesson 15, l. 26) is not obligatory here, perhaps because of the following *no desu*; if one is used, the verb would need to be *sasetagatte ita* (*no desu*).

23 syokugyoo ga mitukeyasui: *ga* is used because the addition of -*yasui* (and -*tai*, -*nikui*, etc.) makes the original verb into an adjective; this then describes what would be the object of an ordinary transitive verb (here, e.g., 'employment is easy to find').

28 aru: qualifies *tomodati*, not *seizi undoo*.

30 hito no ii watasi: as well as 'person', *hito* can mean 'nature, disposition', as here. On this use of *no* in an attributive clause, see n. to Lesson 4, No. 18.

31 nanzenmai to yuu hagaki: see n. to Lesson 13, l. 16.

31-32 ... -tari ... -tari ... -tari simasita: see n. to Lesson 16, ll. 24-27.

34 Goozyoo na kono otoko: this word order puts more emphasis on *goozyoo* than if *kono* came first.

sore de mo: 'even so, nevertheless'.

36 kinodoku-gatte: see n. to Lesson 15, l. 26.

37 Soko de: 'there'.

38 kyooiku site iru: as no subject for this verb is given in the Japanese, a passive form is useful in translation.

47 bakari sika: see n. to Lesson 10, l. 24. The context requires the phrase to be taken with *Eigo to Huransugo* rather than with *sukosi* alone; i.e. the meaning is that he knew a bit of English and French and nothing else, not that he knew only a little of these languages.

48 nantoka site: 'somehow or other, by some means'.

51 site ageru: although, in reported speech, the speaker usually reduces the level of politeness of the forms that have been used to him (see n. to Lesson 14, ll. 20-23) and *yaru* is just such a less polite equivalent for *ageru*, the use of *yaru* tends to be avoided unless it means 'giving' to an animal or brusque language is being used throughout.

53-54 Sore kara ... naratte imasu: 'Since then, I have been learning ...' Cf. n. to Lesson 15, l. 22.

57 yome sae sureba: see n. to Lesson 7, ll. 20-21. *Sae* can be used with a verb itself by inserting it between the base of the verb and *sureba*. The verb here is *yomeru*, potential (hence the use of *ga* with *Doitugo*) from *yomu*.

58 rensyuu o saseraremasu: 'I get a causing to practice', i.e. 'I am made to practice'; *saseraremasu* is the (indirect) passive of the causative *saseru*.

59 Doitugo ga ... yomeru: are subject and verb; see n. to l. 57 above.

60 dekiru dake no koto: 'things to the extent possible', i.e. 'everything possible'. In addition to 'only', *dake* can also mean 'extent, limit'.

十八

わたしはある子どもに、人間とほかの動物とはどんな點でちがふ
か、と聞いた。子どもはしばらく考へてから、人間は二本の足で歩
くが、ほかの動物は四本の足で歩く、と返事した。もちろん、鳥が
二本の足しか持つてゐない事をわすれてゐるが、それは問題にしな
いで、まだほかにちがひがあるか、と聞いた。人間は着物を着てゐ
るが、動物には毛が澤山ある、といふのが次の返事だつた。まだあ
るか、と言へば、人間は手で物を食べるが動物は口で物を取つて食
べる、と言つた。

わたしは質問をつづけたが、子どもは、わたしがしてもらひたい
と思つてゐた返事をしなかつた。そこでわたしは、いぬは話しをす
るか、と聞いた。子どもは、もちろん話しをする、となりのいぬは

百ぐらゐの言葉を知つてゐる、いぬばかりでない、庭のありでさへ話しをする、と言つた。どうしてありが話しをするのを知つてゐるか、と聞けば、庭でありの行列を見てゐると右へ行くのと左へ行くのとがときぐ〈とまつて頭と頭を突き合はせるからだ、と説明した。

わたしは子どもに、自分の考へとか感じとかを言葉で他人に知らせる、つまり本當の意味で話しの出來るのは人間だけだ、といふ事を分からせるつもりだつたのだが、成功しなかつたやうである。う

たがひもなく、責任はわたしにある。わたしの質問の仕方が下手なために、子どもの頭の働きをわたしの思ふ方向へ向ける事が出來なかつたのである。

以上は子どもの場合の例だが、おとなに對しても物を分からせようとして、なかく〈成功しない事がよくある。特に、今まで自分で

考へた事もなく經驗した事もない事とか、目で見たり手でさはつた
りする事が出來ないものとかをはつきり分からせようとするのは非
常にむづかしい。もちろん、學校の先生など、これが專門の仕事と
なつてゐる人は、長い間の經驗で、知識のひくい者とか、物を考へ
る力の余りない者とかに、上手に分からせるやうにする事が出來る
であらう。

むかし、教育の一つの方法として、本を讀む場合、先生は少しも
説明しないで、生徒に何度も何度も同じ所を讀ませた。そして、何
度も讀んでゐるうちに、そこに書いてある事が自然に分かるやうに
なる、と考へたのである。この方法は、生徒の頭が非常にいい場合
には大變結構なものであらう。しかし、普通の生徒は、かりに分か
つたやうに思つても、それは表面的なものだけで、本當の意味は分

からないのである。それを、先生も生徒も分かつたと思つて滿足す
る。その結果、何か話したり書いたりしようとする時、自分の知識
とか意見とかがないか、あつてもそれを分かりやすく、正しく、簡
單に發表する事が出來ないか、どちらかになる。

こういふ頭の使ひ方の練習しかしてゐないのが國民的な一つのく
せとなつて、何か議論をする場合に、話し手も聞き手も早く問題の
中心をつかむ事が出來ないやうになる。議會政治はつまらない議論
に時間をむだにして物事を早く決める事が出來ないのが短所だと人
はよく言ふ。その原因の一つは、經驗が足りない事であらうが、も
つと大事な原因は、自分の考へを他人に分かりやすく發表する事が
出來ないか、下手であるかにある。子どもの時から「意見の發表の
正しい方法」を練習する必要があるわけである。

LESSON 18

ZYUUHATI

WATASI wa aru kodomo ni, ningen to hoka no doobutu to wa donna ten de tigau ka, to kiita. Kodomo wa sibaraku kangaete kara, ningen wa nihon no asi de aruku ga, hoka no doobutu wa sihon no asi de aruku, to henzi sita. Motiron, tori ga nihon no asi sika motte inai koto o wasurete iru ga, sore wa mondai ni sinai de, mada hoka ni tigai ga aru ka, to kiita. Ningen wa kimono o kite iru ga, doobutu ni wa ke ga takusan aru, to yuu no ga tugi no henzi datta. Mada aru ka, to ieba, ningen wa te de mono o taberu ga doobutu wa kuti de mono o totte taberu, to itta.

Watasi wa situmon o tuzuketa ga, kodomo wa watasi ga site moraitai to omotte ita henzi o sinakatta. Soko de watasi wa, inu wa hanasi o suru ka, to kiita. Kodomo wa, motiron hanasi o suru, tonari no inu wa hyaku-gurai no kotoba o sitte iru, inu bakari de nai, niwa no ari de sae hanasi o suru, to itta. Doosite ari ga hanasi o suru no o sitte iru ka, to kikeba, niwa de ari no gyooretu o mite iru to, migi e iku no to hidari e iku no to ga, tokidoki tomatte atama to atama o tukiawaseru kara da, to setumei sita.

Watasi wa kodomo ni, zibun no kangae toka kanzi toka o kotoba de tanin ni siraseru, tumari hontoo no imi de hanasi no dekiru no wa ningen dake da, to yuu koto o wakaraseru tumori datta no da ga, seikoo sinakatta yoo de aru. Utagai mo naku, sekinin wa watasi ni aru. Watasi no situmon no sikata ga heta na tame ni, kodomo no atama no hataraki o watasi no omou hookoo e mukeru koto ga dekinakatta no de aru.

Izyoo wa kodomo no baai no rei da ga, otona ni taisite mo mono o wakaraseyoo to site, nakanaka seikoo sinai koto ga yoku aru. Toku ni, ima made zibun de kangaeta koto mo naku keiken sita koto mo nai koto toka, me de mitari te de sawattari suru koto ga dekinai mono toka o hakkiri wakaraseyoo to suru no wa hizyoo ni muzukasii. Motiron, gakkoo no sensei nado, kore ga senmon no sigoto to natte iru hito wa, nagai aida no keiken de, tisiki no hikui mono toka, mono o kangaeru tikara no amari nai mono toka ni, zyoozu ni wakaraseru yoo ni suru koto ga dekiru de aroo.

Mukasi, kyooiku no hitotu no hoohoo to site, hon o yomu baai, sensei wa sukosi mo setumei sinai de, seito ni nando mo nando mo onazi tokoro o yomaseta. Sosite, nando mo yonde iru uti ni, soko ni kaite aru koto ga sizen ni wakaru yoo ni naru, to kangaeta no de aru. Kono hoohoo wa, seito no atama ga hizyoo ni ii baai ni wa, taihen kekkoo na mono de aroo. Sikasi, hutuu no seito wa, kari ni wakatta yoo ni omotte mo, sore wa hyoomen-teki na mono dake de, hontoo no imi wa wakaranai no de aru. Sore o, sensei mo seito mo wakatta to

[168]

omotte manzoku suru. Sono kekka, nanika hanasitari kaitari siyoo to suru toki, zibun no tisiki toka iken toka ga nai ka, atte mo sore o wakariyasuku, tadasiku, kantan ni happyoo suru koto ga dekinai ka, dotiraka ni naru. Koo yuu atama no tukaikata no rensyuu sika site inai no ga, koku-min-teki na hitotu no kuse to natte, nanika giron o suru baai ni, hanasi-te mo kiki-te mo hayaku mondai no tyuusin o tukamu koto ga dekinai yoo ni naru. Gikai-seizi wa tumaranai giron ni zikan o muda ni site, monogoto o hayaku kimeru koto ga dekinai no ga tansyo da to hito wa yoku yuu. Sono gen-in no hitotu wa, keiken ga tarinai koto de aroo ga, motto daizi na gen-in wa, zibun no kangae o tanin ni wakariyasuku happyoo suru koto ga dekinai ka, heta de aru ka ni aru. Kodomo no toki kara 'iken no happyoo no tadasii hoohoo' o rensyuu suru hituyoo ga aru wake de aru.

Notes

Previous lessons have been in the colloquial -*masu* style, but this and the next lesson are in what is called *de aru* style. This uses the plain forms of verbs and adjectives instead of the -*masu* forms, with *de aru* replacing *desu*. It is the standard modern written style, appropriate for use whenever personal relationships do not require polite forms as they do, for example, in letter-writing. There will not always be absolute consistency, however: while -*masu* forms are never used in *de aru* style, *da* and *datta* are occasionally found in it in informal writing (see, e.g., l. 19 in this lesson).

10–11 **watasi ga site moraitai to omotte ita henzi**: 'the reply which I (was feeling I) wanted to have him make'. *Watasi* is the subject of *omotte ita* (and, secondarily, of *moraitai*), not of *site*. As *omou* often has a wider and more emotional meaning than the English 'think', it may have to be translated as 'feel, wish, hope', etc. (see, e.g., l. 21 below); but -*tai to omou* means much the same as 'would like to . . .'.

13 **de sae**: see n. to Lesson 7, ll. 20–21.

15–16 **. . . no to . . . no to ga**: the subject of the clause; 'the ones . . . and the ones . . . (sometimes stop and . . .)'.

17–19 **kodomo ni . . . koto o wakaraseru**: 'to cause an understanding of . . . by the child', i.e. to make him understand that . . .

21 **tame ni**: 'on account of'; see n. to Lesson 11, l. 11.

23 **otona ni taisite mo**: 'even toward/in regard to adults'.

27–28 **sensei nado . . . hito wa**: 'people such as teachers (for whom . . .)'.

35–36 **kari ni . . . omotte mo**: 'even supposing they think . . .'.

37 **Sore o**: a conjunctive phrase (cf. *sore de*, etc.) with adversative feeling similar to *no ni* (see n. to Lesson 6, No. 10).

39 **sore o**: object of *happyoo suru*.

39–40 **. . . nai ka, . . . dekinai ka, dotiraka ni naru**: 'are they without . . .? (or) are they unable . . .?—it turns out to be one or the other'.

41 **Koo yuu . . . no ga**: 'Doing nothing but (*sika site inai no ga*) this kind of training in the use of the mind'.

十九

信六はまどから入って来る日の光りに目をさまされて、寝台の上に横になりながらきのうの事をぼんやり考えていた。きのうの朝、この町の駅へ着いた時には雨がふっていた。様子が分からないでこ〜まっている信六を見て、親切な駅長は自動車をさがしてくれた。かなり古い車だったが、とにかく大きなかばんを持って雨の中を歩かないですんだ。その上、この家は駅から遠くはなかったが急な坂を上らなければならなかったから、そのためにも自動車で来た事は助かった。

10 　家はかなり大きい西洋式の建物で、道の向こう側にはこれと平行して古い日本式の家がならんでいる。玄関に着くと中から小使らしいおじいさんが出て来た。

「井上ですが……」。

「あ、おまちしていました。どうぞお入り下さい。荷物はわたしが

持って行きます」。

「重いですよ」。

「大丈夫です。慣れていますから」。

やせているこの人は重いかばんを何でもないように持ち上げた。

「お部屋は二階です。では御案内しましょう」。

部屋のまどからは、はい色の屋根がならんでいる先に海が見えた。

きりのような雨がふっているので遠くははっきりしないが、天気が

よければいゝながめだろうと思った。やせたおじいさんはかばんを

床の上に重ねて部屋の外へ出て行った。五分ばかりすると、背が高

い、わかい時にはかなり美しかっただろうと思わせる四十ばかりの

女の人が入って来た。

「よくいらっしゃいました。これはながめが一番いゝ部屋ですから

25 お気に召すと思います。あとで、下へおいでになったら玄関の左側

の小さな部屋へおいでになって下さい。お名前など書き取りたいと

思いますから」。

「かしこまりました。すぐ行きます」。

30 「そんなにお急ぎにならなくてもよろしいんですよ」。

一通り荷物を片付けて下へ行った。小さな部屋は事務所のように

なっていた。もゝ色の洋服を着た二十ばかりの女の人がテーブルの

上で何か書いていたので、信六はかるくあいさつした。

「井上さんでいらっしゃいますね。こゝへちょっとお名前と御住所

35 を書いていただきたいんですの」。

信六は下手な字で名前と住所を書き入れた。

「母はお食事の時間を申上げまして?」

「いゝえ」。

40「おひるは十二時半ですの。食堂はあちら側で、あなたのは五番のテーブルです」。

信六はこれでこのわかい女は背が高い女の人のむすめである事が分かった。

信六は庭に向かっていた。五番のテーブルにはもう二人の人がす

45わっていた。一人は太った頭の毛のうすい男だった。もう一人は和服を着たわかい女だった。女は信六の顔を見ると、

「井上さんでしょう? こゝへおかけなさいな」。

と言ってあいているいすを少しテーブルからはなした。

「わたし、石川道子、道子とよんで下さいね。そしてこれはわたし

しの父」。

と言って太った男を信六に紹介した。信六は、

「わたし井上です。どうぞよろしく……」。

と形式的なあいさつをした。男は、

「あなたがおいでになる事はみんな知っているんですよ。こゝにと

ゞまっている人は全部で十五人ばかりですが、みんな何もする事がな

くてこまっている人ですから新しく来る人に非常に大きな興味を持

つんです」。

とむすめがなぜ信六の名前を知っているかの理由を説明した。

「こゝの奥さんにお会いになったでしょう？とてもいゝ方、わた

したたちの気持をよく察して下さってね」。

道子はこうして、食事中にこの家の家族の事とか、お客の事とかを話した。それで信六は、背が高い女の人がこの女主人である事、小使らしいおじいさんは奥さんの父である事、事務所のわかい女は奥さんの一人むすめである事、奥さんの夫は戦争で死んだ事などを知った。しかし変な事には道子は自分たちの事は何も言わなかった。

信六は午後は自分の部屋で持って来た本を読んだ。晩には雨がやんで空はすっかりはれた。食事のあとで道子は信六を庭に案内した。美しい月が出ていて、海はうすい銀色に光り、白い砂にはまつの木の黒いかげがあった。東京よりはずっと暖かいはずだが、夜はまだかなり寒かった。道子と信六は竹で出来ているいすにこしかけてしばらくだまって景色をながめていた。突然道子は、

「わたしの結婚式のお話ししましょうか」。

と言った。信六は少しおどろいて何と返事していゝか分からなかった。道子は信六の返事をまたないでつづけた。

「簡単なのよ。式が終って夫と家に帰って来て着物を換えたら、それで終りよ。夫は調べる事があると言って自分の部屋へ入って勉強なのよ。わたしは気ちがいにでもなった気がしました。わたしの友だちは結婚式の晩ににげだして愛人の所へ行きました。わたしも愛人があったらそんな事でもしたでしょうに……」。

道子は少しないているようだった。信六はかたくなって聞いているだけだった。

「夫は仕事だけが生活の全部なんです。芝居へ行きましょうと言えば、いそがしいからお前だけだれか友だちと行けと言うのよ。わた

しは自分の考えを通す力がなかったんです。父の命令で結婚したで

⁸⁵しょう。だからとてもさびしくて病気になってしまったわ。お医者

さんがこゝへ来てしばらく休みなさいと言うので来たんですけれど

父はわたしを一人にさせないんです。父はわたしの番人なのよ。か

らだの具合が少しよくなって来るので近く帰らなければならないと

考えると、とてもいやになってしまうのよ」。

⁹⁰　信六は道子がとてもかわいそうだった。けれどもどう言ってい、

のか言葉を知らなかった。つかれているからあした、また会おうと約

束して自分の部屋へ帰って寝たのである。それで今目がさめて、き

ょう道子に会ったらどうしょう、どんな事を言おうと考えているの

だった。

LESSON 19

ZYUUKU

SINROKU wa mado kara haitte kuru hi no hikari ni me o samasarete, sindai no ue ni yoko ni nari-nagara kinoo no koto o bonyari kangaete ita. Kinoo no asa, kono mati no eki e tuita toki ni wa ame ga hutte ita. Yoosu ga wakaranai de komatte iru Sinroku o mite, sinsetu na ekityoo wa zidoosya o sagasite kureta. Kanari hurui kuruma datta ga, tonikaku ooki na kaban o motte ame no naka o arukanai de sunda. Sono ue, kono ie wa eki kara tooku wa nakatta ga kyuu na saka o noboranakereba naranakatta kara, sono tame ni mo zidoosya de kita koto wa tasukatta.

Ie wa kanari ookii seiyoo-siki no tatemono de, miti no mukoo-gawa ni wa kore to heikoo site hurui Nihon-siki no ie ga narande iru. Genkan ni tuku to naka kara kozukai rasii oziisan ga dete kita.

'Inoue desu ga. . . .'

'A, o-mati site imasita. Doozo o-hairi kudasai. Nimotu wa watasi ga motte ikimasu.'

'Omoi desu yo.'

'Daizyoobu desu. Narete imasu kara.'

Yasete iru kono hito wa omoi kaban o nandemo nai yoo ni moti-ageta.

'O-heya wa nikai desu. De wa go-annai simasyoo.'

Heya no mado kara wa, hai-iro no yane ga narande iru saki ni umi ga mieta. Kiri no yoo na ame ga hutte iru no de tooku wa hakkiri sinai ga, tenki ga yokereba ii nagame daroo to omotta. Yaseta oziisan wa kaban o yuka no ue ni kasanete heya no soto e dete itta. Gohun bakari suru to, se ga takai, wakai toki ni wa kanari utukusikatta daroo to omowaseru sizyuu bakari no onna no hito ga haitte kita.

'Yoku irassyaimasita. Kore wa nagame ga itiban ii heya desu kara o-ki ni mesu to omoimasu. Ato de, sita e oide ni nattara genkan no hidari-gawa no tiisa na heya e oide ni natte kudasai. O-namae nado kakitoritai to omoimasu kara.'

'Kasikomarimasita. Sugu ikimasu.'

'Sonna ni o-isogi ni naranakute mo yorosiin' desu yo.'

Hitotoori nimotu o katazukete sita e itta. Tiisa na heya wa zimusyo no yoo ni natte ita. Momoiro no yoohuku o kita hatati bakari no onna no hito ga teeburu no ue de nanika kaite ita no de, Sinroku wa karuku aisatu sita.

'Inoue-san de irassyaimasu ne. Koko e tyotto o-namae to go-zyuusyo o kaite itadakitain' desu no.'

Sinroku wa heta na zi de namae to zyuusyo o kakiireta.

'Haha wa o-syokuzi no zikan o moosiagemasite?'

'Iie.'

'O-hiru wa zyuunizi han desu no. Syokudoo wa atira-gawa de, anata no wa goban no teeburu desu.'

Sinroku wa kore de kono wakai onna wa se ga takai onna no hito no musume de aru koto ga wakatta.

Syokudoo wa niwa ni mukatte ita. Goban no teeburu wa moo hutari no hito ga suwatte ita. Hitori wa hutotta atama no ke no usui otoko datta. Moo hitori wa wahuku o kita wakai onna datta. Onna wa Sinroku no kao o miru to, 'Inoue-san desyoo? Koko e o-kake nasai na,' to itte aite iru isu o sukosi teeburu kara hanasita.

'Watasi, Isikawa Mitiko; Mitiko to yonde kudasai ne. Sosite kore wa watasi no titi,' to itte hutotta otoko o Sinroku ni syookai sita. Sinroku wa, 'Watasi Inoue desu. Doozo yorosiku . . .,' to keisiki-teki na aisatu o sita.

Otoko wa, 'Anata ga oide ni naru koto wa minna sitte irun' desu yo. Koko ni tomatte iru hito wa zenbu de zyuugonin bakari desu ga, minna nanimo suru koto ga nakute komatte irun' desu kara atarasiku kuru hito ni hizyoo ni ooki na kyoomi o motun' desu,' to musume ga naze Sinroku no namae o sitte iru ka no riyuu o setumei sita.

'Koko no okusan ni o-ai ni natta desyoo? Totemo ii kata. Watasitati no kimoti o yoku sassite kudasatte ne.'

Mitiko wa koo site, syokuzi-tyuu ni kono ie no kazoku no koto toka, o-kyaku no koto toka o hanasita. Sore de Sinroku wa se ga takai onna no hito ga koko no onna-syuzin de aru koto, kozukai rasii oziisan wa okusan no titi de aru koto, zimusyo no wakai onna wa okusan no hitori-musume de aru koto, okusan no otto wa sensoo de sinda koto nado o sitta. Sikasi hen na koto ni wa Mitiko wa zibuntati no koto wa nanimo iwanakatta.

Sinroku wa gogo wa zibun no heya de motte kita hon o yonda. Ban ni wa ame ga yande sora wa sukkari hareta. Syokuzi no ato de Mitiko wa Sinroku o niwa ni annai sita. Utukusii tuki ga dete ite, umi wa usui gin-iro ni hikari, siroi suna ni wa matu no ki no kuroi kage ga atta. Tookyoo yori wa zutto atatakai hazu da ga, yoru wa mada kanari samukatta. Mitiko to Sinroku wa take de dekite iru isu ni kosikakete sibaraku damatte kesiki o nagamete ita. Totuzen Mitiko wa, 'Watasi no kekkonsiki no o-hanasi simasyoo ka,' to itta. Sinroku wa sukosi odoroite nan to henzi site ii ka wakaranakatta. Mitiko wa Sinroku no henzi o matanai de tuzuketa.

'Kantan na no yo. Siki ga owatte otto to uti ni kaette kite kimono o kaetara, sore de owari yo. Otto wa siraberu koto ga aru to itte zibun no heya e haitte benkyoo na no yo. Watasi wa kitigai ni de mo natta ki ga simasita. Watasi no tomodati wa kekkonsiki no ban ni nigedasite aizin no tokoro e ikimasita. Watasi mo aizin ga attara sonna koto o sita desyoo ni. . . .'

Mitiko wa suk̇osi naite iru yoo datta. Sinroku wa kataku natte kiite iru dake datta.

'Otto wa sigoto dake ga seikatu no zenbu nan' desu. Sibai e ikimasyoo to ieba, isogasii kara omae dake dareka tomodati to ike to yuu no yo. Watasi wa zibun no kangae o toosu tikara ga nakattan' desu. Titi no meirei de kekkon sita desyoo. Da kara totemo sabisikute byooki ni natte simatta wa. O-isya-san ga koko e kite sibaraku yasumi nasai to yuu no de kitan' desu keredo, titi wa watasi o hitori ni sasenain' desu. Titi wa watasi no bannin na no yo. Karada no guai ga sukosi yoku natte kuru no de tikaku kaeranakereba naranai to kangaeru to, totemo iya ni natte simau no yo.'

Sinroku wa Mitiko ga totemo kawaisoo datta. Keredomo doo itte ii no ka kotoba o siranakatta. Tukarete iru kara asita mata aoo to yakusoku site zibun no heya e kaette neta no de aru. Sore de ima me ga samete, kyoo Mitiko ni attara doo siyoo, donna koto o ioo to kangaete iru no datta.

Notes

3 **yoko ni nari-nagara** : *yoko ni naru* is a common expression for 'lie down'.

4-5 **wakaranai de komatte iru** : 'be troubled by not knowing'. *Komaru* 'be in difficulties' is often used after a *-te* form (see ll. 55–56 below) or *de*, e.g. *byooki de komaru*, 'be inconvenienced by illness'.

6-7 **arukanai de sunda** : 'he finished/got through without walking', i.e. 'he avoided/ was saved walking'.

8 **noboranakereba naranakatta** : see n. to Lesson 16, l. 5.

13 **Inoue** : see n. to Lesson 8, l. 11.

14 **o-mati site imasita** : depreciatory equivalent for *matte imasita*.
o-hairi kudasai : polite imperative from *hairu*.

18 **nandemo nai yoo ni** : 'as if it is not anything at all'. Cf. uses of *nandemo* in Lesson 6, Nos. 3, 6, and 11.

20 **yane ga narande iru saki ni** : 'beyond the rows of roofs'.

24-25 **utukusikatta daroo to omowaseru . . . onna** : 'a woman who makes one think she was probably beautiful'.

26 **Yoku irassyaimasita** : 'Welcome'; a standard greeting to guests.

27 **o-ki ni mesu** : *mesu* is an honorific verb much used by servants with a wide range of meanings, the two most common being 'wear' and 'take (a bath)'. Here the phrase is equivalent to *ki ni iru*, 'be to one's liking', and, since its subject can only be understood as *heya* (or *kore*), it is clearly rather different from ordinary honorific verbs, which always show respect to their subject (see n. to Lesson 16, ll. 34–36 and 'Respect Language' after Lesson 20). It is clearly honorific to the person about whom it is used, but this person will not always be its grammatical subject.

oide ni nattara : honorific equivalent for *kitara* here (rather than *ittara*), since the proprietress would doubtless identify herself with the downstairs part (see n. to Lesson 6, No. 15).

30 **Kasikomarimasita**: 'Yes, certainly'; a polite expression of agreement with a request.

31 **o-isogi ni naranakute mo**: honorific equivalent for *isoganakute mo*.

34 **karuku**: 'lightly', i.e. easily, casually, informally (because, being a young woman member of the staff, she warranted no great formality).

36 **desu no**: this *no*, which is used with a level intonation in women's speech, must be distinguished from the friendly interrogative *no* (see n. to Lesson 9, l. 32) which, like *ka*, has a rising intonation. This *no* is very weak in feeling and is often used with a following exclamatory *yo* (see, e.g., ll. 75 and 83 below).

38 **moosiagemasite?**: the -*te* form of -*masu*, used with *moosiageru*, a depreciatory equivalent for *yuu*. It is equivalent to *moosiagemasita ka*, 'did (my mother) tell you', the -*te* sometimes being used in women's language in place of a final form.

47 **na**: final particle similar to *ne*; when used after an imperative, it has the effect of softening the feeling of command.

49 **Watasi, Isikawa Mitiko**: in speech, the particles *wa* and *o* are often omitted.

62–65 **Sore de, Sinroku wa … koto … koto … koto … koto nado o sitta**: 'From this, Sinroku learned such things as that . . ., . . ., . . ., and . . .

65 **zibuntati**: 'herself and those connected with her'; -*tati* is conveniently described as a 'plural suffix', but it sometimes means rather '—— and those like ——; such people as ——'.

68–69 **tuki ga dete ite, umi wa … hikari, … kage ga atta**: 'the moon being out, the sea shone . . ., and . . . there were shadows'. *Dete ite* is connected in meaning to both the following clauses; *hikari* is a suspensive form.

69 **hazu**: a noun meaning 'likelihood, probability, expectancy', it is often conveniently translated by 'should, ought to (be here soon)', etc. But it must not be confused on that account with the 'should' and 'ought' expressing moral obligation which must be translated by something like -*nakute wa ikenai* (see n. to Lesson 16, l. 5) or by the literary suffix -*beki*.

75 **Kantan na no yo**: a woman's expression, equivalent to *Kantan da yo* in standard speech. On the exclamatory *no yo*, see n. to l. 36 above.

79 **sita desyoo ni**: this *ni* expresses regret that something is not so, and is equivalent to the *no ni* used after plain verbal forms or *desu*, e.g. *ittara yokatta (desu) no ni*, 'I *do* wish I'd gone'.

80 **kataku natte**: 'becoming stiff, formal, ill at ease'.

83 **omae**: a brusque second person pronoun commonly used by a man to his children or wife.
   dareka tomodati to: 'with some friend or other' (cf. *nanika*, Lesson 11, l. 6, etc.).
   ike: brusque imperative of *iku*.

84 **zibun no kangae o toosu**: 'put through one's own ideas', i.e. 'get one's own way'.

85 **wa**: a weak final particle used by women, similar to *no* but a shade more exclamatory in feeling.

87 **watasi o hitori ni sasenai**: 'he won't (allow anyone to) leave me on my own'. Some form of *hitori ni suru* might seem sufficient, but this phrase is, in fact, used only in the meaning 'make it one (person)' when discussing numbers.

90 **kawaisoo**: 'pitiable'; very similar in meaning to (*o-*)*kinodoku*, but, not having the respectful feeling of the latter, is rarely used in addressing the object of pity, unless it is a child or animal.

93 **doo siyoo**: 'what would he do?' Note the different feeling behind *doo simasyoo*, 'how shall we do/go about things?', and the less used *nani o simasyoo*, 'what (from the choice available) shall we do?'

二十

御元気にお過ごし〜の事と存じます。日本に帰って参りまして から

一度御あいさつに参ろうと存じて居りましたが、非常にいそがし〜い

ため時間がなく失礼申し上げました。

さて、私が国際連合の仕事の関係でニューヨークに居りました時、

日本文学に興味を持っているイギリスの青年に出会いました。ロン

ドン大学で日本語を習ったそうですが、私が会った時は米国の大学

で勉強して居りました。私は文学は専門でございませんが、よくこ

の青年と日本の事を中心に語し合いました。

二三日前この青年から近く日本へ行きどこかの大学で明治文学を

勉強したいから適当な先生を紹介してもらいたいと申して参りまし

た。

これには先生にお願するのが一番いゝと存じ、そう返事致すつも
りで居りますが、その前に先生の御承知をいたゞきたいと存じ、こ
の手紙を書きました。
おいそがしい所を失礼でございますが、御返事下さるようお願申
上げます。

土月一日

秋野京一

東山先生

20

お手紙拝見しました。君の子は長井さんから〜ときゝ〳〵驚いてをり
〜た。わたーは外交とか政治とかの事はほとんど興味も知識もあり

[183]

ませんが、日本が国際連合のメンバーになつて色々の仕事をはじめ

た事は非常に結構な事と思つて居ます。

さて、英国青年の事承知しました。日本に着いたらすぐわたーの

所へ連れておいでなさい。出来るだけのお世話をします。ただ、わ

たーは外国語はだめですから会話はみな日本語ですから、勉強以外

の事では全然責任を取る事が出来ない事をよく話して置いて下さい。

ではその青年が着いたら気にもお目にかかれるでせう。

三月三日

東山英治

秋里京一様

[184]

二十

御元気にお過ごしの事と存じます。日本に帰って参りましてから一度御あいさつに参ろうと存じて居りましたが、非常にいそがしいため時間がなく失礼申し上げました。

さて、私が国際連合の仕事の関係でニューヨークに居りました時、日本文学に興味を持っているイギリスの青年に出会いました。ロンドン大学で日本語を習ったそうですが、私が会った時は米国の大学で勉強して居りました。私は文学は専門でございませんが、よくこの青年と日本の事を中心に話し合いました。

二三日前この青年から、近く日本へ行きどこかの大学で明治文学を勉強したいから適当な先生を紹介してもらいたいと申して参りました。

これには先生にお願するのが一番いゝと存じ、そう返事致すつも
りで居りますが、その前に先生の御承知をいたゞきたいと存じ、こ

15

の手紙を書きました。

おいそがしい所を失礼でございますが、御返事を下さるようお願

申し上げます。

　　　五月一日

　　　　　　　　　　　　　　　　　　　　　　　秋野京一

東山先生

20

　お手紙拝見しました。　君の事は長井さんからときぐ〜聞いてゐま

した。。わたしは外交とか政治とかの事はほとんど興味も知識もあり

ませんが、日本が国際連合のメンバーになつて色々の仕事をはじめた事は非常に結構な事と思つてゐます。

さて、英国青年の事承知しました。日本に着いたらすぐわたしの所へ連れておいでなさい。出来るだけのお世話をします。たゞ、わたしは外国語はだめですから会話はみな日本語でする事、勉強以外の事では全然責任を取る事が出来ない事をよく話して置いて下さい。ではその青年が着いたら君にもお目にかゝれるでせう。

　　　　五月三日

　　　　　　　　　東山英治

秋野京一様

NIZYUU

O-GENKI ni o-sugosi no koto to zon-zimasu. Nihon ni kaette mairi-masite kara itido go-aisatu ni mairoo to zon-zite orimasita ga, hizyoo ni isogasii tame zikan ga naku siturei moosiagemasita.

Sate, watakusi ga kokusai-rengoo no sigoto no kankei de Nyuu Yooku ni orimasita toki, Nihon bungaku ni kyoomi o motte iru Igirisu no seinen ni deaimasita. Rondon-daigaku de Nihongo o naratta soo desu ga, watakusi ga atta toki wa Beikoku no daigaku de benkyoo site orimasita. Watakusi wa bungaku wa senmon de gozai-masen ga, yoku kono seinen to Nihon no koto o tyuusin ni hanasiai-masita.

Nisanniti mae kono seinen kara tikaku Nihon e iki dokoka no daigaku de Meizi bungaku o benkyoo sitai kara tekitoo na sensei o syookai site moraitai to moosite mairimasita.

Kore ni wa sensei ni o-negai suru no ga itiban ii to zon-zi, soo henzi itasu tumori de orimasu ga, sono mae ni sensei no go-syooti o itadakitai to zon-zi, kono tegami o kakimasita.

O-isogasii tokoro o siturei de gozaimasu ga, go-henzi kudasaru yoo o-negai moosiagemasu.

Gogatu tuitati   Akino Kyooiti
Higasiyama-sensei

O-tegami haiken simasita. Kimi no koto wa Nagai-san kara tokidoki kiite imasita. Watasi wa gaikoo toka seizi toka no koto wa hotondo kyoomi mo tisiki mo arimasen ga, Nihon ga kokusai-rengoo no menbaa ni natte iroiro no sigoto o hazimeta koto wa hizyoo ni kekkoo na koto to omotte imasu.

Sate, Eikoku seinen no koto syooti simasita. Nihon ni tuitara sugu watasi no tokoro e turete oide nasai. Dekiru dake no o-sewa o simasu. Tada, watasi wa gaikokugo wa dame desu kara kaiwa wa mina Nihongo de suru koto, benkyoo igai no koto de wa zenzen sekinin o toru koto ga dekinai koto o yoku hanasite oite kudasai.

Dewa sono seinen ga tuitara kimi ni mo o-me ni kakareru desyoo.

Gogatu mikka   Higasiyama Eizi
Akino Kyooiti-sama

Notes

4 **siturei moosiagemasita**: *siturei* is exceptional in never taking an honorific prefix. *moosiagemasita* is here a highly deferential equivalent for *simasita*.

    Language tends to be more honorific in letters, especially in more or less set phrases, than it would be in speech between the persons concerned. For example, in replying to Akino, who is apparently a younger man and perhaps a former pupil, the teacher uses what is virtually normal *-masu* language; but, since he refers to Akino as *kimi*, he would probably soon lapse into the use of plain forms on meeting him.

10–12 kono seinen kara . . . moosite mairimasita: 'word came from this young man that . . .', the unquoted part all being a version of what he said—hence the retention of *iki* although the student is *coming* to where the writer himself is.

13–14 itasu tumori de orimasu: depreciatory equivalent for —— *de imasu*; —— *de gozaimasu* (for —— *desu*) could have been used instead, but there is a more personal feeling about the *imasu/orimasu* usage.

14 go-syooti o itadakitai: on this use of *o* with *-tai*, see n. to Lesson 7, ll. 6–7.

25 dekiru dake: see n. to Lesson 17, l. 60.

RESPECT LANGUAGE

THE forms of respect language in Japanese are capable of almost infinite variation and gradation, according to the speaker and the circumstances, but the table below shows the most common and standard verbs within each category and is intended to give help in identifying them when they are encountered.

The *Plain Verbs* are 'neutral' in feeling, in that they have no overtones of either respect or humility. They are used as they stand to and about people to whom it is not necessary to express respect and, in their *-masu* forms showing respect to the person addressed, form the basis of the standard, polite conversational language.

The special verbs which express respect do so either by elevating the status of their subject or, conversely, by depreciating the status of their subject in order to raise the relative standing of someone else concerned. Hence, those of the former type have been called *Honorific Verbs* and those of the latter *Depreciatory* (or *Negative Honorific*) *Verbs*.

The *Honorific Verbs* quite straightforwardly express the speaker's respect for their subject. They can be used as they stand in their plain forms when the subject is not the same as the person addressed, and the speaker does not need to show respect to the latter (e.g. one maid to another: *O-kyaku-san wa moo o-yasumi ni naru*, 'The guest is going to bed now'); and in their *-masu* forms when he does want to show respect to him too or when, of course, the subject and the person addressed are the same (e.g. maid to guest: *Moo o-yasumi ni narimasu ka*, 'Are you going to bed now, sir?').

It should perhaps be mentioned in passing that the plain forms are, in fact, sometimes used to a person who is himself the subject of the verb (e.g. *Irassyaranai?* 'Aren't you coming?'), the feeling then being one combining respect (because of the honorific verb) and intimacy (because of the plain form); but these forms are uncommon except in women's speech.

In the list of honorific verbs *nasaru* is throughout an alternative to *ni naru*, but has been omitted in most cases to save space.

The *Depreciatory (Negative Honorific) Verbs* lower the standing of their subject (usually the speaker or someone associated with him) and thereby elevate proportionately the position of someone or something else concerned. This other person is very often the person addressed, in which case a *-masu* ending will also be needed; but it may be a third person, when a *-masu* form will not always be necessary (e.g. a man talking to a subordinate about being given something by his superior might say *Itadaita*, 'I got it from him').

Where there is no special depreciatory word for a particular verb, the plain form is used instead; and these forms have been added to the list in brackets.

It is necessary at this point to draw attention to the distinctions observed within the noun form (e.g. *benkyoo, renraku, o-kiki*) + *suru* construction, depending on whether the noun is of the *benkyoo* 'study' kind, involving no one but the person carrying out the action, or of the *renraku*, 'connection', and *o-kiki*, 'hearing, asking', type which, from their meaning, necessarily involve two or more people. Logically enough, an honorific *go-* or *o-* is used with the latter in the depreciatory forms to show respect to the other person involved, but is not used with the *benkyoo* type, since there is then no such other person.

The *Deferential Verbs* are a small group of depreciatory verbs of limited application, in that they show respect only to the person addressed. We have already seen that, if appropriate, all depreciatory verbs can be used in their *-masu* forms to show respect to the person addressed, but the deferentials are even more respectful forms which, in normal circumstances, can be used to express respect *only* to the second person. As final verbs, therefore, they will always be in their *-masu* forms; before nouns, etc., they will normally be used in their plain forms (i.e. *mairu* instead of *mairimasu*, etc.) except for the special cases shown in square brackets.

Five of these verbs, marked in the list by asterisks—*de gozaimasu, gozaimasu, orimasu, mairimasu,* and *moosimasu*—are deferential verbs *par excellence*, since they can only ever be used to show respect to the person addressed and are, moreover, applicable to all subjects (except the person addressed, his associates and even more exalted persons), including impersonal ones, e.g. *tenki ga samuku natte mairimasita ne,* 'the weather has turned cold, hasn't it?' The other verbs listed here as deferentials can only have the speaker or some such person as their subject (like the depreciatories), and are forms which, on balance, are so respectful that in normal circumstances they are used only to show respect to the second person. It is possible to imagine situations in which some of these forms might be used by some speakers to show respect to a very esteemed third person instead, and allowance must be made for such extreme cases.

It will be seen from the table that, in this deferential group, *moosia-gemasu* can be used as the verbal element with noun forms of the *go-renraku* and *o-kiki* type; that is, when another person is involved in the action described.

It must be emphasized that the table is intended essentially as an aid to the analysis of Japanese verbal forms used in respect language. It is not given to provide ready-made forms to be used with abandon in one's own Japanese. Although listed, the -*(ra)reru* passive (or potential) forms, for example, need to be treated with great circumspection: they can be ambiguous; some verbs are not commonly used in these forms in ordinary speech; and it is important to distinguish such forms as *o-kyaku ga koraremasita*, 'a (respected) guest came', and *o-kyaku ni koraremasita*, 'I was (inconvenienced by being) visited by a guest'.

The *o* + base + *suru* construction, too, needs care. Primarily a depreciatory form, it is nowadays sometimes used loosely as an honorific, showing respect to its subject. This is no doubt merely a modification of the standard *o* + base + *nasaru* honorific construction unconnected with the *o* + base + *suru* depreciatory construction as such; but it is not generally accepted as a genuine honorific form and is not recommended for the student's own use.

The system of respect language may appear very complicated, and it is true that much experience is necessary to be able to handle it with confidence; but patient identification of different forms as they are met will gradually lead to familiarity with this type of language. In the meantime, the best course is to continue using the widely acceptable -*masu* level of language for your own Japanese and only venture to produce more ambitious forms of respect language when you are quite sure that they are suitable ones.

TABLE OF VERBS USED IN RESPECT LANGUAGE

PLAIN	(1) HONORIFIC	(2) DEPRECIATORY (NEG. HON.)	(3) DEFERENTIAL
Used to and of familiars or inferiors	Respect to subject	Respect to person or thing not the subject	Respect only to person addressed
All verbs except:	o + *base* + ni naru/ nasaru(/suru), -(ra)reru *passive endings*	o + *base* + suru/ itasu	-masu
da	de irassyaru	(da)	*de gozaimasu [no, na, de aru]
aru	o-ari ni naru	(aru)	*gozaimasu [aru]
iru	oide ni naru, irass-yaru	(iru)	*orimasu
iku	oide ni naru, irass-yaru	(iku)	*mairimasu
kuru	yaru	(kuru)	
yuu	ossyaru	moosiageru	*moosimasu
negau	o-negai ni naru	ukagau, o-negai	
kiku	o-kiki ni naru	(etc.) suru/itasu,	o-negai (*etc.*)
tanomu	o-tanomi ni naru	o-ukagai suru/	moosiagemasu
tazuneru	o-tazune ni naru	itasu	
yobu	o-yobi ni naru, mesu, o-mesi ni naru[1]	o-yobi suru/itasu	
suru	nasaru	(suru), itasu	
renraku (*etc.*) suru	go-renraku nasaru	go-renraku suru/ itasu	go-renraku moosia-gemasu
benkyoo (*etc.*) suru	go-benkyoo nasaru	(benkyoo suru)	benkyoo itasimasu
siru	go-zonzi ni naru	(siru)	zon-zimasu
omou	o-omoi ni naru	(omou)	
kureru	kudasaru	—	
kariru	o-kari ni naru	haisyaku suru/ itasu	haisyaku moosiage-masu
morau	o-morai ni naru		
taberu	agaru, o-agari ni naru, mesiagaru	itadaku, tyoodai suru/itasu	*and the* -masu *forms*
nomu	o-nomi ni naru, agaru, o-agari ni naru, mesiagaru		*of verbs under* (2)
miru	goran ni naru	haiken suru/itasu	
miseru	o-mise ni naru	o-me ni kakeru, goran ni kakeru/ ireru	
au	o-ai ni naru	o-ai suru/itasu, o-me ni kakaru '*meet person*' only	
sinu	o-nakunari ni naru	(sinu)	*Applicable to all subjects (including impersonal ones) except the person addressed, his associates and even more exalted persons.
nakunaru	,, ,, ,,	(nakunaru)	
yaru	o-yari ni naru	'*give*' only: ageru,	
ageru	o-age ni naru	sasiageru	
kiru '*wear*'	mesu, o-mesi ni naru [1] *and certain passive forms*		

[1] See n. to Lesson 19, l. 27

TRANSLATIONS

Lesson 1

1. What are over there? Chairs and tables. 2. How many chairs are there? There are four. 3. How many tables are there? There are two. 4. How many forks are there (by you)? There are six. 5. Are there six knives too? There are seven knives. 6. What are those? These are apples. 7. How many are there? There are five. 8. Are those (over there) apples too? Those are oranges. 9. How many oranges are there? There are ten. 10. Whose dog is that? It is my dog. 11. Where is your cat? The cat is here.

Lesson 2

1. Is that your book? It's the book of a good friend of mine. 2. Is your friend an Englishman? He isn't English. He's a Japanese. 3. Who is he? He is Mr. Honda. 4. Where is Mr. Honda? He is in Tokyo. 5. What is he doing in Tokyo? He is studying English. 6. Is this Mr. Honda's book too? That is Mr. Higashi's book. 7. Is Mr. Higashi a good friend of yours too? He is a friend of Mr. Honda. 8. Is he in Tokyo? Not in Tokyo—he's on a journey to England. 9. Whose hat is that over there? That is my child's hat. 10. Do you wear a hat? I do not. 11. Does Mr. Higashi have any children? He has two. 12. Have they gone to England? One has gone to England; one is in Japan. 13. Are there any pencils there? There are not. 14. Are there any writing-brushes? There are some writing-brushes. 15. How many are there? Three. One is my brush; two belong to my child. 16. Are they good brushes? Mine is; my child's aren't.

Lesson 3

1. Are you a reader of the *Chugai Shimbun*? I am not. 2. Do you read any of the newspapers or magazines that are here? M'm, I don't read any. I read that book once. 3. Which book? This one? Yes,

that one. 4. Do you read books in foreign languages? No, I don't. Do you? 5. I read English books and magazines. Don't you read newspapers? 6. No, I don't. Is that your case? Which one? That one there? Yes, that's my case. 7. What's inside it? Some committee papers. 8. What time is the committee? It's at eleven o'clock in the morning. 9. Who is the chairman of the committee? Mr. Nakata. Did you hear his broadcast? 10. No, I didn't. What is he? He's a schoolteacher. He also writes books. Are you going to go somewhere? 11. I'm going to go to Tokyo Station. Are you going away? 12. No, I intend to meet a friend. Will he be waiting inside the station? 13. In front of it. What does he do? 14. He deals in cars and such things. Do you intend to buy a new car? 15. No, I'm going to sell one. Are you going to send someone that magazine? I'm going to send it to a friend abroad.

Lesson 4

1. When is it you go to Mt. Koya? On Thursday of next week. 2. Why are you going there? My idea is to see a friend who is writing a novel there. He's the man who wrote *The Parents of the Consul Maeda*. I intended to go last month. 3. How is it you didn't? My father wouldn't give his permission. 4. Did your mother give hers? Yes, *she* did. 5. My assistant is going to Kyoto on Tuesday or Wednesday of next week. Sightseeing? 6. No. He comes from Kyoto. His father is there. Really? Do you know where he lives? 7. I don't. That's a pity. I may be going to Kyoto too. Have you ever been to Kyoto? 8. Yes. Who is your novelist friend? He is Mr. Miki. He's related to Mr. Miki of the well-known Miki Store. 9. What does the Miki Store sell? Cameras. 10. Does it sell them to foreign countries too? It both imports and exports them. This is a photograph of Mr. Miki's shop. 11. Which is Mr. Miki? He's the small man wearing a hat. His English is very good. 12. Do you know Mr. Miki very well? Yes, I do. I often go to the shop and help him. 13. Where does he live? He lives in a new house in Nakano. 14. Have you ever been inside his house? Of course. It's a big house. Here's a photograph of it. 15. What's this funny thing? That's a hand. Someone put a hand out in front of the camera. Here's another photo. It's Mr. Miki moonwatching in the shadow of a tall tree. 16. What is this? It's a small house in the mountains. 17. Is this a fish? Yes, it is. It's a fish in the water. 18. What's that a photograph of? This is a photo of the house where I was born.

Lesson 5

1. What did you do on Friday? In the morning I went to the bank and to the Ministry of Education, and in the afternoon I went to the park and zoo. 2. When did you go to the Town Hall? I went on Saturday and met the Tayama brothers. I went after phoning to see if it was convenient. 3. Is it the elder brother who is Mr. Tayama the mayor? No, the elder Tayama edits the *Choya Shinron*. 4. Is the *Choya Shinron* a magazine? Yes, it is. He also writes novels. Have you read his *Sister-ship*? 5. I've never even heard of that novel. I've never read it, but my elder brother thinks very highly of it. 6. This has nothing to do with what you were saying, but what's that strange thing? M'm, I don't know what it is. It belongs to my brother's child. He's studying archaeology and buys peculiar old things from time to time. Is that book yours? 7. This? This is my sister's. Your sister's? May I see it? 8. Certainly. This is a very rare book. There is no cover, but the inside paper is very clean. Are you going to read it some time? 9. Yes, I intend to read it on Sunday morning. I often buy old books, but I've never seen this one in a shop. Do you think your sister intends to sell it? 10. Well, I don't know. I wouldn't mind buying it. 11. I'll speak to my sister. Are you going out tonight? 12. No, I'm not. Shall we go to the cinema? 13. I *could* go, but . . . Don't you have the time? 14. The fact is, I was going to sort out my papers this evening. Will it take long? 15. It probably won't take very long. Shall I phone you this afternoon? 16. That would be better. I wouldn't mind if we didn't go. 17. No, let's go. What time does the film start? It starts at eight. You'll be in time even if you leave home at seven. 18. Where shall we meet? In front of the cinema would be all right.

Lesson 6

1. Who are you writing the letter to? An English friend. He has lived in Japan for more than fifteen years and last year he became naturalized. As he used to be a supporter of the Labour Party, for a long time the Japanese Government wouldn't allow him to become naturalized. 2. Do you suppose it thought that everyone who supports the Labour Party has dangerous thoughts? That was it, no doubt. 3. Of course, it's probably necessary to be very careful about questions of ideology, but it's peculiar to think that the ideas of the Labour Party are dangerous, isn't it? Nothing the Government does is

up to the mark. 4. The light is very bad in the museum where I work, and we find it hard because the Government doesn't spend much money on such places. My room in the government offices is very dark too. There was one occasion when the town mayor and Dr. Ueda's eldest son came and it was too dark for them to read the documents. 5. What sort of thing is your English friend doing? Being very interested in Buddhism, he is studying in Kyoto. 6. Won't he go back to England? He feels that Japan is better than England in every respect, so he probably won't go back. 7. I suppose he speaks Japanese well? Yes, he does. 8. Don't you think that Japanese is difficult for foreigners? I suppose it's difficult to read and write it. 9. He'll find Buddhist studies very hard going, don't you think? I think so—though I don't know much about religion. 10. Mr. Yamashita, who lives near my house, has begun to study physics in spite of his age. He has taken on something, hasn't he! 11. He may have the idea that there's nothing to it. Which is more difficult, do you think, physics or chemistry? 12. Chemistry probably isn't as difficult as physics. I don't really know, though. What time is it now? I don't have a watch with me. 13. It's eleven. I've promised to meet a friend at twelve, so I'll leave right away. 14. I shall leave too. The bookshop I always go to is close by, so I'll go along there. I'll wait for a tram going to the station. 15. Will you? You're coming to next week's meeting, aren't you? Yes, I'll certainly be there. 16. Goodbye then. Goodbye.

Lesson 7

Yesterday was Sunday. The weather being fine, all the family were going to go to the park for a walk together. We got up in the morning at the same time as on an ordinary day; but as breakfast was somewhat later than usual, my mother was worried about the lunch and stayed at home with my younger sister. As we went out of the gate, we ran into Mr. Oyama, who works in my father's office. He no doubt had something he wanted to see my father about. As the two of them started to talk, my elder and younger brothers and I had to wait more than fifteen minutes.

We walked for two and a half hours. As we were passing the second-hand shop near the tram terminus, intending to come back along the main road, we saw a collision between a lorry and a bicycle. A crowd gathered immediately. Someone must have notified the police, and they too came before long. Both the lorry and the bicycle were slightly damaged, but fortunately no one was hurt.

When lunch was over I thought I would listen to the news on the radio. Since it was a little early, there was some Western music on. The news broadcast was at two o'clock. The item about the Prime Minister's journey to Hokkaido was too long to be interesting. Everyone was relieved that the earthquake in Kyushu, about which we had been anxious, was not as big as we had gathered from the morning news. My elder sister is living in Kyushu. I wanted to go to her place in Kyushu, if only my father had let me, but from the way things seem now there is probably no need to do so.

My elder brother is worrying about his examination and began to study as soon as he had listened to the news. I, too, read an English book. Being a story of the South Seas, it is very interesting but it was rather difficult in places. I thought of asking my brother, but he was busy with his own work and did not have the time. Being able to hear my sister playing the piano in the next room, I could not go on reading for long. My brother is lucky—his room is farther away.

In the evening I listened to a broadcast by someone who had studied Japanese at the Oriental School in England. He talked for thirty minutes about old Japanese buildings. We were surprised that he should talk in very fine Japanese of things which we did not always know about. There are many foreign students at the university where my brother goes and we have heard them speaking Japanese, but there is not one who speaks it better than this man. His talks are on today and tomorrow too, so I intend to listen without fail.

Lesson 8

It happened in the summer, three years ago. Since the spring of that year I had been writing about democracy in America. Thanks to the kindness of the American ambassador, plenty of material had been collected, but it was very hard work to write the thesis.

One day, a letter came from a friend who had been studying the Wakayama dialect since his student days. He mentioned almost nothing about himself, but seemed to be very worried about his father. His father was the president of a big insurance company, but, the secretary of the company having been a bad lot, he had had to go to court in connection with taxes.

I immediately wrote in reply. Not having a stamp, I went out to the post office to buy one. There I met Mr. Kinoshita, who lives next door. Mr. Kinoshita has in the past been the headman of a country village in Akita prefecture, and he is always ready with a joke. On this day, however, he looked very unhappy. I therefore asked, 'When is your wife coming out of hospital, Mr. Kinoshita?' He said, 'She isn't coming out yet. The operation turned out well, so I didn't worry any more, but she'll have to stay in hospital until the autumn because her stomach isn't right.'

'That is a worry, isn't it? Your wife is always a very healthy-looking person, so I thought she'd probably be able to leave hospital in a week or ten days.'

'I thought so too. Even the doctor at the hospital said so.'

Feeling sorry for Mr. Kinoshita, I thought I wouldn't continue the conversation any further; but he spoke again.

'Mr. Nishimura! They say that even after my wife comes out of hospital she'll have to be careful for quite a while about what she eats and drinks, and must never miss taking her medicine after she's had anything to eat.'

Mr. Kinoshita was certainly not his usual lively self.

'Won't you come over there and have some tea or something?' I said to him.

'Let me see, now. I have somewhere else I must go after this, but let's have a bit of a break, shall we?' With this, he left the post office with me.

That day I thought about my friend's father and Mr. Kinoshita's wife even after I was back at home. I wanted to write a bit more of my thesis before my child, who had been born in the winter of the previous year, was up, but I could not manage it.

Lesson 9

The place where I am living lies between Yokohama and Kanazawa, and has three hundred houses and a population of one thousand seven hundred. In it there are three strange-looking people.

The first is a maths teacher at a high school in Yokohama. He lives alone in an old house beside the shrine to the west of the main street. He seems to be still young, and he is tall and wears a long beard. It is said that he has a very good brain, but he has never talked with the people here. He goes off by bicycle early in the morning and comes back late in the evening. On Sundays he goes into the wood behind the shrine and sings songs in a loud voice. He makes so much noise that the people of the neighbourhood have to close their windows. Some people say that he probably sings in the forest because he has lung trouble.

The second is a white man who lives next door to the church. No one knows where he was born. A Japanese maid looks after his cooking, cleaning, washing, and so on for him. His house is half Japanese style and half Western style. The drawing-room, bedrooms, and lavatory are said to be Western style. People say that he is a philosopher. An advertisement for a book written by him is said to have appeared in a newspaper at some time, but I do not know what book it is. Every day he goes into the nearby forest for a walk. There is a small pond in the forest, and for a long time he stops beside it, saying something in a language no one understands.

The third is a young man who lives in the Toko-ji. He has the use of a six-mat room in the temple. His hair is long and almost reaches his collar. He has broad shoulders and a fine physique. He says he is an artist, but as no one has ever seen his paintings, it may not be true. When he goes out he always wears Japanese *kimono* and divided skirt. On fine days he never fails to be by the side of the primary school playground, gazing vacantly at the children playing there.

It being New Year when we moved here, my elder brother, the head of the house, went to make New Year calls on behalf of all our family at the houses of these people among others. At the maths teacher's place there was no reply. At the Westerner's house the maid came out and said, 'The master isn't at home.' At the young man's place the young man opened the door and shut it fast again as soon as he saw that it was my brother. My brother said that he did not know whether to laugh or lose his temper.

These three all live beside buildings connected with religion, and it is very amusing that they themselves should all be peculiar people completely unconnected with religion. Never a day goes by without the people here talking about them.

Lesson 10

Mr. Nagano is connected with a certain oil company and had been abroad since about 1953. He suddenly came back by plane recently with the object of conferring with the directors. My uncle is an old friend of Mr. Nagano, and my uncle's second son and Mr. Nagano's eldest son are studying economics at the same university. Mr. Nagano is a year younger than my uncle, and since my uncle is a bit older than my father, I suppose Mr. Nagano was born about 1910. My father was born in 1912.

On my uncle's introduction I went last night to the hotel where Mr. Nagano is staying. It was between the library and the telephone exchange. As I did not know the number of his room, I asked the old man in the entrance hall, 'What number is Mr. Sakutaro Nagano's room?' 'It is No. 26. Go up those stairs and turn to the left. Next go to the right and then turn left again. No. 26 is the third on the right,' the kind-looking old man told me. I went up to the first floor as directed, but I was not very clear which way to go. I eventually found No. 26 by asking a maid who was doing some cleaning. Mr. Nagano was on the telephone. Seeing me, he said, 'Just wait a moment, please. I'm just finishing,' and went on with his telephone conversation for about half a minute. After he had finished he turned to me and said, 'Are you in a hurry? I'd like to do a bit of letter-writing—would you mind waiting? It will only take about ten minutes.' Saying, 'I'm in no particular hurry, so please do,' I opened and read a book I had brought with me. The ceiling light was bright, but it was a little dark where I was sitting and a mosquito came flying over. Mr. Nagano took a fountain-pen, note-paper, and envelopes from a very fine box and wrote two letters.

'Do you know the addresses of Mr. Tani and Mr. Okawa?'

'Mr. Tani's is 259 1-chrome, Nogata-machi, Nakano-ku, Tokyo-to. Mr. Okawa's is Aichi Prefecture, but I have forgotten the names of the district and village.'

'I'll ask someone later. Well then, what was it you . . .?'

'I should like to hear about your experiences.'

For about an hour Mr. Nagano kindly talked to me about his experiences abroad.

Lesson 11

Since Mr. Takeda's parents were poor, he had to go and work on a farm in Hokkaido as soon as his compulsory education was over. About five years ago the man who ran the farm died and the responsibility for it passed to Mr. Takeda. Things went well at first, but I understand that for three years now it has been making a loss. With the aim of working out some new scheme, Mr. Takeda is looking into examples not only of Japanese farms but of foreign ones too.

He married last year; and on Wednesday of last week he came up to Tokyo with his wife Itoko. It was my birthday that day, so I invited the Takedas to dinner. As the train they were on had reduced speed because of work on an iron bridge, it was after eight when they arrived at Ueno Station. The meal over, we talked about farming. Mr. Takeda is usually a man of few words, but on farming problems he becomes quite carried away by the conversation.

'Farm work is far from easy. Our work is a war against Nature.

We suffer heavy losses in years when the weather is bad, even though we might work without a break even on Sundays and festival days. And money causes us more anxiety than it need. I can't tell you how often I wish I had a little more money.'

'I hope you won't be offended, but do please discuss money matters with me quite freely. When my father died I received an estate of about 100 million yen. I hate using the fortune left me by my parents to lead a life that is no use at all to society; so I feel I'd like to give you some help financially.'

. 'Thank you very much. However hard it may be for me, I shall go on under my own power as far as possible. But as something may turn up that I can't manage, I should be glad of your help then.'

Mr. and Mrs. Takeda stayed in Tokyo until yesterday. As I had been given three tickets, the three of us went to the theatre together yesterday evening. Then the two of them went off to Kobe on the train leaving at twenty-five minutes past midnight. As Mr. Takeda's cousin is a teacher of agricultural economics at a university in Kobe, he said that he was going there to see him.

Mr. Takeda is having a hard time now, but as he is still young, he will surely make good sooner or later. I feel that Mrs. Takeda too will be helping her husband like the fine wife she is.

Lesson 12

Mr. Akiyama is a young artist. His landscape pictures in particular are very good. He sends pictures to the exhibitions which take place every year at the end of autumn or the beginning of winter, but so far he has never had any success.

Mr. Akiyama's father was an army man. When peace came with the end of the war he worried about not finding a suitable occupation because of his poor hearing, and committed suicide. His mother, who for a long time had had a hard life, no longer had the strength to go on living when she lost her husband, and it was less than a year before she died. Having lost both his parents, Mr. Akiyama worked for a while in a coal-mining company, but it was not work which could give him satisfaction.

Mr. Akiyama has a grandfather who is seventy-eight this year. He used to be a naval man. The story goes that, when he was on a small warship in his young days, he went ashore on an island where the enemy were and killed about ten enemy officers and men with his sword. After leaving the Navy following a disagreement with the

Minister, he came to believe deeply in Shinto. He even, at one time, joined some religious group. Nowadays he lives quietly in a small village near the sea.

Mr. Akiyama has a temperament that is unexpected in a person born to a military family of this kind. Since meeting him by chance on a ferry-boat going to Shikoku, I have thought that, as an artist, he is a fine man. He has, however, one great shortcoming. One day, when he was still a pupil at primary school, his grandfather came to the house in a carriage. His mother cooked some beef and they all had a meal together. His grandfather and his father drank a little rice-wine and, when no one was looking, Mr. Akiyama filled a cup with wine and drank it all down. He suffered greatly for it afterwards and resolved never to touch drink again—but this resolve did not last for very long.

Nowadays Mr. Akiyama says that he could not go on living without drink, cigarettes, and coffee. His shortcoming is that he drinks and gets rowdy. Only the other day, when he and a friend went to a restaurant and Mr. Akiyama had had some drink, he beat his friend severely about the head with a stick or something. Someone nearby tried to stop him, but Mr. Akiyama kicked his legs. The restaurant proprietor went and brought a policeman, and Mr. Akiyama was taken off to the police station. The friend who was hit about the head is still in hospital.

Mr. Akiyama apparently remembers nothing at all of what he did that night. His grandfather, who keeps cattle, horses, pigs, and other animals in the country, must be thinking what a nuisance his grandson is.

Lesson 13

There is a large botanical garden near my house. In former times it was the estate of a feudal lord, but, thanks to Dr. Hayakawa, it became a fine botanical garden. Dr. Hayakawa is a famous botanist, but he has a profound knowledge of chemistry too and is known to the world as the man who discovered a way to lessen the damage caused by caterpillars. Officially, the garden is for the benefit of the students studying botany at the university, but, in fact, anyone is free to go in. The lord's house that was once there fell into ruins and is not there now, but part of the grounds remains just as it was and has come to be one of the best examples of a Japanese-style garden.

There is a round pond in the middle of the botanical garden, and fish can be seen swimming in the water. Around the pond are big rocks, on the outer side of which is a row of shells of various shapes; and between the rocks and the shells pretty flowering plants are always in bloom. There are also buildings planted with rare trees and flowers from places near the equator; big vegetable fields; and many fruit trees which produce delicious-looking fruit. One part on high ground is a grove with many big trees where thousands and thousands of birds sing all day long. It is said that almost every kind of plant there is on the earth can be seen in this garden.

Now, however, something has arisen in connection with the gardens which could turn into a big political question. The original grounds of the lord were more than twice the size of the present botanical garden. At the end of the Meiji period part of the eastern side of the grounds was sold and many small houses were built. At present the road used by trams, cars, and so on lies on the western side of the garden, but this is inconvenient for traffic because it is narrow and steep. The eastern side is unsuitable for the building of a new road because the small houses are in the way. There is a plan, therefore, to cut the garden in half from north to south and to leave the western half as a botanical garden as hitherto; and, by making a new road in the middle of the eastern half, to put up an art gallery and hospital on one side and to build shops, flats, and the like on the other. This plan has given rise to disputes between those who approve of it and those who do not, and has come to be a question taken up not only by the people living in this area but also by the Diet, the newspapers, etc. Those who approve say that it is a very fine thing, but those who oppose it describe it as an unpardonable crime, and are trying to organize a movement against it. It seems that, with the election near, the Government cannot easily decide its attitude. Since I have no direct concern in this question, it does not matter to me how it turns out in the future, but personally I feel it would be a pity if this famous botanical garden were made smaller.

Lesson 14

This morning a parcel was delivered from my aunt in Hiroshima. When I opened it and looked there was an old suit of my uncle's inside. I teach the use of printing machines at a private technical school, and so my clothes get badly soiled with oil. Hence my aunt doubtless sent the suit thinking it would be all right for me to wear at work. In the Hiroshima newspaper in which the suit was wrapped appeared a report that a Mr. Yokoyama had died after being run over by a car. It said that the driver of the car was not only fined but had his licence taken away too.

Mr. Yokoyama was a carpenter who had been working when my house was being built. Already turned sixty, he had hardly any teeth, but he seemed to be strong physically. He was very good with his hands and would take on any job without a sign of reluctance. As he was also quite well up in advanced house-building materials and techniques, I thought what a very handy person he was. But Mr. Yokoyama seemed to have the habit of thinking that, because he could only get the same wages as other people, even though he was far more capable in his work than they were, they were gaining and he was losing. Other people suspected him of being a grasping man always counting money to see that there had not been a mistake of even a farthing.

Three months after I had moved into the new house Mr. Yokoyama's daughter telephoned me. She told me that Mr. Yokoyama was in hospital with injuries to his eyes caused by air getting into an engine and exploding when he was repairing a chimney at a factory somewhere; and that, as they were short of money because of this, she would like me to lend her a little. When I said that I was willing to lend some if I could have it back after six months, she replied that she would like to borrow it on that condition.

It is now five years later. There has been no word at all from Mr. Yokoyama. Late one autumn night last year a man who said he was Mr. Yokoyama's son came to see me and said to me, among other things, 'My father finally became blind. As I work for a fishing company a long way away, I can't look after him. I try to have my young sister take care of him, but my father just gets worked up and won't allow it.' On the surface he seemed a good sort of person, but I could not help feeling that he had some secret or other. Mr. Yokoyama had told me at one time that his son had been led by a friend into becoming a Communist.

On doctor's orders I go to a hot-spring every summer, and this year I was going to go to Kyushu. As I pictured the blind Mr. Yokoyama run over by a car, I came to feel a kind of loss and decided to stop off at Hiroshima on my way to Kyushu.

Lesson 15

When I was passing the village office with Mr. Iguchi on Friday of last week I noticed that something to the following effect was written on a blackboard beside the gate: 'Next Sunday (5 March) there will be a cycle race. Entry is open to any resident of the village aged 16 or over. The distance will be 20 kilometres and the start will be from the primary school playground at 10 a.m. The route has been marked on the map on the blackboard.'

I said to Mr. Iguchi, 'This kind of cycle race seems to be very popular now, doesn't it? You'll be taking part, of course?'

'Yes, I thought I would. I'm not saying anything about the result, though.'

'You've always won, surely?'

'Yes, I've been lucky enough not to have lost yet, but I can't guarantee anything this time—I haven't been practising much lately.'

The weather forecast on Saturday evening said, 'The morning will be cloudy, turning to rain in the afternoon. There will be fairly strong north-westerly winds, and the temperature will be two or three degrees below average.' That evening I attended a farewell party for Mr. Kawamura and Mr. Oishi and came back late at night. The sky was quite clear and the stars were shining like jewels. Mr. Kawamura is a scientist and is due to go to Germany the week after next. Mr. Oishi is a diplomat and will go to India next month. Both of them were born in this village. I have been in the village for four months in order to study the extent of the knowledge of Chinese characters among people of different classes.

On the Sunday morning pitch-black clouds appeared and I wondered if it was not going to snow. On looking at the thermometer, I found that it was as much as 10 degrees below average. With a cold wind blowing, it was not a suitable day for the race. Ono, my assistant, wanted to go to see it, so, grumbling about the wretched weather, I set off with him as my guide. He took fruit and cakes with him, among other things, but all I carried was a small packed lunch.

As the yellow-vested Iguchi came in third, I was very disappointed. Mr. Iguchi told me afterwards that his shoulders and the small of his back had become so painful that he had thought of giving up half-way. Ono was pleased, because the winner was a good friend of his. He is a young man who is very good to his parents and he says that, if he goes to university, he wants to specialize in law. Most work he does well, but as soon as it comes to something a bit involved, he tends to throw in his hand. He has a high regard for the jurist Nagashima Seiji, but seems to be unaware of the irregular life he leads.

Lesson 16

It was a hot summer day. As there was a noisy gramophone on next door, I left my seat and went to close the window. Just then Mr. Hirayama came in carrying a beautiful wreath of flowers. He told me that he would like my help, as he had to write about electric waves, units of wavelength and the like. He is a person who thinks he has a right to ask what he wants without more ado, no matter how busy the other person might be. I talked to him for about an hour, worrying as I did so about missing the train to Nagoya. Having taken a big paper bag off my table, Mr. Hirayama put the wreath of flowers into it and went out.

He is a newspaper reporter and seems to have all kinds of interesting experiences. Once, he was having a meal in the dining-hall of a department store after buying some stationery. On one side of the four-sided table were an old couple dressed in cotton kimono. When the waitress asked what they would like to have, the old man just said, 'We'd like something tasty,' and appeared not to know what he should order. Mr. Hirayama noticed that in the rice he himself was eating there had turned up an old copper coin. Remembering that a friend of his had told him before how, in the kitchens of this dining-hall, knives were used with blood on them, the giant radishes had big grubs in them, potato peelings were in the sugar, boiling and steaming water spilled and made the fuel gas smell and so on, he thought that he would write about these things together with the matter of the copper coin.

Next, there was the time when the President of a small, not very powerful country, came on a visit. Mr. Hirayama received orders to write about events from the entry of the President's ship into Yokohama harbour up to his meeting with the Emperor and Empress in Tokyo. He had a thorough look beforehand at the things likely to catch the President's eye by hiring a sailing-boat and going to look at the view of Yokohama to be seen from aboard ship, and by going to and fro by car between Tokyo and Yokohama. The article of his that appeared in the paper had everything. I understand it was so well done that it was translated and published in newspapers abroad too.

When someone came who was the king of an ancient country in Asia, Mr. Hirayama thought he would go to see a university teacher to find out about the man's ancestors and the history of his country. He telephoned the university, but the teacher was not there. He looked up his home number in the directory and telephoned there.

'Is that Professor Inoue? I am Hirayama, sir, of the *Teikoku Shimbun*.

I have something I should like to consult you about, sir, and I wondered whether I could call on you now. . . .'

'That's not possible. Come another day—I'm busy.'

'The fact is, sir, I have something I should like to show you, but . . .'

'What is it?'

'It's an old Chinese painting. A foreign gentleman who is greatly interested in Oriental art has bought something very rare, and he tells me that as you were once kind enough to allow him to see a picture you had hanging in your alcove, he would like to show this to you, sir, by way of thanks.'

'I'd like to see that, eh? Can you come right away?'

'Yes, I can, sir. I really must apologize for troubling you when you are so busy.'

It goes without saying that Mr. Hirayama was able to ask everything he wanted. This kind of 'nerve' is said to be the very essence of a newspaper reporter.

Lesson 17

Mr. Yasuda and Mr. Hashimoto went to the same schools as I from the time we were children. Mr. Yasuda is now a Civil Servant and Mr. Hashimoto works for a business firm. There was no opportunity to meet for some time after we left university, but we used to hear various things indirectly.

On New Year's Day this year I chanced to meet Mr. Hashimoto. As he said that he was then about to go to Mr. Yasuda's house, I went along with him. Mr. Yasuda lives comfortably with one servant in a big house where his parents lived before they died. The three of us spent a long time talking over old times together, but as Mr. Hashimoto was soon to be married, he talked to us about such things as the awful job he was having to find a house to rent, and how worried he was about having to live on a low salary.

Mr. Hashimoto has a good brain and is fond of study, but he is rather short-tempered. When he was at university his friends all thought that he would become a scholar. He, too, seemed to have that in mind. He gave up all idea of staying on at the university after he had questioned the teacher about trade unions on one occasion. Since he holds rather socialist views, it was no doubt impossible for him to find satisfaction in the conservatism of the teacher.

My father is a rice dealer in a small country town. My uncle, his younger brother, runs a wine-shop next door. This led my elder brother to become a tradesman, but I dislike commerce and was interested in history. My father wanted to have me study economics, but I studied law like Mr. Yasuda and Mr. Hashimoto. To tell the truth, I do not know now why it was I chose law, but it was probably because I believed what people said about it being easy to find suitable employment. I did not do much work on law, but made a detailed study of the connection between a certain famous military ruler of earlier times and a member of his retinue who was a kind of entertainer. I intended to make it into a book later.

Having left university, I went to a broadcasting station for an interview on the introduction of a cousin who was working in the telegraph office, but it was no use. So, as one of my friends, who was engrossed in political activities, said that he would like me to help him organize a new political party, in my good nature I worked for a time as his secretary. Every day I would write thousands of postcards, send telegrams, and make telephone calls. This friend is a clever man, but since he was incapable of grasping clearly the mentality of the people, it was out of the question for him to organize a new political party. This obstinate man nevertheless continued his activity, but it finally ended in failure. Feeling sorry that I had worked and drawn almost no pay, this friend gave me an introduction to the editor of a magazine which specializes in international problems. There I investigated the way in which natives of a low standard of culture are being educated in the colonies of European countries, and wrote a few articles. The material was, of course, foreign books and magazines and, not being very strong on languages, I found it pretty difficult work. While doing this work, I developed an interest in native customs and religions. Since I had studied law at university, questions of custom were not altogether strange to me. I felt, for example, that the most interesting thing was the connection between what the natives thought of as 'God' and the punishment for wrongdoing; and I thought that I would like to go into it more deeply. For this, I felt the necessity of a knowledge of foreign languages. As the only foreign languages I knew were a little English and French, I thought that somehow or other I would like to learn some German.

It was just at this time that I met Mr. Hashimoto and Mr. Yasuda, so I told the two of them what I had in mind. Thereupon Mr. Yasuda told me that, as he knew a good teacher, he would introduce me and that, as it was someone his father had helped earlier, there would be no need for me to give anything to the man in return.

Every day since then I have been going to this man's place and learning German. As he is of mixed Japanese and German parentage, it goes without saying that his German is very good, but he also studies Japanese linguistically and has even told me that I ought to correct my grammar, as it is not that of the standard language. I feel that it would be all right if only I could read German, but he says that I must be able to speak it as well, and every day I am made to do conversation practice. I do not know when I shall be able to read German just by using a dictionary, but at any rate I am doing all I can.

Lesson 18

I asked a certain child, 'In what respect does man differ from other animals?' After thinking for a while, he replied, 'Man walks on two legs, but other animals walk on four.' 'You are forgetting, of course, that birds have only two legs, but, leaving that aside, are there still other differences?' I asked. The next reply was that man wears clothes, but animals are well covered with fur or feathers. When I asked if there was anything else, he said that man eats with his hands, but animals eat by seizing things with their mouths.

I went on with the questions, but the child did not give the answer I was wanting from him. I then asked, 'Do dogs talk?' The child said, 'Of course they talk. The dog next door knows about a hundred words. And not only dogs—even the ants in the garden talk.' When I asked how he knew that ants talked he explained that it was because, when he is watching columns of ants in the garden, the ones going to the right and those going to the left sometimes stop and put their heads together.

My intention had been to get the child to understand that it is only man who tells others in words about his own ideas and feelings, in short, who can talk in the true sense; but I did not appear to have succeeded. Beyond all doubt, the responsibility is mine. Because of my clumsy questioning, I had been unable to turn the working of the child's mind in the direction I had wanted it to go.

This is an example concerning a child, but even efforts to make adults understand something often meets with no success at all. In particular, it is extremely difficult to try to make them understand clearly a matter they have never previously either considered or experienced for themselves, or a thing they can neither see nor touch. Of course, people such as schoolteachers, whose special work this is, can doubtless impart understanding skilfully, through long experience, to people with little knowledge or no great power of thought.

In former times one method of education was for the teacher to give not the slightest explanation when a book was being read, but to make the pupils read the same part time and time again. It was thought that then, while they were reading it innumerable times, they would come naturally to understand what was written there. In the case of extremely intelligent pupils, this method is no doubt very fine; but ordinary pupils gain only a superficial understanding and do not grasp the true meaning, even when they do think that they have understood. But both teacher and pupils think they have understood and are satisfied. The result is that, when they try to talk or write about something, it turns out either that they have no knowledge or opinions of their own, or that, even if they have, they cannot express them accurately and simply, in a way that is easily understood.

Training to use one's mind in no other way but this becomes a national habit, and when something is being discussed this leads to both the speaker and the listener being unable to grasp swiftly the essentials of a problem. People often say that the shortcoming of parliamentary government is its inability to decide things quickly, through wasting time in worthless discussion. One cause of this is no doubt a lack of experience, but a more important cause lies in being unable to express, or in being poor at expressing, one's own ideas in a way readily understandable to others. This means that it is necessary to practise from childhood 'correct methods for the expression of ideas'.

Lesson 19

Awakened by the sunlight coming in through the window, Shinroku lay on his bed and thought vaguely about yesterday. When he arrived at the station of this town yesterday morning it had been raining. Seeing that Shinroku was in some difficulty in not knowing the place, the kindly station-master had been good enough to look for a car for him. It was quite an old vehicle, but at any rate it saved him walking in the rain carrying big cases. What is more, although this house was not far from the station, it was necessary to go up a steep hill and so, on this account too, it was a help to have come by car.

The house was a fairly large Western-style building, and parallel with it on the opposite side of the road was a row of old Japanese-style houses. When he arrived at the entrance an old man who seemed to be the porter came out.

'I am Inoue. . . .'

'Oh, yes; we were expecting you. Please go in. I will take your luggage.'

'They're heavy.'

'That's all right—I'm used to it.'

The frail old man picked up the heavy suitcases as if they were nothing at all.

'Your room is on the first floor. I'll show you the way.'

From the window of the room the sea was visible beyond the rows of grey roofs. The misty rain that was falling made the distant view obscure, but he thought what a fine prospect it must be when the weather was fine. The thin old man put the cases on the floor, one on top of the other, and left the room. About five minutes later there came in a tall woman of about forty who gave the impression that she must have been rather beautiful when she was young.

'We are glad to have you here, sir. This is the room with the best view, so I hope you will like it. Would you please come to the small room to the left of the entrance hall afterwards when you come downstairs? I'd like to take down your name and so on.'

'Certainly. I'll come right away.'

'There's not as much hurry as all that.'

When he had more or less cleared his luggage away he went downstairs. The small room had been made into an office. A woman of about twenty in a rose-coloured dress was writing at the table, so Shinroku gave her a casual greeting.

'You're Mr. Inoue, are you, sir? I wonder if you would just be so kind as to write your name and address here.'

Shinroku entered his name and address in a poor hand.

'My mother told you about the meal times?'

'No.'

'Lunch is at half-past twelve. The dining-room is over there, and yours is table five.'

Shinroku realized from this that this young woman was the daughter of the tall one.

The dining-room faced on to the garden. Two people were already sitting at table five. One was a stout, thin-haired man. The other was a young woman in Japanese dress. When she saw Shinroku she said, 'You're Mr. Inoue? Do come and sit here,' and drew an empty chair away from the table a little.

'I'm Ishikawa Michiko. Please call me Michiko, won't you? And this is my father.' So saying, she introduced the fat man to Shinroku.

'I am Inoue. I would appreciate your kindness,' Shinroku said in formal greeting.

Saying, 'Everyone knew you were coming, you know. In all there are about fifteen people staying here, but they're all at such a loss for something to do that they're very interested in a new arrival,' the man explained why his daughter knew Shinroku's name.

'I suppose you've met the lady of the house? A very nice person. Very understanding towards us, you know.'

Thus, during the meal Michiko talked about the members of the family of the house and about the guests. From this, Shinroku learned, among other things, that the tall woman was the proprietress of the place, that the old man looking like a porter whom he had met at the beginning was her father, that the young woman in the office was her daughter, and that the mother's husband had died in the war. But, strangely enough, Michiko made no mention of anything on her own side.

In the afternoon Shinroku read in his own room a book he had brought with him. In the evening the rain stopped and the sky cleared completely. After the meal Michiko took Shinroku into the garden. With a beautiful moon out, the sea shone pale silver and the pine trees threw black shadows on the white sand. It was probably far warmer than Tokyo, but the nights were still quite cold. Michiko and Shinroku sat down in some bamboo chairs and gazed at the scene for a while in silence. Suddenly, Michiko said, 'Shall I tell you about my wedding?' Rather taken aback, Shinroku did not know what to reply. Michiko went on without waiting for an answer.

'It's very simple. When I went back to the house with my husband after the ceremony to change, that was the finish! My husband said he had something to look up, went into his own room and started work! I felt as if I'd gone mad or something. A friend of mine ran away on her wedding night and went to her lover. If I'd had a lover. I'd probably have done the same. . . .'

Michiko seemed to be crying a little. Shinroku grew uneasy and just listened.

'For my husband, work, and work alone, is his whole life. If I suggest going to the theatre he tells me to leave him and go with some friend or other because he's busy. I wasn't strong enough to get my own way. I suppose I married on my father's orders. The result was that I was terribly lonely and became quite ill. I'm here because the doctor told me to come to rest for a while, but my father doesn't leave me alone. He treats me like a prisoner! When I think I'll have to go back soon, now that I'm getting a bit better, why, I just hate it!'

Shinroku felt very sorry for Michiko, but he did not know what to say. Promising that, as he was tired out, he would meet her again tomorrow, he had come back to his room and gone to bed. That is why, having just woken up, he was wondering what he would do and say when he met her today.

Lesson 20

I trust you are going along in the best of health. Since returning to Japan, I have been meaning to call on you to pay my respects, and I must apologize for not having done so because I have been extremely busy and have not had the time.

Well now, when I was in New York in connection with work for the United Nations I happened to meet a young Englishman who had a great interest in Japanese literature. He told me that he had learned Japanese at London University, but when I met him he was studying at an American university. Literature is not my speciality, but I talked with him a lot, mainly about Japan.

Two or three days ago word came from him that he would soon be coming to Japan and that, as he wants to study Meiji literature at a university somewhere, he would like me to introduce him to a suitable teacher. I feel that the best thing would be to ask you, Professor, and I intend to reply to that effect; but I should like to have your consent before doing so, and am therefore writing to you now.

I must apologize for troubling you when you are so busy, but I should be grateful for your kind reply.

1 May   Akino Kyoichi
Professor Higashiyama

Thank you for your letter. I had heard about you from time to time from Mr. Nagai. I have very little interest or knowledge as far as diplomacy and politics are concerned, but I think it is a very fine thing that Japan has become a member of the United Nations and begun projects of various kinds.

Now, I am agreeable about this matter of the young Englishman. Please bring him to my place as soon as he arrives in Japan. I shall do what I can for him. But please give him clearly to understand that, as I am no good at foreign languages, the conversation will all be in Japanese, and that I can take no responsibility at all for anything outside his studies.

No doubt I shall be able to see you too when this young man arrives.

3 May   Higashiyama Eiji
Mr. Akino Kyoichi

H   [213]

GLOSSARY

Brackets show the part of a word which is written in *kana* when a character is used to write the first part of the word.

A number following a word refers to a lesson in which the word is written in characters.

Abbreviations: *a.*, adjective; *adv.*, adverb; *conj.*, conjunction; *def.*, deferential; *dep.*, depreciatory; *hon.*, honorific; *imp.*, imperative; *int.*, interjection; *n.*, noun; *neg.*, negative; *num.*, numeral; *p.*, pronoun; *part.*, particle; *pref.*, prefix; *suf.*, suffix; *u.*, unit; *vi.*, verb intransitive; *vt.*, verb transitive.

abu(nai) *a.* dangerous
abura 14 *n.* oil, fat, grease
a(garu) 10 *vi.* rise, ascend; *hon.* eat, drink, smoke
a(geru) 11 *vt.* raise, give (*to 'superior'*)
ago n. chin, jaw
aida n. interval, space between
ainoko 17 n. person of mixed blood
aisatu *n.* greeting, salutation
  aisatu suru *vi.*
aite 11 *n.* companion, opponent
aizin 19 *n.* lover
aka(rui) 10 *a.* bright, light
a(keru) 10 *vt.* open
aki 8 *n.* autumn
a(ku) *vi.* become open
ama(ri) 5 *adv.* too (much)
ame 15 *n.* rain
Amerika *n.* America
anata *p.* you
ane 5 *n.* elder sister
ani 5 *n.* elder brother
annai 19 *n.* guidance
  annai suru *vi. and vt.* guide
ano *a.* that
ansin 7 *n.* peace of mind
  ansin suru 7 *vi.* be free from worry
apaato *n.* apartment (house), flat
are *p.* that (over there)
ari *n.* ant
arigatoo *int.* thank you
aru *a.* a certain
a(ru) *vi.* be, exist
aru(ku) 7 *vi.* walk
asa 5 *n.* morning
  asa-gohan 7 *n.* breakfast
asi 12 *n.* leg, foot
asita *n. and adv.* tomorrow
aso(bu) *vi.* play, enjoy oneself
asoko *p.* over there

atama 9 *n.* head, mind
ata(rasii) 3 *a.* new
atata(kai) 19 *a.* warm
ato *n.* remains, time after
  ato de *adv.* afterwards
atu(i) 16 *a.* hot
atu(maru) 7 *vi.* congregate
atu(meru) *vt.* collect
a(u) 3 *vi.* meet
a(u) 5 *vi.* fit, correspond (to)
Azia *n.* Asia

baai 17 *n.* circumstances, case
bai *n.* double
  -bai 13 *u.* times (as much)
baibai 3 *n.* buying and selling
  baibai suru *vt.*
bakari *part.* only; (*after numerals*) about
bakkin 14 *n.* fine, penalty
bakuhatu 14 *n.* explosion
  bakuhatu suru *vi.*
ban 7 *n.* evening
  ban-gohan 11 *n.* evening meal
-ban 15 *u.* No. (*forms ordinal numbers*)
bangoo 10 *n.* number
-banme 10 *suf.* (1)st, (2)nd, *etc.*
bannin 19 *n.* watchman, guard
banti 10 *n.* plot number, house number
basya 12 *n.* horse carriage
batu 17 *n.* punishment
Beikoku 20 *n.* U.S.A.
benkyoo 2 *n.* study
  benkyoo suru *vi. and vt.*
benri na 14 *a.* convenient
bentoo 15 *n.* packed lunch
benzyo 9 *n.* lavatory
binboo 11 *n.* poverty
  binboo na *a.* poor
  binboo suru *vi.* become poor
bizyutu (bizitu) 16 *n.* art, fine arts

GLOSSARY

bizyutukan 13 *n.* art gallery
bonyari (to) *adv.* dimly, distractedly
　bonyari suru *vi.* be dull, be absent-
　　minded
boo 12 *n.* stick, bar, pole
boosi 2 *n.* hat
bukkyoo 6 *n.* Buddhism
bunboogu 16 *n.* stationery
bungaku 20 *n.* literature
bunka 17 *n.* culture
bunpoo 17 *n.* grammar
bunsyoo 16 *n.* sentence, writing
buta *n.* pig
buturigaku 6 *n.* physics
buzi na 7 *a.* safe
-byoo 10 *u.* second (of time)
byooin 8 *n.* hospital
byooki 19 *n.* illness

da *vi.* be
dai- 9 *pref.* No. (*forms ordinal numbers*)
daidokoro 16 *n.* kitchen
daigaku 7 *n.* university
daihyoo 9 *n.* representation
　daihyoo suru *vt.*
daikon 16 *n.* giant radish
daiku 14 *n.* carpenter
daimyoo 13 *n.* Japanese feudal lord
daitooryoo 16 *n.* president (of country)
daizi na 18 *a.* important, momentous
　daizi ni *adv.*
daizin 12 *n.* minister of state
daizyoobu (na) 15 *a.* safe, all right
dake *part.* only; *n.* extent
dama(ru) *vi.* become silent
dame na *a.* no good
danna(san/sama) *n.* the master (of a
　house), husband
dantai 12 *n.* group, body
dare *p.* who
　daredemo *p.* anyone at all
　dareka *p.* someone
　daremo *p.* (*with neg. v.*) no one
da(su) 4 *vt.* send out, take out, put out
de *part.* in, at, by means of
de aru *vi.* (= da) be
dea(u) 7 *vi.* encounter
de gozaimasu *def. vi.* (= de aru) be
de irassyaru *hon. vi.* be (*of animate
　things*)
deka(keru) 5 *vi.* go out, set off
deki(ru) v *vi.* be possible, be made, be
　produced
denpa 16 *n.* electric wave
denpoo 17 *n.* telegram
densin *n.* telegraph
　densinkyoku 17 *n.* telegraph office
dentoo 10 *n.* electric light

densya 6 *n.* tram, electric train
denwa 5 *n.* telephone
　denwatyoo 16 *n.* telephone directory
depaato *n.* department store
de(ru) 5 *vi.* go out, come out, attend
de sae *part.* even
dewa (d'ya, zya) *conj.* well then
Doitu *n.* Germany
　Doitugo 17 *n.* German (language)
　Doituzin 17 *n.* a German
doko *p.* where
　dokodemo *p.* anywhere at all
　dokoka *p.* somewhere
　dokomo *p.* (*with neg. v.*) nowhere
doku 8 *n.* poison
dokuritu *n.* independence
dokusya 3 *n.* reader
donna *a.* what kind of
　donna ni *adv.* in what way, to what
　　extent
dono *a.* which
doo *adv.* in what way, how
　doosite *adv.* why
　doozo *adv.* please
doobutu 12 *n.* animal
　doobutuen 5 *n.* zoo
dooka 16 *n.* copper coin
dore *p.* which
　doreka *p.* any, some
　doremo *p.* (*with neg. v.*) none
dotira *p.* which (of two)
　dotiraka *p.* one or the other
　dotiramo *p.* (*with neg. v.*) neither
dozin 17 *n.* native
d'ya *contraction of conj.* dewa *or parts.*
　de wa

e 9 *n.* picture
　e-kaki 9 *n.* artist
e *part.* to
e *int. of acknowledgement, aggreement*
eiga *n.* film
　eigakan 5 *n.* cinema
Eigo 2 *n.* English (language)
Eikoku 2 *n.* Great Britain
　Eikokuzin 2 *n.* Englishman, the
　　British
eikyoo 14 *n.* influence
eki 3 *n.* railway station
　ekityoo 19 *n.* station-master
-en 11 *n.* yen
enpitu 2 *n.* pencil
enryo *n.* reserve, restraint
　enryo-naku 11 *adv.* without reserve
　enryo suru *vi. and vt.*
entotu 14 *n.* chimney
enzin *n.* engine
era(bu) *vt.* choose

[215]

fooku *n.* fork

ga *nominative part.*
ga *conj.* and, but
gaikoku 3 *n.* foreign country
  gaikokugo 3 *n.* foreign language
  gaikokuzin 6 *n.* foreigner
gaikoo *n.* diplomacy
  gaikookan 15 *n.* diplomat
gaizin 7 *n.* foreigner
gakkari suru *vi.* be disappointed
gakkoo 3 *n.* school
gakumon 17 *n.* learning, studies
gakusei 7 *n.* student
gakusya 17 *n.* scholar
gannen 10 *n.* first year (of reign period)
ganzitu 17 *n.* New Year's Day
-garu *suf. used with certain 'subjective' a.*
gasu *n.* gas
-gawa 13 *suf.* side
geinin 17 *n.* entertainer
geizyutu (geizitu) *n.* art
  geizyutuka 12 *n.* artist
gen-in 13 *n.* cause
genkan 19 *n.* entrance hall
genki 8 *n.* vitality
  genki na *a.* vigorous, healthy
  genki ni *adv.*
genzai 13 *n.* present time
getuyoo-bi 5 *n.* Monday
gikai 13 *n.* Parliament, Diet *etc.*
  gikai seizi 18 *n.* parliamentary government
gimu *n.* duty, obligation
  gimu kyooiku 11 *n.* compulsory education
gin 19 *n.* silver
  gin-iro 19 *n.* silver colour
ginkoo 5 *n.* bank
giron 13 *n.* argument, discussion
gizyutu (gizitu) 14 *n.* technique
go- 7 *hon. pref.*
gogaku 17 *n.* language study, linguistics
gogo 5 *n. and adv.* afternoon, p.m.
gohan 7 *n.* a meal, cooked rice
-goo 10 *u.* No.
goozyoo na 17 *a.* obstinate
-goro (koro) *n.* time; *suf.* about (*of time*)
gozaimasu *def. vi.* (= **aru**) be, exist
gozen 3 *n. and adv.* morning, a.m.
guai 6 *n.* condition
gun 10 *n.* sub-prefecture
gunkan 12 *n.* warship
gunzin 12 *n.* serviceman
gurai *part.* about *n.* extent = **kurai**

guuzen ni 12 *adv.* by chance
gyogyoo 14 *n.* fishery
gyoo *n.* row, column
gyooretu 18 *n.* procession
gyuuniku 12 *n.* beef

ha 14 *n.* tooth
haba *n.* width
hagaki 17 *n.* postcard
haha 4 *n.* mother
hai 9 *n.* lung
hai *n.* ashes
  hai-iro 19 *n.* grey
haiken suru 16 *dep. vt.* see, look at
hai(ru) *v vi.* enter
hakama *n.* formal Japanese skirt
hakase (hakusi) 6 *n.* (*academic*) doctor
hakken *n.* discovery
  hakken suru 13 *vt.*
hakkiri (to) *adv.* clearly, definitely
  hakkiri suru *vi.* become clear
  hakkiri sita *a.* clear
hako *n.* box
haku *vt.* wear, put on (*legs or feet*)
hakubutukan 6 *n.* museum
hakusi = **hakase**
hakuzin 9 *n.* white man
hakuzyoo *n.* confession
  hakuzyoo suru 17 *vi. and vt.*
hamono 16 *n.* edged tool, knife, etc.
han- *pref.* half
  hanbun 9 *n. and adv.* half
-han 7 *suf.* (and a) half
hana *n.* nose
  hanazi *n.* nosebleed
hana 13 *n.* flower
  hanawa 16 *n.* wreath, garland
hana(reru) *vi.* become separated
hana(si) 7 *n.* speech, story, talk
  hana(si)-te 18 *n.* person speaking
hana(su) 5 *vt.* speak
  hana(si)a(u) *vt.* talk over
hana(su) *vt.* separate, let go
happyoo 18 *n.* announcement
  happyoo suru 18 *vt.*
hara(u) 14 *vt.* pay off
ha(reru) *vi.* become clear (weather)
haru 8 *n.* spring (season)
ha(ru) *vt.* stick on, stretch over
hatake *n.* (dry cultivated) field
hatara(ki) 18 *n.* work, function
hatara(ku) 6 *vi.* work
hatyoo 16 *n.* wave-length
haya(i) 7 *a.* early, swift
hayasi 9 *n.* wood, forest
hazi(maru) *vi.* begin
hazi(me) *n.* beginning
hazi(meru) *vt.* begin

GLOSSARY

hazu *n.* likelihood, probability
heikin 15 *n.* average, mean
heikoo suru 19 *vi.* run parallel to
heitai 12 *n.* soldier, troops
heiwa 12 *n.* peace
hen 13 *n.* vicinity
hen na 4 *a.* strange
hensyuu *n.* editing
  hensyuu suru 5 *vt.*
  hensyuutyoo 17 *n.* chief editor
henzi 8 *n.* reply
  henzi suru 18 *vi.*
heta na 18 *a.* unskilful, inexpert
heya 6 *n.* room
hi 7 *n.* sun, day
hi *n.* fire, light
hidari 10 *n.* left
higasi 2 *n.* east
hige *n.* moustache, beard
hi(kareru) *vi.* be run over
hika(ri) 19 *n.* light, ray
hika(ru) 15 *vi.* shine
-hiki 10 *u. for counting animals*
hi(ki)u(keru) 14 *vt.* take on (*work, etc.*)
hikooki 10 *n.* aeroplane
hi(ku) *vt.* pull, play (*stringed instrument*)
hiku(i) *a.* low
himitu 14 *n.* secret
hiro(i) 9 *a.* wide, large
hiru *n.* noon, daytime
  hiru-gohan 7 *n.* midday meal
hito 2 *n.* person, disposition, nature
  hitobito 9 *n.* people
hitori 2 *n. and adv.* one person
  hitori musume 19 *n.* only daughter
hitotoo(ri) 19 *adv.* in a general way, briefly
hito(tu) 8 *num.* one
hituyoo 6 *n.* necessity
  hituyoo na *a.*
hizyoo na *a.* extraordinary
  hizyoo ni 5 *adv.*
ho *n.* sail
  hokakebune 16 *n.* sailing boat
hodo *n.* extent, limit; *part.* (*with numbers*) about
hoka *n.* elsewhere, the rest
  hoka no 16 *a.* other, another
hoken 8 *n.* insurance
ho(meru) 5 *vt.* praise
hon 2 *n.* book
-hon 2 *u. for counting cylindrical objects*
hone *n.* bone
hontoo *n.* truth
  hontoo ni 8 *adv.*
honya 6 *n.* bookshop
hoo 5 *n.* direction, side
hoogen 8 *n.* dialect

hoohoo 13 *n.* method, means
hookoo 10 *n.* direction
hookyuu *n.* salary
hooritu 15 *n.* law
  hoorituka 15 *n.* jurist
hoosoo 3 *n.* broadcast
  hoosookyoku 17 *n.* broadcasting station
hosi 15 *n.* star
ho(sii) *a.* desired, wanted
hosyu *n.* conservativeness
  hosyusyugi 17 *n.* conservatism
hotondo *adv.* almost, (*with negative*) hardly
hu- 11 *pref.* dis-, un- *etc.*
huben 13 *n.* inconvenience
  huben na *a.*
hubo 4 *n.* parents
hude 2 *n.* writing-brush
huhei 15 *n.* complaint
huhituyoo na 11 *a.* unnecessary
huka(i) *a.* deep
hukisoku *n.* irregularity
  hukisoku na 15 *a.*
huku 14 *n.* suit, dress, clothes
hu(ku) *vi.* blow
hukuro 16 *n.* bag, packet, sack
hukuzatu na 15 *a.* complicated
-hun 7 *u.* minute (*of time*)
hune 16 *n.* boat, ship
Huransu *n.* France
  Huransugo 17 *n.* French
huru(i) 5 *a.* old
  huru-doogu *n.* second-hand article
  huru-dooguya 7 *n.* second-hand shop
  huru-hon 5 *n.* second-hand book
husai 11 *n.* man and wife, Mr. and Mrs.
huseikoo 17 *n.* failure
hutari 2 *n.* two persons
huta(tu) 1 *num.* two
hutekitoo na 13 *a.* unsuitable
huto(i) 13 *a.* thick, big
huto(ru) *vi.* grow fat
  hutotta 19 *a.* fat
hutuu no 7 *a.* usual, ordinary
  hutuu ni *adv.*
huu 15 *n.* manner, style
huuhu 16 *n.* husband and wife
hyaku 9 *num. and u.* hundred
hyoomen 14 *n.* surface
  hyoomen-teki na 18 *a.* superficial
hyoosi 5 *n.* cover (*of book*)
hyoozyun 6 *n.* standard, norm
  hyoozyungo 17 *n.* standard language

i 8 *n.* stomach
ie 4 *n.* house
ie (iie) *int. of disagreement*

igai 20 *suf.* beyond, outside
Igirisu *n.* England, Great Britain
i(i) (yo(i)) *a.* good
iinkai 3 *n.* committee
ika 6 *suf.* below, less than
ike 9 *n.* pond
iken 18 *n.* opinion, view
ikenai *neg. vi.* not do, be wrong
i(kiru) 12 *vi.* be alive
i(ku) 2 *vi.* go
iku(tu) *adv.* how many
ima 6 *n. and adv.* present time
imi 16 *n.* meaning
imo *n.* potato, sweet potato
imooto 7 *n.* younger sister
inaka *n.* the country(side)
Indo *n.* India
insatu *n.* printing
   insatu kikai 14 *n.* printing machine
insyokubutu 8 *n.* food and drink
inu *n.* dog
ippai 12 *n.* one vesselful *adv.* full
irassyaru *hon. vi.* (= **iru**) be
i(reru) 12 *vt.* put in
iroiro na 13 *a.* various
iru *vi.* be
isi 13 *n.* stone
isoga(sii) *a.* busy
iso(gu) 10 *vi.* hurry
isu *n.* chair
issyo ni 8 *adv.* together
isya 8 *n.* doctor, physician
itada(ku) *dep. vt.* receive
ita(i) *a.* painful
ita(su) *dep. vt. and vi.* do
iti 1 *num.* one
itiban 13 *adv.* most
itibubun 13 *n.* one part
itido (ni) 3 *adv.* one time, once
itoko *n.* cousin
itu *adv.* when
   itudemo *adv.* (at) any time at all
   ituka *adv.* at some time
   itumo *adv.* always
itu- *pref.* five
   ituka 15 *n. and adv.* fifth day, five days
   itutu *num.* five
iya (iiya) *int. of disagreement* = **ie**
iya na *a.* repugnant
   iya ni *adv.*
izyoo 6 *suf.* above, more than; *n.* the above(-mentioned), finis

ka 10 *n.* mosquito
ka *interrog. part.*; or
-ka 12 *n. suf.* -er, -ist
kaban *n.* case, bag, trunk

kabu(ru) *vt.* wear, put on (*the head*)
kae(ru) 6 *vi.* return
ka(eru) 19 *vt.* change, alter
kae(su) 14 *vt.* give back
kagaku 6 *n.* chemistry
kagaku *n.* science
   kagakusya 15 *n.* scientist
kage *n.* shadow, shade
-kagetu 14 *u.* months
kai 6 *n.* meeting, association
   kaityoo 3 *n.* chairman, president
kai 13 *n.* shell(-fish)
kaidan 10 *n.* steps, stairs
kaigun 12 *n.* navy
kaikyuu 15 *n.* class, grade
kaisya 8 *n.* company, firm
   kaisyain 17 *n.* company employee
kaiwa 8 *n.* conversation
ka(karu) *vi.* cost, take (*time, money etc.*); hang
ka(keru) *vt.* hang up, put up, spend, sit (= **kosikakeru**)
ka(ki)i(reru) 19 *vt.* write in
ka(ki)to(ru) 19 *vt.* take down (*from dictation*)
kako 11 *n.* the past
ka(ku) 3 *vt.* write, draw
kakugo 12 *n.* resolve
   kakugo suru *vi.* be resolved
kama(u) 13 *vi.* care (about)
kami 5 *n.* paper
kami (kamisama) 17 *n.* god
kamotu *n.* goods, cargo
   kamotu zidoosya 7 *n.* goods van, lorry
-kan 11 *suf.* period, duration
kanai 8 *n.* (*one's own*) wife
kanara(zu) 6 *adv.* without fail
kanari *adv.* fairly, considerably
kana(sii) *a.* sad
kandankei 15 *n.* thermometer
kane 6 *n.* metal, money
   kanemoti *n.* wealthy man
kanga(e) 17 *n.* thought, idea
kanga(eru) 8 *vt.* consider
kankei 9 *n.* relation, connection
   kankei suru *vi.*
kanoosei 13 *n.* possibility
kansetu (ni) 17 *adv.* indirectly
kantan na *a.* simple, easy
   kantan ni 13 *adv.*
kanzen na 16 *a.* complete, perfect
   kanzen ni *adv.*
kanzi 15 *n.* Chinese character
kanzi 14 *n.* feeling, sensation
kan-ziru 17 *vt.* feel
kanzyoo 14 *n.* bill, account
   kanzyoo suru *vt.* count

kanzyoo *n.* emotion, sentiment
kanzyoo-teki na 14 *a.* emotional
kao 8 *n.* face, expression
kara *part.* from, since, after
karada *n.* body, health
kari ni *adv.* provisionally, (even) supposing
ka(riru) 14 *vt.* borrow
karu(i) *a.* light(weight)
kasa(neru) 19 *vt.* pile up
kasi 15 *n.* cake, sweets
kasiko(maru) *vi.* assent (with respect)
kasiya 17 *n.* house to let
ka(su) 14 *vt.* lend, let (*room etc.*)
kata 16 *n.* person (*hon.*)
kata *n.* shoulder
kata- *pref.* one of two
katagawa 13 *n.* one side
-kata 14 *suf.* way of -ing
kata(i) *a.* hard, firm
kataku naru *vi.* become nervous, ill at ease
katana 12 *n.* sword
katati 13 *n.* shape, form
katazu(keru) 19 *vt.* clear away, finish off
katei 12 *n.* home, family
ka(tu) 15 *vi.* win
ka(u) 3 *vt.* buy
ka(u) *vt.* keep (*animals*)
kawa *n.* river
kawa 16 *n.* skin, peel, leather, bark
kawaisoo na *a.* pitiable
kawaisoo ni *adv.*
kayoo-bi *n.* Tuesday
kaze 15 *n.* wind; a cold
kazoku 7 *n.* family, members of a family
ke 9 *n.* hair, fur, feathers
kega *n.* injury
-kei 15 *n. suf.* -meter
keikaku 11 *n.* plan
keikaku suru *vt. and vi.*
keiken 10 *n.* experience
keiken suru *vt.*
keikoo 15 *n.* tendency
keisatu 7 *n.* police
keisatusyo 12 *n.* police station
keisiki 13 *n.* form, formality
keisiki-teki na *a.* formal
keisiki-teki ni *adv.*
keizai *n.* economy
keizaigaku 10 *n.* economics
kekka 8 *n.* result
kekkon 11 *n.* marriage
kekkonsiki 19 *n.* wedding
kekkoo na 13 *a.* excellent
kemusi 13 *n.* caterpillar
ken 8 *n.* prefecture

-ken 9 *u. for counting buildings*
kenbutu 4 *n.* sightseeing
kenbutu suru *vt.*
kenka *n.* quarrel
kenka suru *vi.*
kenkoo 8 *n.* health
kenkoo na *a.*
kenri 16 *n.* right, claim
kerai 17 *n.* retainer
keredo, keredomo *conj.* but
ke(ru) *vt.* kick
kesiki 12 *n.* scenery
kes(site) 12 *adv.* definitely; never (*with neg. v.*)
ki 4 *n.* tree, wood (substance)
ki 8 *n.* spirit, feeling
ki ga suru 19 *vi.* have a feeling
ki ga tu(ku) 15 *vi.* notice
ki ni iru *vi.* be to one's liking
ki-iro no/na 15 *a.* yellow
kika 6 *n.* naturalization
kika suru *vi.* become naturalized
kikai 14 *n.* machine
kiki-te 18 *n.* listener, audience
kiko(eru) 7 *vi.* be heard
kikoo 15 *n.* climate, weather
ki(ku) 5 *vt.* listen, hear, ask
ki(meru) 13 *vt.* decide
kimi 20 *p.* you (*familiar*)
kimono 9 *n.* Japanese dress, kimono, clothes
kimoti 14 *n.* feeling
kinodoku na 8 *a.* to be pitied
kinoo *n. and adv.* yesterday
kinyoo-bi 5 *n.* Friday
kinzyo 6 *n.* neighbourhood
kippu 11 *n.* ticket
kirai na *a.* repugnant
kiraku na 17 *a.* easy, comfortable
kirei na *a.* pretty, clean
kiri *n.* mist, fog
ki(ri)koro(su) 12 *vt.* stab, slash to death
ki(ru) 13 *vt.* cut
ki(ru) 9 *vt.* wear, put on
kisoku 15 *n.* rule, regulation
kisya 11 *n.* steam train
kita 13 *n.* north
kitiga(i) 19 *n.* madman
kitte 8 *n.* stamp
kiyoo na 14 *a.* dexterous, skilful
ko 5 *n.* child
kobo(reru) *vi.* spill
kodomo 2 *n.* child
koe 9 *n.* voice
koko *p.* here
kokoro *n.* heart, mind, spirit
kokuban 15 *n.* blackboard
kokumin 17 *n.* nation, the people

kokumin-teki na *a.*

kokusai(-teki na) 17 *a.* international

kokusai rengoo 20 *n.* United Nations

koma(ru) *vi.* be in difficulties, feel embarrassed

koma(tta) *a.* awkward, annoying

kome *n.* (uncooked) rice

komeya 17 *n.* rice merchant('s)

konaida = konoaida

konban 5 *n. and adv.* this evening

kondo 15 *n. and adv.* this time, next time

konna *a.* this sort of, such a —— as this

konna ni *adv.* to this extent

kono *a.* this

konoaida (konaida) *adv.* recently

konogoro *adv.* lately, nowadays

koo *adv.* in this way, like this

koo yu(u) *a.* this sort of, such a ——

kooen 5 *n.* park

koogoo 16 *n.* empress

koogyoo *n.* industry

koogyoo gakkoo 14 *n.* technical school

koogyoo 12 *n.* mining industry

koohii *n.* coffee

kookankyoku 10 *n.* telephone exchange

kookogaku 5 *n.* archaeology

kookoku 9 *n.* advertisement

kookoku suru *vi.*

kookoo 15 *n.* filial piety

koori *n.* ice

koosen 6 *n.* (beam of) light

kootoo gakkoo 9 *n.* high school

kootuu 13 *n.* traffic, communications

koozi 11 *n.* construction work

koozyoo 14 *n.* factory, workshop

kore *p.* this

koro *n.* time; *see* -goro

kosi *n.* waist, small of the back

kosika(keru) *vi.* sit down

kosyu 9 *n.* head of family

koto 4 *n.* (*abstract*) thing, matter

kotoba 9 *n.* word, language

kotosi 17 *n. and adv.* this year

kowa(i) *a.* frightening, frightened

kowa(reru) *vi.* break, be smashed

kozin 13 *n.* individual

kozukai 19 *n.* porter, messenger

kozutumi 14 *n.* parcel

ku 9 *num.* nine

ku 10 *n.* urban district

kubi 9 *n.* neck

kudamono 13 *n.* fruit

kuda(saru) 10 *vt.* give, condescend

kumiai 17 *n.* association, (trade) union

kumo 15 *n.* cloud

kumo(ru) *vi.* cloud over

-kun 15 *suf.* Mr.

kuni 17 *n.* country, one's native place

kurai *n.* rank, extent; *part.* about (= gurai)

kura(i) *a.* dark

ku(rasu) *vi.* live

ku(reru) *vt.* give

kuro(i) 19 *a.* black

kuro *n.*

ku(ru) 4 *vi.* come

kuruma 19 *n.* vehicle, car

kuru(sii) 11 *a.* painful, hard

kuru(simu) 11 *vi.* suffer

kusa *n.* grass, plant (*other than trees and crops*)

kusabana 13 *n.* flowers, flowering plants

kuse *n.* habit

kusin 11 *n.* anxiety, hard work

kusin suru *vi.*

kusuri 8 *n.* medicine

kuti 18 *n.* mouth

kuuki 14 *n.* air

kuwa(sii) *a.* detailed

kyaku 19 *n.* guest (= o-kyaku)

kyakusitu 9 *n.* drawing-room

kyonen 6 *n. and adv.* last year

kyoo *n. and adv.* today

kyoodai 5 *n.* brothers, brothers and sisters

kyooiku 11 *n.* education

kyooiku suru *vt.*

kyookai 9 *n.* church

kyoomi 6 *n.* interest

kyoosan *n.* common property

kyoosansyugi 14 *n.* communism

kyoosoo 15 *n.* competition, race

kyoosoo suru *vi.*

kyori 15 *n.* distance

kyuu- *num.* nine

kyuu na 13 *a.* sudden

kyuu ni 10 *adv.*

kyuuryoo 14 *n.* salary

kyuuzi 16 *n.* waiter, waitress, office boy

ma 5 *n.* interval of time; *u. for counting rooms*

ma ni a(u) 5 *vi.* be in time, be adequate

mada *adv.* still

made *adv.* until, up to

mado *n.* window

mae 3 *n.* front part; *suf.* ago, before

mae ni *adv.* previously

maga(ru) *vi.* turn, twist

mago *n.* grandchild

-mai 11 *u. for counting flat thing.*

GLOSSARY

mai- *pref.* every
  mainen 12 *n. and adv.* every year
  mainiti 9 *n. and adv.* every day
mai(ru) 16 *def. vi.* go, come
ma(keru) 15 *vi.* be defeated
makkuro na 15 *a.* completely black
mama *n.* unchanged state
mamonaku 7 *adv.* shortly
mannenhitu 10 *n.* fountain pen
manzoku 12 *n.* satisfaction
  manzoku na *a.* satisfactory
  manzoku suru *vi.* be satisfied
  manzoku saseru *vt.* satisfy
maru(i) 13 *a.* round
mata *adv.* again
mati (tyoo) 10 *n.* town
matiga(i) *n.* mistake
  matiga(i) naku *adv.* without fail
ma(tu) *vt.* await
matu *n.* pine
mawa(ri) *n.* area around
me 14 *n.* eye
  me ga sa(meru) 19 *vi.* awake
  me ni tu(ku) 16 *vi.* catch the eye
-me *suf. for making ordinal numerals*
meirei 14 *n.* order, command
  meirei suru *vt.*
Meizi 10 *n. reign period* 1868–1911
mekura *n.* blindness, blind person
menkai 14 *n.* interview
  menkai suru *vi.* give interview
menzyoo 14 *n.* licence, diploma
me(si)a(garu) *hon. vt.* eat, drink
mesitukai 17 *n.* servant
me(su) *hon. vt. and vi.* wear, take (*bath*), ride in, *etc.*
mi- *pref.* three
  mit(tu) *num.* three
mi 13 *n.* fruit, seed
mi(eru) 13 *vi.* be visible
migi 10 *n.* right(-hand)
mimi 12 *n.* ear
mina (minna) *adv.* all
minami 13 *n.* south
minato 16 *n.* harbour, port
mi(ru) 4 *vt.* see, look at
mise 4 *n.* shop
mi(seru) *vt.* show
minsyu *n.* democracy
  minsyusyugi 8 *n.* democratism, democracy
miti 13 *n.* road, street, way
  miti-annai 15 *n.* guide
mitu(karu) 10 *vi.* be found
mitu(keru) 17 *vt.* find, discover
mizu 4 *n.* water
mo *part.* also, even
mokuteki 10 *n.* aim, object

mokuyoo-bi 4 *n.* Thursday
momen 16 *n.* cotton
momo *n.* peach
  momoiro 19 *n.* pink
mon 7 *n.* gate(way)
monbusyoo 5 *n.* Ministry of Education
mondai 6 *n.* problem, question
mono 4 *n.* (*concrete*) thing
mono 7 *n.* person
monogoto 18 *n.* things
moo *adv.* already, by now; more
moo(su) 16 *def. vt.* say
moo(si)a(geru) *dep. vt.* say, do
mora(u) *vt.* receive, be given
mori 9 *n.* grove, wood
motiron *adv.* of course
moto 13 *n.* origin
motto *adv.* more
mo(tu) 17 *vt.* hold, possess
mu- *pref.* six
  mu(tu) *num.* six
muda na *a.* useless, futile
mukasi *n.* former times
mu(kau) 19 *vi.* face
mu(keru) 18 *vt.* turn towards
mu(koo) *n.* opposite (side)
  mu(koo)gawa 19 *n.* opposite side
mu(ku) 10 *vt. and vi.* face (*a direction*)
mura 10 *n.* village
  mura yakuba 15 *n.* village office
muri na 17 *a.* unreasonable
  muri ni *adv.*
musi 16 *n.* insect
musuko *n.* son
musume *n.* daughter
muzuka(sii) *a.* difficult

na 10 *n.* name (= **namae**)
na *relative part.*
na *neg. imp. part.*
nado *part.* and so on
naga(i) 5 *a.* long
nagame *n.* view
naga(meru) *vt.* gaze at
-nagara *suf.* while
na(ge)da(su) *vt.* throw out, throw away
nai *a.* non-existent
-nai *neg. suf.*
naihu *n.* knife
naka 3 *n.* middle, inside
nakanaka *adv.* considerably
na(ku) *vi.* cry, weep
na(ku) 13 cry (*of animals, etc.*)
na(kunaru) *vi.* disappear, die
na(kusu) *vt.* lose
namae 19 *n.* name
nan 2 *p.* what (= **nani**)

[221]

nandemo *p. and adv.* anything at all
nan- *pref.* what
    nando mo 18 *adv.* any number of times
    nanzi 6 *n. and adv.* what time
nana- *pref.* seven
    nana(tu) 1 *num.* seven
nani 2 *p.* what
    nani(ka) *p.* something
    nani(mo) *p.* (*with neg. v.*) nothing
nan(toka) *adv.* something or other
    nan(toka) site 17 *adv.* somehow or other
nan-yoo 7 *n.* South Seas
nao(su) 14 *vt.* cure, mend, repair
nara *part.* if (it is)
nara(beru) *vt.* put in line
nara(bu) *vi.* get in line
naranai *neg. vi.* not do
nara(u) 17 *vt.* learn
na(reru) 19 *vi.* become used to
na(ru) *vi.* become
nasaru *hon. vt. and vi.* do
    nasai *imp.*
natu 8 *n.* summer
naze *adv.* why
    nazeka *adv.* for some reason or other
ne (nee) *int.* is it not so? *etc.*
ne *n.* root
neesan 5 *n.* elder sister (polite)
nega(i) *n.* request
nega(u) 11 *vt.* request
neko *n.* cat
-nen 6 *u.* years
nenryoo 16 *n.* fuel
ne(ru) 19 *vi.* lie down, go to bed
nettyuu suru 11 *vi.* get absorbed in
ni *part.* in, at, on
ni 2 *num.* two
niga(i) *a.* bitter
ni(ge)da(su) *vi.* run away
nigo(ru) *vi.* become cloudy (*of liquid*)
Nihon 2 *n.* Japan
    Nihongo 6 *n.* Japanese
    Nihon-siki no 9 *a.* Japanese style
    Nihonsyu 12 *n.* sake, rice wine
    Nihonzin 2 *n.* Japanese
niisan 5 *n.* elder brother (polite)
nikai 10 *n.* upstairs, first floor
niku *n.* meat, flesh
    nikuya *n.* butcher('s)
nimotu 15 *n.* luggage
-nin *u.* persons
ningen 18 *n.* human being
nioi *n.* smell, scent
Nippon = **Nihon**
nisi 9 *n.* west
-niti *u. and suf.* day

nitiyoo-bi 7 *n.* Sunday
niwa 13 *n.* garden
no *possessive part.; interr. part.; final part. in women's speech*
no *p.* the (one) *etc.*
nobo(ru) 10 *vi.* go up, climb
no ka *interr. part.*
noko(ru) 4 *vi.* remain behind
noko(su) 11 *vt.* leave behind
no(mu) 8 *vt.* drink
noogyoo 11 *n.* agriculture
noozyoo 11 *n.* farm
no(ri)oku(reru) 16 *vi.* be late (*for catching train, etc.*)
no(ru) 11 *vi.* ride on, go aboard
no yo *exclam. part. in women's language*
nyuuin 8 *n.* entering hospital
    nyuuin suru *vi.*
nyuumon *n.* introduction, guide
nyuusu *n.* news

o *accusative part.*
o- *hon. pref.*
oba *n.* aunt
obo(eru) 12 *vt.* learn, memorize
odoro(ku) *vi.* be surprised
o-hiru *n.* lunch
oide ni naru, oide nasaru *hon. vi.* go, come, be
oisii *a.* tasty, delicious
okaasan 4 *n.* mother (*polite*)
okage(sama) de *adv.* thanks to (*another*)
o-kane 11 *n.* money
o-ki ni mesu, *see* **ki ni iru**
o(kiru) *vi.* rise, get up
okona(u) *vt.* act, carry out
oko(ru) *vi.* get angry
oko(ru) *vi.* arise, happen
oku 11 *num. and u.* hundred million
o(ku) 13 *vt.* put, place, leave
oku(reru) *vi.* become late, become backward
oku(ru) 3 *vt.* send
okusan 8 *n.* another's wife
o-kyaku 19 *n.* guest
omae 19 *p.* you (*brusque*)
o-me ni ka(keru) *dep. vt.* show
omo(i) 19 *a.* heavy
omo(i)da(su) 16 *vt.* call to mind
omosiro(i) *a.* interesting, amusing
omo(u) 6 *vt.* think, feel
onazi 7 *a.* same
ondo 15 *n.* temperature
ongaku 7 *n.* music
onna 17 *n.* woman
    onna syuzin 19 *n.* proprietress
oo- *pref.* great, large
    oodoo(ri) 9 *n.* main road

oo(i) 13 *a.* many, much
  ooku *adv.* mostly
oo(kii) (oo(ki) na) 4 *a.* big, large
  oo(kisa) 13 *n.* size
oo-sama 16 *n.* king
o-rei 16 *n.* thanks, payment
orenzi *n.* orange
o(reru) *vi.* snap, break (off)
o(ru) *vt.* snap, break (off)
o(ru) *def. vi.* be
o-sake 12 *n.* rice wine, alcoholic drink
osi(eru) 10 *vt.* teach, tell
oso(i) *a.* late, slow
oto *n.* sound, noise
otoko 8 *n.* man, male
otona *n.* adult
otoosan 4 *n.* father (*polite*)
otooto 7 *n.* younger brother
otto 11 *n.* husband
o-tya 8 *n.* tea
owa(ri) 12 *n.* end
owa(ru) 7 *vi. and vt.* end, finish
oya 11 *n.* parent
  oya kookoo 15 *n.* filial piety
oyo(gu) *vi.* swim
ozi *n.* uncle
oziisan *n.* grandfather, old man

pan *n.* bread
pen *n.* pen
penki *n.* paint
piano *n.* piano

rai- *pref.* next
  raigetu 15 *n. and adv.* next month
  raisyuu 6 *n. and adv.* next week
raku na 11 *a.* easy, comfortable
  raku ni *adv.*
ranboo 12 *n.* violence, rowdyism
  ranboo na *a.*
rasii *a.* looking like
razio *n.* radio
rei 11 *n.* example
rei *n.* thanks, *see* o-rei
rei *n.* zero
  reizi 11 *n. and adv.* 12 o'clock mid-
    night
rekisi 16 *n.* history
rengoo 20 *n.* combination, league
renraku *n.* communication, connection
  renraku suru *vi.*
  renrakusen 12 *n.* ferry-boat
rensyuu 15 *n.* practice
  rensyuu suru *vt.*
ressya 16 *n.* train
retaa peepaa *n.* writing paper
rikoo na 17 *a.* clever
rikugun 12 *n.* army

ringo *n.* apple
rippa na 9 *a.* splendid, fine
riyuu 19 *n.* reason
roku 6 *num.* six
ronbun 8 *n.* essay, article, thesis
roodoo *n.* labour
  roodoo kumiai 17 *n.* trade union
  roodootoo 6 *n.* Labour Party
rusu 9 *n.* absence from home
ryokan 10 *n.* (Japanese-style) hotel
ryokoo 2 *n.* travel
  ryokoo suru *vi.*
ryoo- *pref.* both
  ryoohoo *n.* both (sides, directions)
ryoori 12 *n.* cooking, preparation of
    food
  ryoori suru *vi.*
  ryooriya 12 *n.* restaurant
ryoosin 11 *n.* parents
ryoozi 4 *n.* consul
ryuukoo 15 *n.* fashion
  ryuukoo suru *vi.* be in fashion

-sa *suf. for making nouns*
saa *int. used when pondering*
sabi(sii) *a.* lonely
sae *part.* even; (*with* -eba) if only
saga(su) *vt.* search for
saiban *n.* trial
  saibansyo 8 *n.* law court
saizitu 11 *n.* festival day, public holiday
saka 13 *n.* slope, hill
sakana *n.* fish
sakaya 17 *n.* wine merchant('s)
sake 12 *n.* rice wine, alcoholic drink
saki 19 *n.* (pointed) end, tip, part
    beyond
sa(ku) *vi.* bloom, flower
sakuban 10 *n. and adv.* last evening
-sama 9 *suf., hon. form of* -san
sa(masu) *vt.* wake
sa(meru) *vi.* wake
samu (i) 15 *a.* cold (*of weather*)
san 3 *num.* three
-san *suf.* Mr., Mrs., Miss, *etc.*
sangatu 15 *n.* March
sanpo 7 *n.* walk, stroll
  sanpo suru *vi.*
sansei 13 *n.* agreement
  sansei suru *vi.*
sarai- *pref.* one after next
  saraisyuu 15 *n.* week after next
sas-suru 19 *vt.* conjecture, be under-
    standing about
satoo 16 *n.* sugar
-satu 10 *u. for counting books*
sawa(ru) *vi.* touch
sayonara (sayoonara) *int.* goodbye

se 9 *n.* back (of body), stature
seihoku 15 *n.* northwest
seihu 6 *n.* government
seikatu 11 *n.* life, living
    seikatu suru *vi.*
seikoo 11 *n.* success
    seikoo suru *vi.*
seinen 9 *n.* young man
seiri 5 *n.* putting in order
    seiri suru *vt.*
seiryoku 16 *n.* power, energy
seisin 16 *n.* spirit, mind
seisitu 12 *n.* nature, character
seito 12 *n.* pupil
seitoo 17 *n.* political party
seiyoo 7 *n.* the West
    seiyoo-siki 9 *n.* Western style
seizi 13 *n.* politics
    seizi undoo 17 *n.* political activity
sekai 13 *n.* world
seki 16 *n.* seat
sekidoo 13 *n.* equator
sekinin 18 *n.* responsibility
    sekininsya 11 *n.* person responsible
sekitan 12 *n.* coal
sekiyu 10 *n.* oil, petrol, paraffin
sema(i) *a.* narrow
sen *n.* line
sen 9 *num. and u.* thousand
-sen 14 *u.* sen, 1/100 of yen
sen- *pref.* last
    sengetu 4 *n. and adv.* last month
    sensyuu 15 *n. and adv.* last week
senkyo 13 *n.* election
senmon 15 *n.* speciality
sensei 3 *n.* teacher
sensoo 11 *n.* war
sentaku 9 *n.* washing
    sentaku suru *vt.* launder
setumei 18 *n.* explanation
    setumei suru *vt.*
sewa 9 *n.* assistance, care
    sewa suru *vi.* look after, care for
si 5 *n.* city, town
si 4 *num.* four
-si 15 *suf.* Mr.
sia(wase) 7 good fortune
    sia(wase) na *a.*
    sia(wase) ni *adv.*
sibai 11 *n.* play, the theatre
sibara(ku) *adv.* (for) a while
sigoto 15 *n.* work
sika *part.* (*with neg. v.*) only
sikaku 16 *n.* quadrilateral, square
sikasi *conj.* but
sikata 18 *n.* method, way of doing
siken 7 *n.* examination
siki 19 *n.* ceremony

-siki *suf.* style
sima 12 *n.* island
simai *n.* sisters
    simaisen 5 *n.* a sister-ship
sima(u) *vt.* finish
si(meru) *vt.* shut, close
sina 16 *n.* article, goods
    sinamono *n.* goods
Sina *n.* China
sinbun 3 *n.* newspaper
    sinbun kisya 16 *n.* newspaper reporter
sindai 19 *n.* bed
sinnen 9 *n.* New Year
sinpai 7 *n.* anxiety
    sinpai suru *vi.*
sinpo 14 *n.* progress
    sinpo suru *vi.*
sinri 17 *n.* mentality, psychology
sinrui 4 *n.* relative(s)
sinsetu na 8 *a.* kind
sinsitu 9 *n.* bedroom
Sintoo 12 *n.* Shinto
si(nu) 11 *vi.* die
sinyuu 2 *n.* good friend
sin(-ziru) 12 *vt.* believe in
sinzoo 19 *n.* heart (*organ*)
sira(beru) 11 *vt.* investigate, search, study
sira(seru) *vt.* inform
si(reru) 4 *vi.* become known
siritu (no) 14 *a.* private, non-governmental
siro(i) 19 *a.* white
si(ru) 4 *vt.* (get to) know
sirusi *n.* mark, sign
sisoo 6 *n.* thought, idea
sitaku *n.* preparation
    sitaku suru *vi.*
situmon 17 *n.* question
    situmon suru *vt.*
siturei 11 *n.* rudeness
    siturei suru *vi.* be impolite, excuse oneself
sityoo 5 *n.* city mayor
siyakusyo 5 *n.* Town Hall
sizen 11 *n.* nature
    sizen ni 18 *adv.*
sizi 6 *n.* support
    sizi suru *vt.*
sizu(ka) na *a.* quiet
soba *n.* side
soko *p.* there
    soko de *conj.* then, thereupon
sokuryoku 11 *n.* speed
son 11 *n.* loss
songai 13 *n.* damage
sonkei 15 *n.* respect

sonkei suru *vt.*
sonna *a.* that sort of, such a —— as
  that
sonna ni *adv.* to that extent
sono *a.* that
sontyoo 8 *n.* village mayor
sontyoo *n.* respect, esteem
  sontyoo suru *vt.*
soo *adv.* so, in that way
soo *n.* (iku —— desu *etc.*) it is said
  that
-soo na *a.* -looking
soobetu *n.* farewell, parting
  soobetukai 15 *n.* farewell party
soodan 7 *n.* consultation
  soodan suru *vi.*
soozi 9 *n.* sweeping, cleaning
  soozi suru *vt.*
soozoo 14 *n.* imagination
  soozoo suru *vt.*
sora 15 *n.* sky
sore *p.* that (by you)
  sore de *conj.* (that being) so
  sore de mo *conj.* even so
sosen 16 *n.* ancestors
sosiki 13 *n.* system, organization
  sosiki suru *vt.*
sositara *conj.* then, thereupon
sosite *conj.* (and) then
sotira (sotti) *p.* you, your place; the one
  (of two) by you
soto 5 *n.* outside
  sotogawa 13 *n.* outside
-su(gi) *suf.* past
su(gosu) *vt.* spend (*time*), pass (*time*)
sugu (ni) *adv.* immediately
suiyoo-bi *n. and adv.* Wednesday
suki na *a.* liked, favourite
sukkari *adv.* completely
suko(si) 7 *adv.* a little
suku(nai) 11 *a.* few, small
su(mu) 4 *vi.* reside
su(mu) *vi.* finish
suna 19 *n.* sand
suru *vt. and vi.* do
su(teru) *vt.* abandon, throw away
suugaku 9 *n.* mathematics
suwa(ru) *vi.* sit
-sya 3 *n. suf.* -er, -ist
syakai 11 *n.* society
  syakaisyugi 17 *n.* socialism
syasin 4 *n.* photograph
  syasinki 4 *n.* camera
syatu *n.* vest
syatyoo 8 *n.* president, chairman (of
  company)
syoki 8 *n.* secretary
syokubutu 13 *n.* plant, vegetation

syokubutuen 13 *n.* botanical garden
syokubutugaku 13 *n.* botany
syokubutugakusya 13 *n.* botanist
syokudoo 16 *n.* dining-room
syokugyoo 12 *n.* profession, occupation
syokumin *n.* colonists, colonialization
  syokuminti 17 *n.* colony
syokuzi 7 *n.* meal
syoobu 15 *n.* victory and defeat, result
syoogakkoo 9 *n.* primary school
syoogatu 9 *n.* the New Year, January
syoogun 17 *n.* military ruler of Japan,
  general
syoogyoo 17 *n.* commerce
syookai 10 *n.* introduction
  syookai suru *vt.*
syookoo 12 *n.* officer
syoonin 17 *n.* tradesman
syoorai 13 *n.* future
syoosetu 4 *n.* novel
  syoosetuka 4 *n.* novelist
syooten 4 *n.* shop, store
syooti 4 *n.* consent, acknowledgement
  syooti suru *vt.*
syoototu 7 *n.* collision
  syoototu suru *vi.*
Syoowa 10 *n. reign period* 1926–
syorui 3 *n.* documents, papers
syugi 17 *n.* principle, doctrine, -ism
syuppatu *n.* departure
syurui 13 *n.* kind, sort
syusyoo 7 *n.* Prime Minister
syuu *n.* week
  -syuukan 8 *u.* weeks
syuukan 14 *n.* custom, habit
syuukyoo 6 *n.* religion
syuuten 7 *n.* terminus
syuzin 11 *n.* master of house, shop, *etc.*,
  husband
syuzyutu (syuzitu) 8 *n.* surgical operation

ta *n.* rice-field
tabako *n.* cigarette, tobacco
ta(beru) 8 *vt.* eat
tabitabi *adv.* often
tabun 7 *adv.* perhaps, probably
tada *adv.* only; *conj.* but
tada(sii) 18 *a.* correct
-tai *suf.* want to
taido 13 *n.* attitude
taihen 4 *adv.* very
  taihen na *a.* exceptional, what a ——
taiin 8 *n.* leaving hospital
  taiin suru *vi.*
taisi 8 *n.* ambassador
taisite 18 *adv.* against, towards

Taisyoo 10 *n. reign period* 1912–25
taitei no 15*a.* most, general
taka(i) 4 *a.* high, dear
take 19 *n.* bamboo
takusan 7 *adv.* much, a lot
tama 15 *n.* jewel
tama *n.* ball
tame *n.* benefit, purpose
tani 10 *n.* valley
tan-i 16 *n.* unit
tanin 14 *n.* other people
tanki na 17 *a.* short-tempered
tansyo 12 *n.* shortcoming
tanzyoo-bi 11 *n.* birthday
tao(reru) *vi.* collapse
ta(riru) 14 *vi.* be enough
tassya na 14 *a.* strong, healthy
tasu(karu) 19 *vi.* be helped, be saved
tasu(keru) 11 *vt.* help, rescue
tasyoo 7 *adv.* somewhat
tatemono 7 *n.* building
ta(teru) 11 *vt.* erect
-tati *pluralizing suf.*
tato(eba) 17 *adv.* for example
ta(tu) 11 *vi.* stand (up); *vt.* depart from
ta(tu) *vi.* elapse
tayo(ri) 14 *n.* news; trust
te 4 *n.* hand
　te ni hai(ru) 11 *vi.* come into one's possession
teeburu *n.* table
tegami 6 *n.* letter
teido 15 *n.* extent, degree
teikoku 16 *n.* empire
teki 12 *n.* enemy
-teki na (ni) *suf. forming a. (adv.)*
tekitoo na 12 *a.* suitable
tekkyoo 11 *n.* iron bridge
ten 18 *n.* point, spot, mark
tenki 7 *n.* weather
　tenki yohoo 15 *n.* weather forecast
tennoo 16 *n.* emperor
tenrankai 12 *n.* exhibition
tenzyoo 10 *n.* ceiling
tera 9 *n.* (Buddhist) temple, monastery
tetuda(i) 4 *n.* help
tetugaku *n.* philosophy
　tetugakusya 9 *n.* philosopher
ti 16 *n.* blood
tiga(tta) *a.* different
tiga(u) *vi.* differ
tii(sai) (tii(sa) na) 4 *a.* small, little
tika(i) 6 *a.* near
　tikagoro *adv.* recently
　tika(ku) 17 *adv.* soon; *n.* neighbourhood
tikara 11 *n.* strength
tikuonki 16 *n.* gramophone

tikyuu 13 *n.* the earth, globe
tisiki 13 *n.* knowledge
titi 4 *n.* father
tizu 15 *n.* map
to 9 *n.* door
to 10 *n.* metropolis
to *part.* and, with
to(bu) 10 *vi.* fly, jump
todo(keru) *vt.* deliver, report
todo(ku) *vi.* be delivered, reach
toka *part.* and
tokei 6 *n.* watch, clock
toki 7 *n.* time
tokidoki *adv.* occasionally
toko(no)ma 16 *n.* alcove for pictures, flowers, etc.
tokoro 7 *n.* place, moment, aspect (of character)
tokorodokoro *adv.* here and there
tokoro(ga) 8 *conj.* however
toku 14 *n.* gain, profit
toku ni 10 *adv.* especially
to(maru) *vi.* stay, stop
to(meru) *vt.* stop, put (*person*) up
-tomo 15 *suf.* both, all; (*with neg.*) neither, none
tomodati 2 *n.* friend
tonari *n.* next door
tonikaku *adv.* at any rate
too 1 *num.* ten
too(i) *a.* distant
　too(ku) 14 *n.* the distance
tooka 8 *n. and adv.* ten days, tenth day
too(ri) *n.* street, road, way
　too(ri) ni (-doo(ri) ni) 10 *adv.* in accordance with, as ——
too(ru) 7 *vi.* go through, go along
too(su) 19 *vt.* send through, send along
tootoo *adv.* finally
tooyoo 7 *n.* the Orient
tori 13 *n.* bird
to(ru) 14 *vt.* take
tosi 8 *n.* year, age
　tosisita no 10 *a.* younger
　tosiue no 10 *a.* older
　tosiyori 6 *n.* old person
tosyokan 10 *n.* library
totemo *adv.* very
totuzen (ni) 19 *adv.* suddenly
totyuu 14 *n.* midway
tugi *n.* next one
　tugi ni 10 *adv.* next
tugoo 5 *n.* convenience, one's situation
tuka(mu) *vt.* catch, grab
tuka(reru) *vi.* become tired
tuka(u) 9 *vt* use
tu(keru) 15 *vt.* affix, attach
tuki 4 *n.* moon, month

GLOSSARY

tu(ki)a(waseru) 18 *vt.* put together, bring (*one thing*) against (*another*)
tu(ku) 11 *vi.* arrive, reach
tu(ku) 15 *vi.* become attached
tuku(ru) 13 *vt.* make, cultivate
tuma 11 *n.* wife
tu(maranai) *a.* insignificant, trivial, worthless
tu(mari) *adv.* that is, in short
tumi *n.* crime, sin
tumo(ri) *n.* intention
tu(reru) *vt.* take (*person, dog, etc.*) with one
tutu(mi) *n.* parcel
tutu(mu) 14 *vt.* wrap, pack
tuyo(i) 12 *a.* powerful
tuzu(keru) *vt.* continue
tuzu(ku) *vi.* continue
tyawan 12 *n.* tea-bowl, rice-bowl
tyokusetu (ni) 13 *adv.* directly
tyoo (mati) *n.* town
tyoodo 17 *adv.* just, exactly
tyoome 10 *n.* district
tyoonan 6 *n.* eldest son
tyoosi 11 *n.* tone, condition
tyootyoo 6 *n.* town mayor
tyooya 5 *n.* government and people, the nation
tyotto *adv.* just, a little
-tyuu 19 *suf.* during
tyuugai (no) 3 *a.* internal and external, domestic and foreign
tyuui *n.* attention, care
　tyuui suru 6 *vi.*
tyuumon *n.* (shopping, *etc.*) order
　tyuumon suru 16 *vt.*
tyuuoo 13 *n.* centre
tyuusin 18 *n.* centre

ue 12 *n.* upper part, top
ue(ru) 13 *vt.* plant
ukaga(u) *dep. vt. and vi.* visit, ask *etc.*
u(keru) 16 *vt.* receive
uma 12 *n.* horse
uma(reru) 4 *vi.* be born
umi 12 *n.* sea
u(mu) *vt.* bear (*young*)
undoo 13 *n.* exercise, movement, activity
　undoozyoo 9 *n.* playground, sports field
unten *n.* driving (*car, etc.*)
　unten suru *vt.*
　untensyu 14 *n.* driver
ura *n.* rear, back
u(ru) 3 *vt.* sell
usi 12 *n.* cow, bull, ox
usu(i) *a.* thin (*cloth, etc.*), light (*colour*)

uta 9 *n.* song
utaga(i) *n.* doubt
　utaga(i) mo naku *adv.* without doubt
utaga(u) *vt.* doubt
uta(u) 9 *vt.* sing
uti 19 *n.* home, house
uti ni 8 *adv.* while, within
u(tu) *vt.* strike, send (*telegram*)
utuku(sii) 16 *a.* beautiful
utu(ru) *vi.* change position, move (house)

wa *n.* wheel, ring
wa *part.* indicating subject about which something is to be said, *etc.*; final part. in women's language
wahuku 19 *n.* Japanese dress
waka(i) *a.* young
wa(karu) 9 *vi.* be clear, be understandable
wake *n.* reason, meaning
wa(ku) *vi.* boil
wara(u) *vt. and vi.* laugh
waru(i) *a.* bad, wrong
wasu(reru) *vt.* forget
watakusi 16 *p.* I (*formal equivalent of* watasi)
watasi *p.* I

ya- *pref.* eight
　yat(tu) *num.* eight
-ya 7 *n. suf. indicating shop or trader*
yabu(reru) *vi.* become torn, break, burst
yakama(sii) *a.* noisy, fault-finding
yaku *n.* duty, office, service
　yakuba 15 *n.* (local government) office
　yakunin 17 *n.* government official
　yaku ni ta(tu) 11 *vi.* be of use
　yakusyo 6 *n.* government office
yaku 16 *n.* translation
yakusoku 6 *n.* promise, appointment
　yakusoku suru *vi.*
yama 4 *n.* mountain
ya(meru) *vt.* cease, resign
ya(mu) *vi.* cease
yane 19 *n.* roof
yasai 13 *n.* vegetables
ya(seru) *vi.* become thin
　ya(seta), ya(sete) iru *a.* thin
yasu(i) 17 *a.* cheap
-yasu(i) *suf.* easy to ——
yasu(mu) 8 *vi.* rest
yatto *adv.* at long last
yo *emphatic final part.*
yo- *pref.* four
　yot(tu) 1 *num.* four

[227]

yo(bu) *vt.* call, invite, send for
yogo(reru) *vi.* become dirty
yohoo 15 *n.* forecast
yo(i) = ⁱi(i)
yokei na 5 *a.* unnecessary, uncalled-for
yoko 9 *n.* side
  yoko ni na(ru) 19 *vi.* lie down
yoku 14 *n.* greed
yo(mu) 3 *vt.* read
yoo *n.* likeness, appearance
yoohuku 19 *n.* Western clothes
Yooroppa *n.* Europe
yoosu 7 *n.* appearance, state
yoozi 10 *n.* business, thing to be done
yori *part.* than
yoroko(bu) *vi.* rejoice
yoro(sii) *a.* = i(i); *int.* Right!
yoru 14 *n.* night
yo(ru) *vi.* call in (*at*)
yu 16 *n.* hot water
yuka 19 *n.* floor
yuki 15 *n.* snow
-yu(ki) 16 *suf.* bound for
yunyuu 4 *n.* importation
  yunyuu suru *vt.*
yuru(meru) *vt.* slacken, loosen
yuru(su) *vt.* forgive, permit
yusyutu 4 *n.* exportation
  yusyutu suru *vt.*
yu(u) 8 *vt. and vi.* say, tell
yuubin *n.* mail
  yuubinkyoku 8 *n.* post office
yuumei na 4 *a.* famous

zaimoku *n.* timber
zairyoo 8 *n.* material
zaisan 11 *n.* property, fortune
zannen na 4 *a.* regrettable
zassi 3 *n.* magazine
zei *n.* tax
  zeikin 8 *n.* taxes
zenbu 12 *n.* the whole
zenzen 17 *adv.* completely

zi 19 *n.* character, letter (of alphabet *etc.*)
-zi 3 *suf.* o'clock
zibiki 17 *n.* dictionary
zibun 7 *n.* self
zidai 13 *n.* period
zidoosya 3 *n.* motor-car
zikan 5 *n.* time
-zikan *u.* hours
ziken 13 *n.* incident, affair
zimusyo 7 *n.* office (of firm, *etc.*)
zinan 10 *n.* second son
zinkoo 9 *n.* population
zinzya (zinsya) 9 *n.* Shinto shrine
zisatu 12 *n.* suicide
  zisatu suru *vi.*
zisin 7 *n.* earthquake
zissai 13 *n.* truth, practice
zitensya 7 *n.* bicycle
zitu 16 *n.* truth
ziyuu 13 *n.* freedom
zon(-ziru) *def. vt. and vi.* know, think
zunoo 9 *n.* brain
zutto *adv.* far more
zya = **dewa** *or* **de wa**
zyama *n.* obstacle, hindrance
  zyama suru *vi.* be in the way
-zyoo 9 *u.* (*approx.* 6 *feet by* 3 *feet*) *of size of room*
zyoobu na *a.* strong
zyoodan 8 *n.* joke
zyooken 14 *n.* condition, proviso
zyooki 16 *n.* steam
zyooriku 12 *n.* going ashore, landing
  zyooriku suru *vi.*
zyoozu na 6 *a.* skilful
zyosyu 4 *n.* assistant
zyotyuu 9 *n.* maid
zyunzyo 15 *n.* order, sequence
zyunsa 12 *n.* policeman
zyuu 10 *num.* ten
zyuusyo 4 *n.* address, residence
zyuuyaku 10 *n.* company director

INDEX TO NOTES ON GRAMMATICAL POINTS

INDEX OF CHARACTERS
IN STANDARD USE (*TOOYOO KANZI*)

THIS list contains the 1,878 Chinese characters in standard use in Japan (*tooyoo kanzi*), together with older full forms and common variants.

The characters are arranged in groups according to the total number of strokes in them and, within each group, in *a-i-u-e-o* order according to their Sino-Japanese ON readings or, in the case of the 35 characters for which ON readings are not used, according to their *kun* readings. (The 162nd radical, known as *sinnyuu*, has been entered only under its present three-stroke form, as in 通 , and not under its older form with four strokes, as in 通 , where this is the only point of difference between the two forms of a character.)

The official *tooyoo kanzi* forms have been taken as the standard. This means that, where a *tooyoo kanzi* form is listed first, any old or variant forms have been added in brackets, thus: 万 (萬); but where an old or variant form is listed first, the *tooyoo kanzi* has been added without brackets, thus: 萬 万 , so that the modern forms are easily distinguishable. They are, in any case, always the simpler forms except for the following: 歩 (歩); 渉 (渉); 賓 (賓); 涼 (涼); 糾 (糾).

The numbers against the characters refer to the radical and stroke numbers according to Nelson's *The Modern Reader's Japanese–English Character Dictionary*, shown thus: 12/5; to the traditional radical and stroke numbers (where these differ from the above), shown thus: (12/5); and, in the case of the characters used in this book, to the number of the Lesson in which the character was first used, given in bold type before the radical number, thus: **6**.

The following 28 characters were those in the original list of 1,850 *tooyoo kanzi* which were recommended in March 1954 for exclusion from the list:

且 丹 但 劾 叉 唐 嚇 堪 奴 寡 悦 朕 濫 煩
爵 璽 箇 罷 脹 虞 謁 迅 逓 遵 錬 附 隷 頒

and the following 28 were recommended at the same time for inclusion in the list:

杉 桟 殼 汁 泥 洪 涯 渦 溪 矯 酌 釣 斉 竜
亭 俸 偵 僕 厄 堀 壌 宵 尚 戻 披 挑 据 朴

1			寸		41/0	氏	15	83/0	予(豫)	15	6/3	司		30/2
一	1	1/0	夕		36/0	尺		44/1	六	1	8/2 (12/2)	四	1	31/2
乙		5/0	千	9	4/2	手	4	64/0	**5**			市	5	8/3 (50/2)
2			川	10	47/0	収(收)		29/3	圧(壓)		27/3 (32/14)	示		113/0
九	1	4/1	大	4	37/0	少	7	4/3 (42/1)	以	6	9/3	失	11	4/4
七	1	5/1	土	5	32/0	升		4/3 (24/2)	右	10	30/2	写(寫)	4	14/3
十	1	24/0	亡		8/1	冗	8	14/2	永		3/4	主	8	8/3 (3/4)
丁	10	1/1	凡		16/1	心	7	61/0	央	13	2/4	囚		31/2
刀	12	18/0	万(萬)	10	1/2	仁		9/2	加		19/3	汁		85/2
二	1	7/0	与(與)		1/2	水	4	85/0	可	13	1/4	出	4	2/4 (17/3)
入	4	11/0	**4**			井	10	4/3 (7/2)	囘 回		31/3	処(處)		34/2
人	2	9/0	引	14	57/1	切	8	18/2	外	3	36/2	召	16	18/3
八	1	12/0	円(圓)	11	13/2	双(雙)		29/2 (172/10)	且		1/4	申	16	2/4 (102/0)
又		29/0	王	16	96/0	太	10	37/1	刊		51/2 (18/3)	生	3	100/0
力	11	19/0	火	4	86/0	丹		4/3 (3/3)	甘		99/0	世	9	2/4
了		6/1	化	6	9/2 (21/2)	中	3	2/3	旧(舊)		2/4	正	9	1/4 (77/1)
3			介	10	9/2	弔		2/3	丘		4/4 (1/4)	石	10	112/0
干		51/0	刈		18/2	天	7	1/3 (37/1)	去	6	32/2 (28/3)	斥		4/4 (69/1)
丸	13	4/2 (3/2)	及		4/2 (29/2)	斗		68/0	巨		22/2 (48/2)	占		25/3
久		4/2	牛	12	93/0	内	8	2/3	玉	15	96/0	他	14	9/3
弓		57/0	凶		17/2	日	2	72/0	句		20/3 (30/2)	打		64/2
下	6	1/2	斤		69/0	反	13	27/2 (29/2)	兄	5	30/2 (10/3)	代	9	9/3
己		49/0	区(區)	10	22/2	比		81/0	穴		116/0	台(臺)	16	28/3
口	9	30/0	欠(缺)		76/0	匹	10	22/2	玄	10	95/0	庁(廳)		53/22
工	11	48/0	月	4	74/0	不	11	1/3	古	5	24/3 (30/2)	田	2	102/0
才		6/2 (64/0)	犬		94/0	夫	11	4/3 (37/1)	功	11	48/2 (19/3)	奴		38/2
三	1	1/2	元	8	6/2 (10/2)	父	4	88/0	広(廣)	9	53/2	冬	8	34/2 (15/3)
山	4	46/0	幻		52/1	仏(佛)	6	9/2	巧		48/2	尼		44/2
士	6	33/0	戸	9	63/0	分	7	12/2 (18/2)	甲		2/4 (102/0)	白	9	106/0
子	2	39/0	五	1	1/3 (7/2)	文	5	67/0	号(號)	10	30/2 (141/7)	半	7	3/4
勺		20/1	午	3	4/3 (24/2)	片	13	91/0	込		162/2	犯		94/2
女	9	38/0	互		1/3 (7/2)	方	5	70/0	左	10	48/2	皮	16	107/0
小	4	42/0	公	5	12/2	乏	11	4/2 (4/4)	冊(册)	10	2/4 (18/3)	必	6	3/4
上	6	25/1 (1/2)	孔		39/1	毛	9	82/0	札		75/1	氷		3/4
丈	15	4/2	今	5	9/2	木	4	75/0	仕	7	9/3	付	10	9/3
			支	6	65/0	勿		4/3 (20/2)				布		50/0
双	16	4/2 (18/1)	止		77/0	厄		27/2	史	16	2/4	払(拂)	14	64/2
						友	2	29/2				平	12	1/4 (51/2)

丙		1/4
辺(邊)	**13**	162/2
弁(辯)	**15**	28/3
〃(辨)		28/3
〃(瓣)		28/3
母	**4**	80/0
包	**14**	4/4
北	**7**	21/3
本	**2**	2/4
末		4/4
未		4/4
民	**8**	1/4 (83/1)
矛		110/0
目	**10**	109/0
矢		111/0
由	**13**	2/4 (102/0)
用	**10**	101/0
幼		52/2
立	**9**	117/0
令	**14**	9/3
礼(禮)	**11**	113/1

6

安	**7**	40/3
衣		145/0
芋		140/3
印	**14**	2/5
因	**13**	31/3
宇		40/3
羽		124/0
汚		85/3
仮(假)		9/4
会(會)	**3**	9/4 (73/9)
回(囘)		31/3
灰		27/4 (86/2)
各		34/4 (30/3)
汗		85/3
気(氣)	**7**	84/2

企		9/4
危		4/5
机		75/2
吉		32/3 (30/3)
休	**8**	9/4
朽		75/2
共	**14**	12/4
叫		30/2
仰		9/4
凶		2/5 (73/2)
刑		18/4
血	**16**	143/0
件	**13**	9/4
交	**10**	8/4
光	**6**	42/3 (10/4)
后	**16**	4/5 (30/3)
向	**10**	2/5
行	**2**	144/0
考	**5**	125/2
江		85/3
好		38/3
合	**5**	9/4 (30/3)
再	**15**	1/5 (13/4)
在	**13**	32/3
死	**11**	78/2
至		133/0
糸(絲)	**11**	120/0
旨		21/4 (72/2)
字	**15**	40/3
寺	**9**	32/3 (41/3)
次	**10**	15/4
耳	**12**	128/0
自	**3**	132/0
式	**9**	56/3
色	**12**	139/0
芝	**11**	140/2
守	**9**	40/3

朱		4/5
州	**7**	2/5 (47/3)
収(收)		66/2
舟		137/0
充		8/4 (10/4)
旬		20/4 (72/2)
巡	**12**	162/3 (47/4)
如		38/3
匠		22/4
迅		162/3
尽(盡)		44/3
西	**7**	146/0
成	**11**	62/2
舌		135/0
先	**3**	10/4
全	**12**	9/4
早	**7**	72/2
争(爭)	**11**	4/5
壮(壯)		90/3 (33/4)
存	**16**	39/3
多(夛)	**7**	36/3
宅		40/3
団(團)	**12**	31/3
地	**7**	32/3
池	**9**	85/3
竹	**11**	118/0
虫(蟲)	**13**	142/0
仲		9/4
兆		15/4
伝(傳)		9/4
吐		30/3
当(當)	**8**	42/3
灯(燈)	**10**	86/2
同		13/4 (30/3)
弐(貳)		1/5 (154/5)
肉	**12**	130/0
任	**11**	9/4

年	**6**	4/5 (51/3)
伐		9/4
帆	**16**	50/3
妃		38/3
百	**9**	1/5 (106/1)
伏	**8**	119/0
米		61/3
朴		75/2
毎(每)	**9**	80/2
名	**4**	36/3 (30/3)
有	**4**	130/2 (74/2)
羊		123/0
吏		4/5
両(兩)	**11**	1/5
列	**16**	78/2 (18/4)
劣		4/5 (19/4)
老		125/0

7

亜(亞)		1/7 (7/6)
扱		64/4
囲(圍)		31/4
位	**16**	9/5
医(醫)	**8**	22/5
壱(壹)		32/4
応(應)		53/4
沖		85/4
何	**2**	9/5
花	**13**	140/4
我		4/6
快		61/4
改		49/4 (66/3)
戒		62/3
貝	**13**	154/0
角	**16**	148/0
完	**16**	40/4
肝		130/0

含		9/5 (30/4)
希		50/4
汽	**11**	85/4
忌		49/4 (61/3)
岐		46/4
技	**14**	64/4
却		26/5
求		3/6 (85/2)
究		116/2
吸		30/4
糺(糾)		120/1
狂		94/4
局	**8**	44/4
近	**6**	162/4
均	**15**	32/4
吟		30/4
君	**15**	30/4
形	**13**	59/4
系		4/6 (120/1)
芸(藝)	**12**	140/4
迎		162/4
決	**12**	85/4
見	**4**	147/0
言	**8**	149/0
呉(吳)		12/5 (30/4)
孝	**15**	24/5 (39/4)
抗		64/4
坑		32/4
攻		48/4 (66/3)
更		1/6 (73/4)
告	**9**	30/4
谷	**10**	150/0
克		24/5 (10/5)
困		31/4
佐		9/5
災		47/4 (86/3)
材	**8**	75/3
作	**10**	9/5

志 32/4 (61/3)	但 9/5	妙 38/4	怪 61/5	国(國) 2 31/5
私 14 115/2	男 6 102/2	戻(戾) 63/3	劾 19/6	刻 18/6
伺 9/5	町 6 102/2	役 5 60/4	学(學) 3 39/5	妻 11 38/5
似 9/4	沈 85/4	余(餘) 5 9/5	岳 4/7	刷 14 4/7
児(兒) 10/5	低 9/5	抑 64/4	官 15 40/5	参(參) 16 28/6
車 3 159/0	弟 5 12/5 (57/4)	来(來) 4 4/6	岸 46/5	使 8 9/6
社(社) 8 113/3	呈 30/4	卵 4/6	岩 46/5	姉 5 38/5
寿(壽) 4/6	延 54/4	乱(亂)12 5/13	季 115/3 (39/5)	始 38/5
住 4 9/5	努 19/5	利 14 115/2 (18/5)	奇 37/5	枝 75/4
初 145/2	投 64/4	里 166/0	祈(祈) 113/4	刺 18/6
助 4 19/5	豆 151/0	良 138/1	宜 40/5	祉 祉 113/4
序 15 53/4	尿 44/4	冷 15/5	泣 85/5	事 4 6/7
抄 64/4	妊 38/4	励(勵) 4/6	居 11 44/5	兒(児) 134/2 (10/6)
床 16 53/4	忍 61/3	労(勞) 6 19/5	拒 64/5	治 10 85/5
肖 42/4 (130/3)	売(賣) 3 32/4		拠(據) 64/5	侍 9/6
状(狀)14 90/4	伯 9/5	**8**	供 9/6	実(實)13 40/5
条(條)14 34/4	麦(麥) 199/0	亞 亜 1/7 (7/6)	京 2 8/6	舎(舍) 9/6
臣 12 131/0	抜(拔) 64/4	委 3 115/3 (38/5)	協 24/6	社 社 8 113/3
身 158/0	判 8 18/5	依 9/6	況 85/5	者(者) 3 125/4
伸 9/5	坂 13 32/4	育 11 8/6 (130/4)	享 8/6	邪 92/2 (163/4)
辛 160/0	伴 9/5	雨 15 173/0	金 5 167/0	若 140/5
図(圖)10 31/4	否 1/6	泳 85/4	苦 11 140/5	取 14 128/2 (29/6)
吹 30/4	批 64/4	英 2 140/5	具(具) 6 109/3	受 14 87/4
杉 75/3	尾 44/4	易 72/4	空 14 116/3	周 13/6 (30/5)
声(聲) 9 32/4	扶 64/4	延 54/5	屈 44/5	宗 6 40/5
赤 13 155/0	佛 仏 6 9/5	沿 85/5	径(徑) 60/5	秀 115/2
折 64/4	兵 12 4/6	炎 86/4	茎(莖) 140/5	叔 29/6
走 15 156/0	別 15 18/5	往 60/5	券 18/6	述 162/5
壮(壯) 90/3 (33/4)	返 8 162/4	押 64/5	肩 63/4 (130/4)	所 4 63/4
足 12 157/0	歩步 7 77/3	欧(歐) 76/4	弦 57/5	尚 42/5
束 6 4/6 (75/3)	邦 163/4	殴(毆) 79/4	固 31/5	招 64/5
即(卽) 138/2	芳 140/4	卸 26/6	孤 39/5	承 4 4/6 (64/4)
村 8 75/3	防 170/4	果 8 2/7	弧 57/5	松 75/4
妥 87/3 (38/4)	坊 32/4	河 85/5	呼 30/5	昇 72/4
体(體)12 9/5	妨 38/4	価(價) 9/6	効 19/6	沼 85/5
対(對)13 67/4	忘 8/5 (61/3)	佳 9/6	幸 32/5 (51/6)	狀 状 14 90/4 (94/4)
沢(澤) 7 85/4	没(沒) 85/4	芽 140/4	拘 64/5	炊 86/4
択(擇) 64/4	毎 每 9 80/3	画(畫) 5 1/7 (102/7)	肯 77/4 (130/4)	垂 4/7 (32/5)
	免(免)14 10/6			

字	級	索引
枢(樞)		75/4
制		18/6
性	12	61/5
青	9	174/0
征		60/5
姓		38/5
齐(齊)		210/0
祈		75/4
肯		72/4
拙		64/5
阻		170/5
争争	11	87/4
卒		8/6(24/6)
拓		64/5
卓		25/6(24/6)
批		64/5
知	4	111/3
忠		61/5
注	6	85/5
宙		40/5
抽		64/5
長	3	168/0
直	13	24/6(109/3)
坪		32/5
定	14	40/5
底		53/5
邸		163/5
抵	15	64/5
泥		85/5
的	10	106/3
迭		162/5
典		12/6
店	4	53/5
東	2	4/8
到		133/2(18/6)
毒(毒)	8	80/4
突(突)	7	116/3
届(屆)		44/5
乳		5/7
念	4	9/6(61/4)
波	16	85/5
拜(拜)	16	64/5
杯	12	75/4
拍		64/5
迫		162/5
泊		85/5
拔拔		64/5
板	15	75/4
版		91/4
肥		130/4
非	5	175/0
披		64/5
彼		60/5
泌		85/5
表	5	2/7
苗		140/5
府	6	53/5
附		170/5
怖		61/5
武		1/7(77/4)
侮(侮)		9/6
服	14	130/4(74/4)
拂払	14	64/5
沸		85/5
物	4	93/4
並		12/6(1/7)
併		
步(步)	7	73/3
放	3	70/4(66/4)
法	13	85/5
宝(寶)		40/5
奉		4/7
抱		64/5
房	16	63/4
肪		130/4
牧		93/4
奔		37/5
妹	5	38/5
枚	11	75/4
昧	6	30/5
命	14	9/6(30/5)
明	10	72/4
茂		140/5
盲		8/6(109/3)
戾戾		63/4
門	7	169/0
夜	14	8/6(36/5)
油	10	85/5
來来	4	4/7(75/4)
林	9	75/4
兩両	11	1/7(11/6)
例	11	9/6
炉(爐)		86/4
和	8	115/3(30/5)

9

字	級	索引
哀		8/7(30/6)
胃	8	102/4
威		62/5(38/6)
為(爲)		3/8
姻		38/6
栄(榮)		75/5
映	5	72/5
疫		104/4
屋	6	44/6
音	7	180/0
科	15	115/4
架		75/5
界	13	102/4
香		186/0
海(海)	7	85/6
悔(悔)		61/6
皆		81/5(106/4)
革		177/0
活	11	85/6
括		64/6
巻		49/6
冠		14/7
看		48/4
祈祈		113/4
紀		120/3
軌		159/2
客	9	40/6
逆		162/6
虐		141/3
急	10	61/5
糾(糾)		120/3
峡(峽)		46/4
狭(狹)		94/6
軍	12	14/7(159/2)
係	9	9/7
型		32/6
計	5	149/2
契		37/6
研(研)		112/4
建	7	54/6
県(縣)	8	42/6
限		170/6
故		66/5
枯		75/5
後	5	60/6
皇	16	106/4
厚		27/7
洪		85/6
恒恒		61/6
荒		140/6
郊		163/6
候		9/7
紅		120/3
拷		64/6
恨		61/6
查(查)	12	75/6
砂	16	112/4
砕(碎)		112/4
昨	10	72/5
削		18/7
咲		30/6
思	6	102/4(61/5)
祉祉		113/4
指		64/6
姿		38/6
施		70/5
持	6	64/6
室	9	40/6
者者	3	125/4
首	7	185/0
狩		94/6
秋	8	115/4
拾		64/6
臭(臭)		132/3
重	10	4/8(166/2)
柔		110/4(75/5)
祝(祝)		113/5
春	8	72/5
俊		72/5
盾		4/8(109/4)
叙(敍)		4/8
昭	10	72/5
省	5	4/8(109/4)
乗(乘)	11	4/8
城		32/6
浄(淨)		85/6
食	7	184/0
信	12	9/7
神(神)	9	113/5
侵		9/7
帥		2/8(50/6)
是		72/5
政	6	66/5
星	15	72/5

牲 93/5	亭 8/7	面 **14** 176/0	鬼 194/0	宰 40/7
窃(竊) 116/4	討 149/3	約 **6** 120/3	飢 184/2	栽 24/8 (75/6)
宜 40/6	貞 25/7 (154/2)	勇 19/7	宮 40/7	財 **11** 154/3
浅(淺) 85/6	点(點) **7** 25/7	幽 2/8 (52/6)	級 **15** 120/4	剤(劑) 210/2 (18/14)
専(專)**15** 41/6	度 **3** 53/6	洋 **7** 85/6	挙(擧)**13** 64/6	索 24/8 (120/4)
染 75/5	怒 61/6	要 **6** 146/3	恐 61/6	殺 **12** 79/6
洗 **9** 85/6	逃 162/6	律 **15** 60/6	峡 狭 46/7	蚕(蠶) 1/9
泉 **14** 106/4 (85/5)	峠 46/6	柳 75/5	狭 狭 94/7	桟(棧) 75/6
前 **3** 12/7 (18/8)	毒 毒 **8** 80/5	厘 27/7	恭 61/6	残(殘) **4** 78/6
祖(祖)**16** 113/5	独(獨) 94/6	郎(郞)**10** 163/7	脅 19/8 (130/6)	師 2/9 (50/7)
草 **13** 140/6	突 突 **7** 116/4	**10**	胸 130/6	紙 **5** 120/4
相 **7** 75/5 (109/4)	南 **7** 24/7	案 **15** 40/7 (75/6)	訓 149/3	脂 130/6
送 **3** 162/6	派 **9** 85/6	員 **3** 30/7	郡 **10** 163/7	時 **3** 72/6
奏 37/6	肺 **9** 130/5	院 **8** 170/7	径(徑) 60/7	疾 104/5
荘(莊) 140/6	拝 拝 **16** 64/5	益(益) 12/8 (108/6)	茎(莖) 140/7	射 158/3 (41/7)
則 **15** 154/2 (18/7)	背 **9** 130/5	悦 61/7	恵(惠) 61/6	借 **14** 9/8
即 即 26/7	畑 86/5 (102/4)	宴 40/7	兼(兼) 12/8	酌 164/3
促 9/7	発(發)**13** 105/4	翁 12/8 (124/4)	倹(儉) 9/8	弱 15/8 (57/7)
俗 9/7	飛 **10** 183/0	桜(櫻) 75/6	軒 **9** 159/3	酒 **12** 85/7 (164/3)
待 60/6	卑 4/8	恩 61/6	剣(劍) 18/14	珠 96/6
退 **8** 162/6	美 **13** 123/4	夏 **8** 1/9 (35/7)	原 **13** 27/8	殊 78/6
耐 126/3	秒 **10** 115/4	家 **4** 40/7	個 **13** 9/8	修 9/8
胎 130/6	品 **16** 30/6	荷 **15** 140/7	庫 53/7	臭 臭 132/4
怠 28/7 (61/5)	負 **15** 154/2	華 140/7	娯(娛) 38/7	従(從) 60/7
炭 **12** 46/6 (86/5)	赴 156/2	蚊 **10** 142/6	悟 **12** 61/7	祝 祝 113/5
単(單)**13** 3/8	風 **15** 182/0	悔 悔 61/7	校 **3** 75/6	純 120/4
胆(膽) 130/5	封 **10** 41/6	海 海 **7** 85/7	耕 127/4	殉 78/6
段 **10** 79/5	侮 侮 9/7	害 **13** 40/7	候 **15** 9/8	准 15/8
茶 **8** 140/6	柄 75/5	格 75/6	航 137/4	書 **3** 129/4 (73/6)
柱 75/5	変(變) **4** 8/7 (149/15)	核 75/6	高 **4** 189/0	除 **9** 170/7
昼(晝) 1/8	勉 **2** 4/9	株 75/6	降 170/6	徐 60/7
衰 2/8 (145/4)	便 **8** 9/7	陥(陷) 170/7	貢 48/7 (154/3)	消 85/7
挑 64/6	保 **8** 9/7	記 **8** 149/3	剛 18/8	宵 40/7
勅 19/7	胞 130/5	気 气 **7** 84/6	骨 188/0	称(稱) 115/5
珍 96/6	冒 72/5 (18/7)	起 156/3	根 **16** 75/6	笑 118/4
津 85/6	某 99/4 (75/5)	帰(歸) **6** 58/7 (77/14)	差 123/4 (48/7)	症 104/5
追 162/6	盆 12/7 (108/4)	既(旣) 138/5	唆 30/7	将(將)**12** 90/7 (41/11)
帝 **16** 8/7 (50/6)	迷 162/6		座 53/7	渉 沙 85/7